An Annotated
Critical Bibliography of
Langland

An Annotated Critical Bibliography of Langland

Derek Pearsall

THE UNIVERSITY OF MICHIGAN PRESS
Ann Arbor

Ref.

First published in the United States of America in 1990
by The University of Michigan Press

© 1990 Derek Pearsall

Printed and bound in Great Britain.

Library of Congress Cataloging-in-Publication Data applied for.
Library of Congress Catalog Card No. 90–50103

ISBN 0–472–10185–4

Contents

157230

Advice to the reader

This *Annotated Critical Bibliography of Langland* is necessarily selective. It aims to provide a guide to the history of Langland scholarship and criticism in English from 1900 up to the end of 1988, and also to provide information on editions, selections and translations. The great editions of *Piers Plowman* by W. W. Skeat were done before 1900, but they are included here because of their intrinsic importance and because they mark the beginning of serious *Piers Plowman* studies. What Skeat did with the poem, and what he said about it, provided a platform of knowledge which enabled any reader, if he so wished, to be well informed. 1900 is an arbitrary date, but it corresponds roughly to the point in history when readers began to respond to Skeat's invitation, and to the inspiration of Skeat's most fervent reader, J. J. Jusserand.

For the years covered by the present *Bibliography*, there is a fairly full listing of editions, selections and translations. It hardly needs to be pointed out how large a part these works, with their accompanying apparatus, play in shaping response to the poem. Among secondary works, those books and articles are included which seem to be important in themselves or which have had an important influence in Langland studies. (The almost complete exclusion of works in foreign languages, unless translated, and of dissertations, unless published, is by contrast an arbitrary decision made out of practical necessity.) Accounts of *Piers Plowman* in general histories of literature and passing references to the poem in general critical works are not included unless the writers or what they said have proved to be particularly influential (as did the few remarks of C. S. Lewis). Short notes on textual and other points are included only if what they have to say has a relevance to the poem beyond the immediate elucidation of a word or allusion.

The space devoted to the description of a work is generally an indication of its importance, though of course there is inevitably a great difference of proportion in the space given to the summary of a book, on the one hand, and that given to the summary of an article or essay, on the other. Conveying the essential argument of a well-packed essay often takes as many words as summarising, necessarily more broadly, the content of a book. The opinion of the present compiler as to the intrinsic value of a particular book or essay is not necessarily to be construed from its presence in this *Bibliography*: many studies are here only because they are important in the development of Langland scholarship and criticism, and thus part of that history which it is the purpose of a chronological bibliography to record. Particular care has been taken to indicate those studies which have contributed significantly to that history. Otherwise, I have tried not to indulge too much in wanton evaluation, though inevitably there are times when the merits or defects of a particular book or essay need to be pointed out. Entries for which no description is provided relate to books or articles that I have not been able to see but which seem to be of importance.

I should stress that this book, though I have tried to make it convenient for reference as well as possible to read for those who want to get some sense of the sweep of Langland criticism, is not a comprehensive reference guide. It includes perhaps half the possible items: the bibliographies of Colaianne, DiMarco and Middleton are more comprehensive for the period that they cover (though Middleton has virtually no annotation).

Entries are grouped under a series of headings which I have taken care to define as closely as possible. The alternatives – a chronological listing (as in DiMarco), or a listing in alphabetical order of author within a few broad categories (as in Colaianne) – have their merits, and thematic subdivision certainly has its disadvantages and problems of demarcation, especially if it is made on any theoretical basis. But Langland criticism has its well-established traditions, and it is remarkable how readily the very large potential category of 'Interpretative Studies' allows itself to be whittled down, as studies of subjects that have come to be the subjects of study continue to arrange themselves more or less neatly into existing categories. Within the categories so defined, arrangement is chronological. There are advantages in the practice of grouping all works by the same writer at the point of that writer's entry into the chronology of publication (as is the practice in the *Cambridge Bibliography of English Literature*), particularly in the sense that it gives of the individual scholar's contribution to the subject; but these advantages are already partly dissipated because of the extensive subdivision of entries, and in any case are out-weighed, I think, by the importance of recording the potentially significant historical moment of a particular contribution.

Cross-references are given where they are immediately neces-sary or specially helpful, but most of the work of thematic cross-reference is done in the Index. Items are always cited by author and date, for purposes of ease of recognition, but are also numbered on a single system throughout so as to make finding and looking-up easier. Collections of essays on *Piers Plowman*, or collections that contain more than one essay on *Piers Plowman*, are cited, under the individual entry for the essay, by editor (or author, or title) and date, and listed in the Abbreviated References. Important reviews of important books, especially reviews by scholars themselves distinguished in the field of Langland scholarship, are briefly listed. *Piers Plowman* and Langland are abbreviated as *PP* and L throughout the annotation. Passus and line references are as given by the writer whose work is being summarised: it should be remembered that the passus numbering of C is different in those who cite Skeat and in those, after 1978, who cite Pearsall. Skeat has Passus I–XXIII, Pearsall has Prologue and Passus I–XXII.

*

Some reference has been made above to certain patterns in the history of Langland scholarship and criticism. The existence of such patterns is no more than one would expect, given that the patterns are the product of history. Skeat had his own views on the merits of *Piers Plowman* as a religious poem, but he mostly kept them to himself, and acquiesced in the general nineteenth-century view of the poem as a work of satire, an attack on corruption in Church and State and a criticism of the abuses in society, and primarily a document of social history. This was the way in which an old religious poem could be made to seem relevant in an enlightened and progressive age. With his very influential edition of the B *Visio* in 1869 (the standard university textbook for over a century), as well as his own opinion on the matter, Skeat encouraged that concentration on the *Visio*, at the expense of the remainder of the poem, which was early on such an important factor in the history of Langland criticism.

The late nineteenth century saw *Piers Plowman*, as a document of social history, flower into a prophecy of the constitutional reforms which led to 'modern democracy', a passionate rebuke to tyranny and a cry from the heart of England for reform. Piers Plowman becomes the symbol of the idealised English labourer, a people's Christ who walked English fields and inspired men to throw off the shackles of a corrupt Church and State. Langland is closely associated with the Peasants' Revolt, with Wyclif, with the Reformation and with the common people of England. Jusserand is the most enthusiastic advocate of this historical fantasy, which had important issue, for instance in a series of school textbooks called 'The Piers Plowman Histories', each volume of which was prefaced with the story of Langland's dreamer roaming the Malvern Hills and envisioning a time when English people would be freed from oppression and would be truly part of a democratic common-wealth. That time of course was now, and it was not until after the Second World War that *Piers Plowman* ceased to be employed for the purposes of congratulating Englishmen on what they had made of themselves.

It was an American, J. M. Manly, who first disturbed this English myth of *Piers Plowman* with his theory of multiple authorship, sprung upon the world in 1906. No theory so completely groundless can ever have occupied scholars for so long. The arguments that Manly put forward to support his theory nevertheless found a willing audience in those who had long been convinced that the *Visio* was the only part of the poem worth reading anyway. The theory accommodated their opinion nicely. Fifty years of conflict followed, some of it bitter; R. W. Chambers, an excellent scholar, had to fight a running battle to protect the author he was desper-ately trying to edit from being divided into five. J. E. Wells and Anne Middleton have suggested that the authorship controversy was useful in making scholars pay close attention to the text of the poem, but the attention that was paid, being part of the weaponry of polemic, was mostly of a kind that the poem could well have done without.

There was little that could be done with the poem, it seemed, while it was under such siege, but a number of writers (H. W. Wells, Coghill, Dunning) tried to set aside the authorship debate and see the poem whole. There were attempts to evolve an explanation of the structure of the poem, at least of the B text (C was generally thrown to the wolves howling for 'more authors' until Donaldson came to its rescue), and in particular to see the *Vita* as something more than a series of confused and rambling digressions. The schemes that were evolved were premature, and the emphasis they gave to the interpretation of the Three Lives proved unrewarding, but they have contributed importantly to what must be considered the major school of modern Langland criticism. Members of this school, from Robertson and Huppé and Frank, through Bloomfield, Kaske and Vasta, to Hill, Schmidt, Baldwin, Goldsmith, Stokes, Murtaugh, Adams, Alford, Simpson, Morgan, among many others, believe that the poem has a coherent design, that careful enquiry into its background in intellectual, scriptural and patristic tradition will gradually elucidate that design, that Langland is a learned and careful as well as inspired poet. The stabilisation of the text of the poem and the laying of the ghost of multiple authorship, both largely the work of Kane, have encouraged this view of the poem as a structural masterpiece and as an expression of the central orthodoxies of the Christian faith.

Others, particularly those working under the stimulus of the New Criticism, saw the traditional structural problems of the poem – the abrupt transitions, digressions, apparent *non sequiturs* – in a new way, as a representation of the experience of the dreamer in his quest for truth (Lawlor, Salter, Kirk) or indeed as an expression of the problems of Langland himself, and of an age in crisis (Muscatine, Aers). What had been bad became good: the poem's difficulty was the measure of its truthfulness to the experience of spiritual quest and exploration. The handling of the dream and the dreamer, the question of the *persona* of the dreamer, the enigmatic handling of allegory – all these became important issues. The sense of internal conflict within the poem became part of its meaning.

From being part of its meaning it has become all of its meaning.

The allegory breaks down because it is designed to break down, to reveal the inadequacies of the form (Martin); words slip and slide, not because Langland is struggling to communicate, but because he is demonstrating the inherent powerlessness of words to communicate (Finke). The problem of the text is not in the author nor the reader but in the text. *Piers Plowman* is an old poem, and serious scholars have admitted that it is difficult and enigmatic. Nothing could have been better designed, it seems, for the practice of modern techniques of textual manipulation: the poem virtually self-deconstructs.

*

It remains only to confess to the increasingly frantic nature of the entries for 1988, to acknowledge the invaluable assistance I received from the previous studies of Colaianne, DiMarco, and Middleton and to thank Beth Ortner for her help in the Widener Library and with the typing.

Abbreviations

ABR	American Benedictine Review
AnnM	Annuale Mediaevale
CE	College English
ChauR	Chaucer Review
CL	Comparative Literature
CQ	Critical Quarterly
CUP	Cambridge University Press
DQR	Dutch Quarterly Review
EA	Etudes Anglaises
EC	Essays in Criticism
ELH	English Literary History
ELN	English Language Notes
ES	English Studies
E & S	Essays & Studies
HLB	Huntington Library Bulletin
HLQ	Huntington Library Quarterly
JEGP	Journal of English and Germanic Philology
JWCI	Journal of the Warburg and Courtauld Institutes
L	Langland
LMS	London Mediaeval Studies
LSE	Leeds Studies in English
MÆ	Medium Ævum
MLN	Modern Language Notes
MLQ	Modern Language Quarterly
MLR	Modern Language Review
MP	Modern Philology
MS	Mediaeval Studies
MSE	Massachusetts Studies in English
Neoph	Neophilologus
NM	Neuphilologische Mitteilungen

NQ	Notes and Queries
OUP	Oxford University Press
PBA	Proceedings of the British Academy
PP	Piers Plowman
PQ	Philological Quarterly
PMLA	Publications of the Modern Language Association of America
REL	Review of English Literature
RES	Review of English Studies
RP	Romance Philology
SAC	Studies in the Age of Chaucer
SN	Studia Neophilologica
TLS	Times Literary Supplement
UP	University Press
YES	Yearbook of English Studies

Abbreviated references

Alford (1988)
Alford, John A. (ed.), A COMPANION TO *PIERS PLOWMAN* (Berkeley, Los Angeles and London: University of California Press, 1988).

Adams, Alford, Baldwin, Barney, Hudson, Kane, Lawton, Middleton, Samuels, Wenzel, Yunck

Bennett (1981)
Heyworth, P. L. (ed.), MEDIEVAL STUDIES FOR J. A. W. BENNETT, AETATIS SUAE LXX (Oxford: Clarendon Press, 1981).

Burrow, Dronke, Kane

Benson and Wenzel (1982)
Benson, Larry D. and Wenzel, Siegfried (eds.), THE WISDOM OF POETRY: ESSAYS IN EARLY ENGLISH LITERATURE IN HONOR OF MORTON W. BLOOMFIELD, Medieval Institute Publications (Kalamazoo: Western Michigan University, 1982).

Donaldson, Kane, Middleton

Bethurum (1960)
Bethurum, Dorothy (ed.), CRITICAL APPROACHES TO MEDIEVAL LITERATURE: SELECTED PAPERS FROM

THE ENGLISH INSTITUTE, 1958–9 (New York: Columbia UP, 1960).

Donaldson, Kaske

Blanch (1969)
Blanch, Robert J. (ed.), STYLE AND SYMBOLISM IN *PIERS PLOWMAN*: A MODERN CRITICAL ANTHOLOGY (Knoxville: University of Tennessee Press, 1969).

Bloomfield 1939, Burrow 1965, Coghill 1945, Donaldson 1966, Dunning 1956, Kaske 1963, Kean 1964, Lawlor 1957, Macguire 1949, Mitchell 1956, Smith 1951, Troyer 1932, Zeeman 1958

Brahmer (1966)
Brahmer, Mieczyslaw *et al.* (eds.), STUDIES IN LANGUAGE AND LITERATURE IN HONOUR OF MARGARET SCHLAUCH (Warsaw: Polish Scientific Publishers, 1966).

Donaldson, Mroczkowski

Burrow (1984)
Burrow, J. A., ESSAYS ON MEDIEVAL LITERATURE (Oxford: Clarendon Press, 1984).

Burrow 1957, 1965

Carruthers and Kirk (1982)
Carruthers, Mary J. and Kirk, Elizabeth D. (eds.), ACTS OF INTERPRETATION: THE TEXT IN ITS CONTEXTS 700–1600. ESSAYS ON MEDIEVAL AND RENAISSANCE LITERATURE IN HONOR OF E. TALBOT DONALDSON (Norman: Pilgrim Books, 1982).

Carruthers, Russell

Collins, Price and Hamer (1985)
Collins, Marie, Price, Jocelyn and Hamer, Andrew (eds.),
SOURCES AND RELATIONS: STUDIES IN HONOUR OF
J. E. CROSS, *LSE*, NS 16 (1985).

Collins, Goldsmith

Glasscoe (1980)
Glasscoe, Marion (ed.), THE MEDIEVAL MYSTICAL
TRADITION IN ENGLAND. Papers read at the Exeter
Symposium, July 1980 (University of Exeter, 1980).

Schmidt, Windeatt

Groos (1986)
Groos, Arthur, *et al* (eds.), MAGISTER REGIS: STUDIES IN
HONOR OF ROBERT EARL KASKE (New York: Fordham
UP, 1986).

Szittya, Wittig

Hussey (1969)
Hussey, S. S. (ed.), PIERS PLOWMAN: CRITICAL
APPROACHES (London: Methuen, 1969).

Bennett, Burrow, Dunning, Elliott, Evans, Jenkins, Kean,
Knight, Mills, Raw, Russell, Woolf

Kellogg (1972)

Kellogg, Alfred L., CHAUCER, LANGLAND, ARTHUR:
ESSAYS IN MIDDLE ENGLISH LITERATURE (New
Brunswick, NJ: Rutgers UP, 1972).

Kellogg 1949, 1958, 1960

Kennedy, Waldron and Wittig (1988)
Kennedy, Edward Donald, Waldron, Ronald and Wittig, Joseph
S. (eds.), MEDIEVAL ENGLISH STUDIES PRESENTED TO
GEORGE KANE (Woodbridge: D. S. Brewer, 1988).

Adams, Alford, Fisher, Kaske, Middleton, Pearsall, Russell

Kratzmann and Simpson (1986)
Kratzmann, Gregory and Simpson, James (eds.), MEDIEVAL
ENGLISH RELIGIOUS AND ETHICAL LITERATURE:
ESSAYS IN HONOUR OF G. H. RUSSELL (Cambridge: D.
S. Brewer, 1986).

Donaldson, Doyle, Simpson, Waldron

Lawton (1982)
Lawton, David (ed.), MIDDLE ENGLISH ALLITERATIVE
POETRY AND ITS LITERARY BACKGROUND: SEVEN
ESSAYS (Cambridge: D. S. Brewer, 1982).

Middleton, Pearsall

McGann (1985)
McGann, Jerome J. (ed.), TEXTUAL CRITICISM AND
LITERARY INTERPRETATION (Chicago and London:
University of Chicago Press, 1985).

Patterson, Pearsall

Newstead (1968)
Newstead, Helaine (ed.), CHAUCER AND HIS
CONTEMPORARIES: ESSAYS ON MEDIEVAL
LITERATURE AND THOUGHT (Greenwich, Conn.: Fawcett
Publications, 1968).

Coghill 1962, Spearing 1964

Pearsall (1983)
Pearsall, Derek (ed.), ESSAYS IN MEMORY OF
ELIZABETH SALTER, *LSE*, NS 14 (1983).

Aers, Donaldson, Spearing

Quirk (1968)
Quirk, Randolph, ESSAYS ON THE ENGLISH LANGUAGE,
MEDIEVAL AND MODERN (London: Longman, 1968).

Quirk 1953, 1954

Russell (1988)
Russell, J. Stephen (ed.), ALLEGORESIS: THE CRAFT OF
ALLEGORY IN MEDIEVAL LITERATURE (New York:
Garland, 1988).

Allen, Blythe, Green, Holloway, Manning

Stokes and Burton (1987)
Stokes, Myra and Burton, T. L. (eds.), MEDIEVAL
LITERATURE AND ANTIQUITIES: STUDIES IN
HONOUR OF BASIL COTTLE (Cambridge: D. S. Brewer,
1987).

Bishop, Goldsmith, Wirtjes

Vasta (1965)
Vasta, Edward (ed.), MIDDLE ENGLISH SURVEY;
CRITICAL ESSAYS (Notre Dame: University of Notre Dame
Press, 1965).

Frank 1951, Wells 1929, Zeeman 1958

Vasta (1968)
Vasta, Edward (ed.), INTERPRETATIONS OF PIERS
PLOWMAN (Notre Dame: University of Notre Dame Press,
1968).

Bloomfield 1961, Coghill 1933, Dunning 1956, Frank 1960,
Hussey 1956, Kaske 1960, Lawlor 1957, Wells 1929, Wells 1938,
and portions extracted from Donaldson 1949, Frank 1957,
Robertson–Huppé 1951

Woolf (1986)
O'Donoghue, Heather (ed.), ART AND DOCTRINE:
ESSAYS ON MEDIEVAL LITERATURE, by Rosemary
Woolf (London and Ronceverte: The Hambledon Press, 1986).

Woolf 1962, 1969

YLS 1 (1987)
Alford, John A. and Tavormina, M. Teresa (eds.), THE
YEARBOOK OF LANGLAND STUDIES, vol. 1 (East
Lansing: Colleagues Press, 1987).

Cooper, Duggan, Hill, Lawton, Matheson, Middleton, Revard,
Sherbo, Shoaf, Simpson

YLS 2 (1988)
Alford, John A. and Tavormina, M. Teresa (eds.), THE
YEARBOOK OF LANGLAND STUDIES, vol. 2 (East
Lansing: Colleagues Press, 1988).

Bland, Cable, Davlin, Dolan, Kirk, Tarvers, Von Nolcken

Bibliographical Studies

1. Wells, John Edwin
    A MANUAL OF THE WRITINGS IN MIDDLE
    ENGLISH 1050–1400 (New Haven: Connecticut Academy
    of Arts and Sciences, 1916). With 9 Supplements (to
    1941).

    PP is discussed (pp. 244–67) in Chapter IV, 'Works dealing
    with Contemporary Conditions', under subheading 2, 'Sat-
    ire and Complaint'. There is an account of MSS and of the
    relationship and date of the three versions, a history of the
    authorship controversy (which Wells thinks has been valu-
    able in winning the poem the close study it merits) and a brief
    appreciation of the poem that stresses its dynamic and
    uncontrollable power, its passionate sincerity, its realism, its
    urge to reform. There is a brief bibliography, pp. 800–8.
    [Now superseded by Middleton 1986 [9].]

2. Bloomfield, Morton W.
    'Present State of *Piers Plowman* Studies' *Speculum* 14:2
    (April 1939) 215–32. Reprinted in Blanch (1969) 3–25.

    Sums up thirty-five years of research on *PP*, dealing in turn
    with material on the authorship controversy, on the author's
    name and life and on the influences at work upon L.

3. Hussey, S. S.
    'Eighty Years of *Piers Plowman* Scholarship: A Study of
    Critical Methods' unpublished MA Thesis, University of
    London, 1952.

1

An extremely valuable, informative and thorough critical review of scholarship over eighty years.

4.   Zesmer, David M.
GUIDE TO ENGLISH LITERATURE, FROM
BEOWULF THROUGH CHAUCER AND
MEDIEVAL DRAMA. With bibliographies by Stanley
B. Greenfield (New York: Barnes & Noble, 1961).

Brief account of *PP* (pp. 166–72) and selective bibliography, judiciously annotated (pp. 347–50).

5.   Fowler, David C.
'*Piers Plowman*', in Severs, J. Burke (ed.), RECENT
MIDDLE ENGLISH SCHOLARSHIP AND
CRITICISM: SURVEY AND DESIDERATA
(Pittsburgh: Duquesne UP, 1971) 9–27.

Survey of scholarship from 1940, with some comments that Fowler allows himself as 'an embattled participant in the intense, exhilarating conflict now taking place on the darkling plain of *Piers Plowman* scholarship' (p. 9).

6.   Proppe, Katherine
'*Piers Plowman*: An Annotated Bibliography for 1900–
1968', *Comitatus* 3 (1972) 33–90.

Lists 265 books and articles, divided into three sections (authorship, date, MSS, sources, language; critical studies; dissertations). Selective and inaccurate: it should be recognised that this bibliography is the work of a graduate student and appears in a journal published by graduate students.

7. Colaianne, A. J.
PIERS PLOWMAN: AN ANNOTATED
BIBLIOGRAPHY OF EDITIONS AND CRITICISM,
1550–1977 (Garland Reference Library of the Humanities
vol. 121) (New York: Garland, 1978).

Selective annotated bibliography, fuller for the period after
1875, with items arranged alphabetically by author under
four headings: Authorship (73 items); Editions, Textual
Studies, Selections and Translations (102 items); Critical
Interpretation (449 items); Style, Metre and Language (48
items). Six hundred and seventy-two items in all. Works in
foreign languages and some dissertations are included. A
brief essay summarising the main issues addressed in the
different areas of study introduces each of the four sections,
and an epilogue outlines directions for the future. Non-
evaluative summary is provided, but not for items of lesser
significance; there is ample cross-reference between items.
Less comprehensive in its listings and less full in its annota-
tions than DiMarco [8], but a solid work of bibliographical
scholarship.

Bourquin 1970 [555] has an unusually full bibliography (pp.
825–902) of 923 items, especially good on the intellectual
and theological background to *PP*.

8. DiMarco, Vincent
PIERS PLOWMAN: A REFERENCE GUIDE (Boston:
G. K. Hall, 1982).

A list of writings about *PP*, 1395–1979, arranged chronologically and including early allusions as well as later critical
commentary. Editions are listed but not translations or
selections. Dissertations are included, and there is a Table of
Manuscripts. A brief Introduction surveys the history of the
reception of *PP*, with special attention to the early centuries,
and analyses some major trends in modern criticism. For

each of the 1,007 items listed a quite full précis is given, and cross-reference, where appropriate, indicates the relation of the item to other criticism. There is an extensive index. A monumental work of bibliographical scholarship.

9.   Middleton, Anne
       'XVIII. *Piers Plowman*', in Hartung, Albert E. (ed.), A MANUAL OF THE WRITINGS IN MIDDLE ENGLISH 1050–1500, vol. 7 (New Haven: Connecticut Academy of Arts and Sciences, 1986) 2,211–34, 2,417–43.

In accordance with the usual practice of the revised *Manual* (see Wells 1916 [1]), there is here a brief description of the poem (pp. 2,211–34) and a full bibliography (pp. 2,419–48). The former gives a sharp and succinct account of familiar matters, with much that gives freshness of perspective in what Middleton adds (she is unexpectedly positive in giving reasons for the usefulness of the authorship debate). The latter is superb. It covers material up to 1985, and includes important unpublished dissertations, works in foreign languages, including Japanese and Eastern European languages, general works that have had an important influence on the reception of the poem and notes of selected reviews of major books. Contents of pieces with specific subject-matter are sometimes briefly indicated, and works closely associated are entered under the same heading. The bibliography is set out under twenty headings, which is in many ways useful, but also involves some repetition, arbitrary categorisation and inconsistency. Within the categories, items are listed chronologically, with works by the same author at the appropriate chronological point but with works after the first cited by surname only without initials. Finding out what has been written on a particular subject is easier than looking things up.

Annual bibliographies for 1985, 1986 and 1987 may be found in *YLS* 1 (1987) and 2 (1988)[602].

10. Middleton, Anne
'Introduction: The Critical Heritage', in Alford (1988)
[606] 1–25.

'An attempt to define the main perspectives from which the poem has been approached, and to situate its critical fortunes within some of the broader interpretative agendas in literary, social and intellectual history that have affected its reception' (pp. 1–2). By far the best survey of the course of *PP* criticism. [There are quite full bibliographies to all the essays in this collection: see Alford 1988 [606] and list of Abbreviated References, above.]

Editions (of a whole text); discussions of manuscripts, text and editorial practice

11.   Wright, Thomas (ed.)
THE VISION AND CREED OF PIERS
PLOUGHMAN, 2 vols. (London: Wm. Pickering, 1842;
2nd edn, Library of Old Authors, London: J. R. Smith,
1856).

Text from Trinity College, Cambridge MS B.15.17 of the B
text, printed in short continuously enumerated lines, with
Introduction largely devoted to summary of content and
historical generalisation. There are Notes that Skeat found
very useful, and a glossary somewhat expanded in the second edition. Wright believed that the poem existed in two
versions: he prints extensive variant passages from
Whitaker's edition of the C text in his Notes. The edition is a
good one for its time. The title derives from the inclusion of
the poem of *Piers Ploughman's Creed*, though Wright does
not attribute this poem to L.

12.   Skeat, Revd Walter W.
PARALLEL EXTRACTS FROM FORTY-FIVE
MANUSCRIPTS OF PIERS PLOWMAN, WITH
NOTES UPON THEIR RELATION TO THE
SOCIETY'S THREE-TEXT EDITION OF THIS POEM
(EETS, OS 17) (London: Kegan Paul, Trench, Trübner,
1866; 2nd edn with alterations and additions, 1885).

Skeat prints parallel extracts (generally corresponding to C
IV 77–85) from twenty-nine MSS in order to demonstrate

that the poem exists in three versions, rather than two, as previously thought. In the second edition (in Part IV, Section II of the EETS edition: see below) he adds a further sixteen MSS, to make a total of forty-five.

13. Skeat, Revd Walter W. (ed.)
THE VISION OF WILLIAM CONCERNING PIERS PLOWMAN, TOGETHER WITH VITA DE DOWEL, DOBET ET DOBEST, SECUNDUM WIT ET RESOUN. BY WILLIAM LANGLAND. THE 'VERNON' TEXT: OR TEXT A (EETS, OS 28) (London: Trübner, 1867).

The Introduction describes the poem briefly. The Preface gives an account of the forms of the poem, the MSS of the A text and the editorial method, and offers brief remarks on versification and on the author's name and life. The text is printed from the Vernon MS, with variants from six other MSS. Textual notes.

14. Skeat, Revd Walter W. (ed.)
THE VISION OF WILLIAM, etc. [as above]. IN FOUR PARTS – PART II. THE 'CROWLEY' TEXT; OR TEXT B (EETS, OS 38) (London: Trübner, 1869).

The Preface describes the MSS of B and the method of editing, relates B to A, discusses date and dialect and gives an account of the printed editions. The text is printed from Bodleian Library MS Laud misc. 581, with variants from five other MSS. Textual notes.

15. Skeat, Revd Walter W. (ed.)
THE VISION OF WILLIAM, etc. [as above]. IN FOUR PARTS – PART III. THE 'WHITAKER' TEXT; OR TEXT C. [A second title page announces the inclusion of]

RICHARD THE REDELES, BY THE SAME
AUTHOR. THE CROWNED KING, BY ANOTHER
HAND. (EETS, OS 54) (London: Trübner, 1873;
reprinted, with omissions, 1959).

The very long Preface deals with the form of C and its
relation to A and B, the MSS of C and the method of editing,
the date and dialect of C, and previous editions; also with the
two additional poems. The text is printed from Phillipps MS
8231 (now Huntington Library MS HM 137), with variants
from seven other MSS. Textual notes. In the reprint, super-
vised by J. A. W. Bennett, the Preface is omitted, as well as
the additional poems (the former no longer attributed to L),
and a list of corrections to Skeat's representation of his basic
MS appended (derived from Bennett 1948 [30]).

16.   Skeat, Revd Walter W. (ed.)
THE VISION OF WILLIAM, etc. [as above]. PART IV,
SECTION I – NOTES TO TEXTS A, B, AND C.
(EETS, OS 67) (London: Trübner, 1877).

Extensive explanatory notes, ingeniously conflated so as to
deal with the three texts concurrently; still a mine of information, and in some respects unsuperseded. Index III gives
a list of biblical and other Latin quotations.

17.   Skeat, Revd Walter W. (ed.)
THE VISION OF WILLIAM, etc. [as above]. IN FOUR
PARTS – PART IV (SECTION II). GENERAL
PREFACE, NOTES, AND INDEXES. (EETS, OS 81)
(London: Trübner, 1885).

The title-page is misleading. The Preface is comparatively
short, dealing with the form and meaning of the poem, the
author's name and life, the dialect and metre of the poem,

and with the comments of previous critics. The bulk of the volume is the glossary, still the fullest and best there is. Index VII reprints the revised parallel extracts, etc. of Skeat 1866 [12] above. Index IX prints eighty 'Notices' of *PP* by various authors. There are lists of additions and corrections to previous volumes, and several general indexes.

18. Skeat, Revd Walter W. (ed.)
THE VISION OF WILLIAM CONCERNING PIERS THE PLOWMAN, IN THREE PARALLEL TEXTS, TOGETHER WITH RICHARD THE REDELESS, BY WILLIAM LANGLAND, 2 vols. Vol. I, text; Vol. II, introduction, notes, and glossary (London: OUP, 1886; reprinted 1924; 3rd impression, with addition of Bibliographical Note by J. A. W. Bennett, 1954).

The great two-volume edition in which Skeat brought together the materials from the six volumes published by the EETS, as listed above. The three texts are set out on a single opening, so that the relationships between the texts are made evident to the eye. Only a selection of textual notes from the EETS volumes is given. The Introduction is an updating of the General Preface, with some material added from the earlier Prefaces: it contains accounts of the form and meaning of the poem, of the form and date of the three versions, of the author's name and life, of the dialect and metre of the poem and of the manuscripts and their classification, as well as a description of the printed editions and a few selections from criticisms by previous writers. The notes and glossary are reprinted, with some abridgement, from Part IV of the EETS series. This has been the standard edition of the poem for over a hundred years: it is only now being superseded by the Athlone Press editions (Kane 1960 [36]; Kane–Donaldson 1975 [42]), and that not in every respect. It is still invaluable for comparative study of the three versions of the poem. Skeat's view of the poem, though he generally has little time for critical evaluation, is expressed as clearly in the Preface as anywhere. He sees it principally as a document illustrative of the life and history of L's times, as a protest against tyranny and hypocrisy in Church and State and as a poem of Christian exhortation. He writes with unaccustomed eloquence in rebuke of those who view the ending as pessimistic: 'What other ending can there be? or rather, the end is not yet. We may be defeated, yet not cast down; we may be dying, and yet live. We are still pilgrims upon earth. *That* is the truth which the author's mighty genius would impress upon us in his parting words' (p. lvi). See also Warton 1871 [504] (Skeat's chapter on *PP*) and Skeat 1905 [83].

19.   Chambers, R. W. and Grattan, J. H. G.
'The Text of *Piers Plowman*', *MLR* 4:3 (April 1909) 357–89.

The arguments about misplacements and misunderstandings (Manly 1906 [101]) cannot be resolved while the degree of authority of the received A text (namely the print of the Vernon manuscript in Skeat 1867 [13]) remains unclear. Only when A is edited from better manuscripts will it be possible to talk about stylistic and metrical differences from B and their supposed bearing upon the question of authorship.

20.   Knott, Thomas A.
'An Essay toward the Critical Text of the A-Version of "Piers the Plowman" ', *MP* 12:7 (January 1915) 129–61.

Offers a description of the fourteen MSS of A, and a classification of their family relationships, as they descend from a hypothetical archetype (not the author's copy); criticises (in a remarkably acerbic piece of writing, pp. 150–5) the earlier work on the text of A by Chambers and Grattan 1909 [19], which differs in its conclusions from his, as being based on inadequate scholarship and faulty methods; ends with an analysis of standard types of scribal error and discussion of some individual textual problems.

21. Chambers, R. W. and Grattan, J. H. G.
'The Text of *Piers Plowman*: Critical Methods', *MLR* 11:3 (July 1916) 257–75.

The division of A, B and C was a triumph for the genealogical method, but it is a method that cannot be used to classify the MSS of the three recensions into 'trees'. There is too much contamination and 'mixture' between MSS: the phenomena are so complicated that no possible genealogical tree could express them. This is an answer to the method argued for by Knott 1915 [20] and to his attack on Chambers and Grattan 1909 [19]. The authors comment that they 'are closely engaged on war-work' (p. 264), which seems doubly true.

22. Blackman, Elsie
'Notes on the B-Text MSS. of *Piers Plowman*', *JEGP* 17:4 (October 1918) 489–545.

Chambers and Grattan 1909 [19] show how the establishment of a correct text of A (and of B) is necessary for the resolution of the authorship controversy. Blackman, in a remarkably scholarly and important essay, analyses the relationships of the B text MSS as the first step to establishing the text of B. She confirms in detail the argument of Chambers 1910 [113] that many readings of the accepted B text were corrupt, and were indeed corrupt in the archetypal MS of B (as may be seen from, e.g., agreement of A and C against B). Furthermore, 'the writer of the C-text worked from a B-text MS, which, in certain respects, was better than the ancestor of the extant B-text MSS' (p. 530).

23.   Chambers, R. W. and Grattan, J. H. G.
'The Text of *Piers Plowman*', *MLR* 26:1 (January 1931) 1–
51.

The nature of the archetypes of A, B and C, and the
difficulty of establishing a sound text of *PP*, owing to the
large amount of coincidental variation in the MSS (scribal
freedom in handling the text was encouraged by lack of fixity
of language, and fluidity of metre). But sound texts would
not in any case resolve the authorship question, which must
be settled on other grounds. Meanwhile, the arguments of
Day 1928 [128] concerning differences in the practice of
revision are answered: it is quite possible that L might
sometimes make things worse (as in C), that he might be
working with corrupt exemplars of his own poem, that he
might reintroduce from A material not in B. The arguments
of Day 1922 [127] are demolished: it is demonstrated that the
logical application of her method could equally generate
eight authors for B. A note (pp. 50–1) gives an up-to-date list
of MSS.

24.   Carnegy, F. A. R.
AN ATTEMPT TO APPROACH THE C-TEXT OF
PIERS THE PLOWMAN (London: University of London
Press, 1934).

A University of London MA Thesis of 1923, reprinted
without alteration. The Introduction gives a classification of
C text MSS based on the work of B. F. Allen, concluding
that BL MS Add. 35157 is the best MS of the best group, and
far superior to the MS used by Skeat 1873 [15]. A critical
edition of C II–IV (corresponding to C III–V in Skeat)
follows, with full corpus of variants. [Carnegy was unfortu-
nate in not being able to take advantage of the discovery of
Huntington Library MS HM 143 in 1924.]

25. Chambers, R. W.
     'The Manuscripts of *Piers Plowman* in the Huntington
     Library, and Their Value for Fixing the Text of the
     Poem', *HLB* 8 (1935) 1–25, with a 'Note on the
     Inscription in HM 128' by R. B. Haselden and H. C.
     Schulz, 26–7.

     General remarks on the question of authorship, the text and
     the versions of the poem, and textual criticism. Relates the
     Huntington MSS of B (HM 114, HM 128) and C (HM 137,
     HM 143) to their respective textual traditions; concludes
     that HM 143, which Skeat (who used HM 137 as his copy-
     text for C) did not know, is clearly the most important
     manuscript of C and the one to be used as the basis for a
     critical edition.

26. Chambers, R. W. (Introduction by)
     PIERS PLOWMAN. THE HUNTINGTON LIBRARY
     MANUSCRIPT (HM 143) REPRODUCED IN
     PHOTOSTAT. With an introduction by R. W. Chambers
     and technical examination by R. B. Haselden and H. C.
     Schulz (San Marino, California: Henry E. Huntington
     Library and Art Gallery, 1936).

     Chambers declares MS HM 143, unknown until 1924, to be
     the best extant MS of the C text, and the one that should be
     used in a future edition.

27. Coffman, George R.
     'The Present State of a Critical Edition of *Piers Plowman*',
     Speculum 20:4 (October 1945) 482–3.

     Coffman prints here a letter from J. H. G. Grattan which
     explains why the long-awaited A text edited by himself and
     R. W. Chambers has not appeared (the decision not to print
     all three texts parallel, Chambers' death, his own ill-health),

the further problems caused by the war ('The bulk of the *Piers Plowman* material is, for the duration of the War in Europe, stored underground in Central Wales', p. 483) and the hopes for the future (they sound rather desperate). Coffman adds an interesting note on the present state of *PP* in the literary world at large, quoting from a review of the Wells translation of the poem by D. V. Wineman in the *New York Times Book Review* of 2 September 1945, p. 2: 'Unlike Chaucer, *Piers Plowman* has small value as a literary work. It is a piece of popular literature that the people have long since outgrown. It remains a literary milestone, to be revered historically; but like most milestones, it is irrevocably dead'.

28.   Grattan, J. H. G.
'The Text of *Piers Plowman*: Critical Lucubrations with Special Reference to the Independent Substitution of Similars', *SP* 44:4 (October 1947) 593–604.

Analyses and classifies examples of this kind of scribal variation in eight MSS of A, showing how it is due to standard kinds of coincidental error rather than to contamination, with the consequence that this has for the organisation of MSS into families.

29.   Kane, George
'*Piers Plowman*: Problems and Methods of Editing the B-Text', *MLR* 43:1 (January 1948) 1–25.

The authorship controversy has distracted attention from the need to establish the text. The special problem of B is the corruption of the archetype and the consequent need to collate the C archetype.

30.   Bennett, J. A. W.
'A New Collation of a *Piers Plowman* Manuscript (HM
137)', *MÆ* 17 (1948) 21–31.

Collation of Skeat's text of C against his copy-text, Huntington Library MS HM 137 (formerly Phillipps 8231). Skeat
was very accurate.

31.   Kane, George
'The Textual Criticism of Piers Plowman', *TLS* (17 March
1950) 176.

Objects to an anonymous review of Donaldson 1949 [521]
that viewed the biographical references in the poem as
wholly conventional, and that suggested that the classification of the fifty-two MSS into three versions had something
arbitrary and artificial about it and took no account of the
influence of oral transmission. On the contrary, texts in MSS
of the poem that differ in 'shape' from A, B and C are clearly
scribal in origin. There is no evidence of oral transmission.
[The reviewer has a reply in which he maintains his position.]

32.   Fowler, D. C.
'Contamination in Manuscripts of the A-Text of *Piers
Plowman*', *PMLA* 66:4 (June 1951) 495–504.

Determination of the relationships of MSS must make al-
lowance for contamination, i.e. importation into a MS copied from one type of exemplar of readings derived, by
collation and correction in the exemplar, from another.
There are examples in A.

33.   Brooks, E. St. John
'The *Piers Plowman* Manuscripts in Trinity College,
Dublin', *The Library*, 5th series, 6:3/4 (December 1951)
141–53.

Trinity College, Dublin MS D. 4. 12, containing an A text, probably came from the library of Archbishop Ussher. The provenance of MS D. 4. 1, containing a C text and the famous memorandum recording detail of the poet's parentage, is unknown: it is not (*pace* Cargill 1935 [131]) the MS of *PP* known to have been in Ireland in the early fifteenth century in the possession of Walter de Brugge. Brooks gives an account of the biographical memorandum in the context of the brief series of annals that precede it in the MS, in the same hand.

34.   Knott, Thomas A, and Fowler, David C. (eds.)
PIERS THE PLOWMAN. A CRITICAL EDITION OF
THE A-VERSION (Baltimore: The Johns Hopkins Press,
1952).

Begun by Knott in 1907, left off after 1915, and completed by Fowler. Text based on Trinity College, Cambridge MS R.3.14, with select variants from sixteen MSS; editorial method criticised by Kane (Kane 1960 [36]) for use of recension. The Introduction presents but does not press the argument that the first part of A (to VIII 131) is by a different author from the rest of A, and that neither of these two authors was responsible for B, which is regarded as rambling and confused. There is also a list of MSS, an account of date, dialect, metre and textual matters and a long section on historical background (A being regarded as chiefly 'a satire of contemporary conditions', p. 56). Explanatory notes (brief), textual notes (very long), and glossary. [The edition has suffered because of the view that the editors' opinions on authorship are eccentric. The explanation of editorial practice is very brief.]

Reviews: F. Mossé, *EA* 6:1 (February 1953) 56–7.
R. Quirk, *JEGP* 52:3 (July 1953) 400–1.

35.   Donaldson, E. Talbot
'MSS R and F in the B-Tradition of Piers Plowman'.
*Transactions of the Connecticut Academy of Arts and
Sciences* 39 (September 1955) 177–212.

MSS R (Bodleian Rawlinson Poet. 38) and F (Corpus Christi
College, Oxford 201) seem to belong to a separate textual
tradition of B, and to be in some respects superior to other
MSS. After a lengthy discussion, Donaldson concludes that
'RF represent a stage in the B-text slightly older than that
represented by the rest of the B-MSS', in other words, a
version of the poem intermediate between A and B. We
know that L was constantly revising his poem: 'I sometimes
wonder whether the C-text, the B-text, and even the A-text
are not merely historical accidents, haphazard milestones in
the history of a poem that was begun but never finished,
photographs that caught a static image of a living organism at
a given but not necessarily significant moment of time' (p.
211). [But cf. Kane–Donaldson 1975 [42].]

36.   Kane, George (ed.)
PIERS PLOWMAN: THE A VERSION. WILL'S
VISIONS OF PIERS PLOWMAN AND DO-WELL
(University of London: The Athlone Press, 1960).

The first volume of the critical edition of the three versions of
the poem done under the general editorship of Kane (see
Kane–Donaldson 1975 [42]; the edition of C, and the volume
of apparatus, are still awaited). The text is based on Trinity
College, Cambridge MS R.3.14, which is shown to be much
superior to the base MS chosen by Skeat 1867 [13]. A full
corpus of variants from all known MSS (with the exception
noted, p. 14) is provided, and there is extensive emendation
of a radical kind, based on the principles outlined in the
Introduction. This Introduction (pp. 1–172), a monument of
textual scholarship, contains a full description of seventeen
MSS, an account of the integrity of the A version, a classi-

fication of the MSS and a description of editorial resources and methods. Kane's principal argument, now widely accepted, is that 'recension is not a practicable method' (p. 115) for the editor of a vernacular poem so subject to scribal corruption and interference and therefore to convergent variation. He rejects the arguments of Knott and Fowler for the genealogical method. He proposes that each variant must be considered on its merits, and on the basis of an intimate knowledge of the poet's way of writing and a systematic understanding of the types of error introduced by scribes. His statement of method marks an epoch in the history of the theory and practice of textual criticism, not only in relation to *PP*. His text supersedes Skeat.

Reviews: J. A. W. Bennett, *RES*, NS 14:53 (January 1963) 68–71.
J. B. Bessinger, *JEGP* 60:3 (July 1961) 571–6.
M. W. Bloomfield, *Speculum* 36:1 (January 1961) 133–7.
N. Davis, *NQ* 8 (206):3 (March 1961) 115–16.
A. I. Doyle, *ES* 43:1 (1962) 55–9.
D. C. Fowler, *MP* 58:3 (February 1961) 212–14.
P. M. Kean, *Library*, 5th series, 6:3 (September 1961) 218–24.
J. Lawlor, *MLR* 56:2 (April 1961) 243–5.
G. Mathew, *MÆ* 30:2 (1961) 126–8.
T. F. Mustanoja, *Anglia* 80:1/2 (1962) 172–6.
C. L. Wrenn, *MLN* 76:8 (December 1961) 856–63.

37.   Russell, G. H.
'The Evolution of a Poem: Some Reflections on the Textual Tradition of *Piers Plowman*', *Arts* (University of Sydney, Faculty of Arts) 2 (1962) 33–46.

All MSS of B are corrupt: the archetype may derive from a revision of A not authorised for circulation by L, who subsequently embarked on a further revision, which he did not finish. The retention of scribal errors from B in C may be due to the fact that he died in the midst of C, and it was prepared for publication by someone else. Russell will edit C from HM 143, a MS much superior to that used by Skeat.

38. Russell, G. H. and Nathan, Venetia
'A *Piers Plowman* Manuscript in the Huntington Library',
HLQ 26:2 (February 1963) 119–30.

Hitherto thought to be a corrupt text of B, Huntington Library MS HM 114 actually contains 'a carefully edited version of the poem made by one who had before him all three texts of the poem and who sought to produce from their conflation a composite version which would incorporate what he regarded as the best material from all three' (p. 119).

39. Kane, George
'Conjectural Emendation', in Pearsall, D. A. and Waldron, R. A. (eds.), MEDIEVAL LITERATURE AND CIVILIZATION: STUDIES IN MEMORY OF G. N. GARMONSWAY (University of London: The Athlone Press, 1969) 155–69. Reprinted in Kleinhenz, Christopher (ed.), MEDIEVAL MANUSCRIPTS AND TEXTUAL CRITICISM (North Carolina Studies in the Romance Languages and Literature, vol. 173: Symposia, No. 4) (Chapel Hill: University of North Carolina, Department of Romance Languages, 1976) 211–25.

Conjectural emendation (incorporation in the edited text of a reading not evidenced in any MS) is not a form of self-indulgence and unrestrained subjectivity on the editor's part. It is a necessary activity of editing, not capable of certainty but not for that reason to be eschewed. Editing a poem like *PP* that exists in many copies, where classification

of typical error makes reconstruction of the archetype possible, affords 'an ideal occasion for reexamining the relation
between the theory of conjectural emendation and its practice' (p. 225).

40.   Russell, G. H.
'Some Aspects of the Process of Revision in *Piers
Plowman*', in Hussey (1969) 27–49.

There are three and only three versions of the poem; blurring of this fact in the MSS is due to scribes. The C revision
(the chief subject of the essay), based on a scribal copy of B –
though one better than any extant MS – is not thoroughgoing
like B's revision of A, but grows out from local areas of
dissatisfaction. Though intensely engaged and often min-
utely attentive, it is sporadic and unfinished, and B XIX–XX
are not touched.

41.   Poole, Eric
'The Computer in Determining Stemmatic Relationships',
Computers and the Humanities 8:4 (July 1974) 207–16.

Stemmatic relationships do of course exist, though the practical difficulties of recovering them, given the frequency of
coincidental variation, may be great. Computer-aided analysis of masses of individually trivial data enables the 'signal'
of the true stemma to be distinguished from the 'noise' or
'static' of coincidental variation. The theory is tested with A
V 105–58.

42.   Kane, George and Donaldson, E. Talbot (eds.)
PIERS PLOWMAN: THE B VERSION. WILL'S
VISIONS OF PIERS PLOWMAN, DO-WELL, DO-
BETTER AND DO-BEST (University of London: The
Athlone Press, 1975).

The second volume of the critical edition of the three versions of the poem done under the general editorship of Kane (see Kane 1960 [36]). The text is based on Trinity College, Cambridge MS B.15.17, with a full corpus of variants from all known MSS (with the two exceptions noted, pp. 14–15), and extensive emendation of a radical kind. The Introduction (pp. 1–224) contains a description of eighteen MSS, a classification of the MS, an account of the archetypal B MS and of the C reviser's B MS, and description of the editor's practice in the editing of B. As in A (Kane 1960 [36]), recension is rejected, and each variant is considered on its merits. The situation with B is complicated, however, by the corrupt nature of the scribal archetype of all extant copies, and by the fact that C, which might be thought to be a source of good readings in passages that correspond closely, was itself done from a poor copy of B. In these circumstances, the editors resort to a more than usually radical practice of textual reconstruction. Their assumptions about the regularity of L's alliterative practice, and their use of these assumptions as a means for detecting inauthentic readings, have not met with universal favour. All the material for criticising their editorial methods is made available, of course, by the editors in what is by any account a monumental work of textual scholarship, but there has been criticism of the lack of relation between the text, with its corpus of variants, and the explanation of editorial practice in emendation in the Introduction. In the absence of textual notes, the reason for any particular emendation has to be sought laboriously in the thickets of lists of examples in the Introduction. For such reasons, the Kane–Donaldson edition of B has not established itself with quite the authority of the Kane edition of A.

Reviews: J. A. Alford, *Speculum* 52:4 (October 1977) 1,002–5.
J. A. W. Bennett, *RES*, NS 28:111 (July 1977) 323–6.
G. Bourquin, *EA* 30:4 (October 1977) 474–5.

J. Burrow, *TLS* (21 November 1975) 1380.
B. Cottle, *JEGP* 75:4 (October 1976) 589–92.
D. C. Fowler, *YES* 7 (1977) 23–42.
D. Pearsall, *MÆ* 46:2 (1977) 278–85.
E. G. Stanley, *NQ* 23 (221):10 (October 1976) 435–47.
T. Turville-Petre, *SN* 49:1 (1977) 153–5.

See also the comments of Anne Hudson, 'Middle English', in Rigg, A. G. (ed.), EDITING MEDIEVAL TEXTS ENGLISH, FRENCH, AND LATIN, WRITTEN IN ENGLAND, Papers given at the Twelfth Annual Conference on Editorial Problems, University of Toronto, 1976 (New York: Garland, 1977), pp. 34–57 (pp. 41–5).

43.   Pearsall, Derek (ed.)
PIERS PLOWMAN, BY WILLIAM LANGLAND. AN EDITION OF THE C-TEXT (York Medieval Texts, second series) (London: Edward Arnold, 1978; Berkeley and Los Angeles: University of California Press, 1979).

Based on Huntington Library MS HM 143, with record of all departures from the base MS, and selected variants from four other MSS. There is a short Introduction dealing with the contents, nature and form of the poem, with its historical and literary background, and with the character of the C text and of the edition; very extensive notes (the main feature of the edition), with translation of difficult passages and much cross-reference to draw out the complex patterns of internal allusion within the poem; and a full glossary.

Reviews: S. A. Barney, *Speculum* 56:1 (January 1981) 161–5.
D. Fowler, *Review* 2 (1980) 211–69 (see below).
D. Fowler, *YES* 11 (1981) 224–6.

N. Jacobs, *English* 28:131:2 (Summer 1979) 151–60.
A. V. C. Schmidt, *NQ* 27 (225):2 (April 1980) 102–10.
T. Turville-Petre, *RES*, NS 30:120 (October 1979) 454–6.

44. Schmidt, A. V. C. (ed.)
WILLIAM LANGLAND, THE VISION OF PIERS
PLOWMAN. A CRITICAL EDITION OF THE
B-TEXT (Everyman's Library) (London: J. M. Dent;
New York: E. P. Dutton, 1978).

Critical text based on Trinity College, Cambridge MS B.15.17, the same as that used by Kane–Donaldson 1975 [42], with textual notes recording departures from the base MS. Practice in emendation is much more conservative than that of Kane–Donaldson, though Schmidt uses their edition extensively. There is no glossary: hard words are glossed at the side of the page, and difficult passages translated at the foot. There are two parts to the extensive Commentary, the first Textual and Lexical, the second Literary and Historical. A concise Introduction deals with L's poetic excellence (emotional range rather than visualising power), the structure of the poem (a completely integrated whole, based on the theme of the quest and on the dramatic urgency of the sequence of dreams) and its theme (to show the purpose and value of life, for the individual and the community, in the search for grace and spiritual truth through the power of the Incarnation), as well as textual matters. The volume is a marvel of compression.

Reviews: S. A. Barney, *Speculum* 56:1 (January 1981) 161–5.
D. Fowler, *Review* 2 (1980) 211–69 (see below).
N. Jacobs, *English* 28:131:2 (Summer 1979) 151–60.

T. Turville-Petre, *RES*, NS 30:120 (October 1979) 454–6.

45.   Fowler, David C.
'Editorial "Jamming": Two New Editions of *Piers Plowman*', *Review* 2 (1980) 211–69.

An enormously long review of the editions of Pearsall 1978 [43] and Schmidt 1978 [44], done in the form of a passage-by-passage commentary on each edition. The review is a work of meticulous care and great erudition, and displays an unrivalled knowledge of the poem. Sometimes the editors are blamed for not being more sceptical, like Fowler himself, about the hypothesis of single authorship.

46.   Pearsall, Derek
'The "Ilchester" Manuscript of *Piers Plowman*', *NM* 82:2 (1981) 181–93.

University of London Library MS [S.L.] V.88, generally a very good MS of C, contains an unusual version of the Prologue, A with C text additions and material also interpolated from C IX. One of the C text additions is in a textual form that has been argued to represent a version of the author's original. This essay argues that this passage, like the reorganised Prologue as a whole, is the work of a scribe (a Langland enthusiast).

47.   Russell, George H.
'The Poet as Reviser: The Metamorphosis of the Confession of the Seven Deadly Sins in *Piers Plowman*', in Carruthers and Kirk (1982) 53–65.

Russell shows, in an analysis of the Confession scenes, the truth of the position he has stated before: that the C revision is 'selective, sporadic and local' (p. 56), and that the reviser's activity is 'unmistakeably authorial' (p. 62).

48.   Rigg, A. G. and Brewer, Charlotte (eds.)
WILLIAM LANGLAND, PIERS PLOWMAN: THE Z
VERSION (Studies and Texts 59) (Toronto: Pontifical
Institute of Mediaeval Studies, 1983).

Bodleian Library MS Bodley 851 contains a version of a portion of A quite different from any other, with many unique passages, lines and readings as well as extensive omissions. It was long dismissed (e.g. by Kane–Donaldson 1975 [42], pp. 14–15) as a worthless product of scribal corruption, interpolation and contamination. The editors present the case that Z (the sigil long and, as it turns out, felicitously ascribed to the MS) 'represents a version of the poem *anterior* to the A-text' (p. 1). They also present an edition of the relevant portion of Z, with variations from A in bold type, and with extensive textual notes. The case is based on the early date of the Z portion of the MS, the 'Langlandian' quality of the passages and lines unique to Z and the general closeness of Z in language and style to L's way of writing. [Most would accept that the editors' case is worth making, though Kane 1985 [55] is bitterly dismissive.]

Reviews: R. Adams, *SAC* 7 (1985) 233–7.
G. Kane, *Speculum* 60:4 (October 1985) 910–30
(see below).
D. Pearsall, *Archiv* 222:137:1 (1985) 181–4.
H. White, *MÆ* 53:2 (1984) 290–5.

49.   Schmidt, A. V. C.
'The Authenticity of the Z Text of *Piers Plowman*: A
Metrical Examination', *MÆ* 53:2 (1984) 295–300.

Compares lines and half-lines unique to Z with a scheme of
ten types of line derived from analysis of all lines in A, B and
C, and finds confirmation for the hypothesis that Z is an
authorial draft.

50.   Pearsall, Derek
'Texts, Textual Criticism, and Fifteenth Century
Manuscript Production', in Yeager, Robert F. (ed.),
FIFTEENTH-CENTURY STUDIES: RECENT ESSAYS
(Hamden, Connecticut: Archon Books, 1984) 121–36.

Argues for closer attention to MSS (including those of *PP*),
even those declared to be textually valueless, for purposes of
understanding the reception of the poem.

51.   Brewer, Charlotte
'Z and the A- B- and C-Texts of *Piers Plowman*' *MÆ* 53:2
(1984) 194–219.

Follows up Rigg–Brewer 1983 [48] with some comments on
the way comparison of other versions with Z (which is
argued to be an early authorial draft) throws light on L's
creative processes, e.g., in the shifting roles of Meed and
Conscience in relation to each other and in the increasing
drama and vividness in the portrayal of the Sins.

52.   Adams, Robert
'The Reliability of the Rubrics in the B-Text of Piers
Plowman' *MÆ* 54:2 (1985) 208–31.

The divisions in the poem in Skeat's edition (*Visio*, *Vita de
Dowel*, *Dobet*, *Dobest*), made on the basis of MS rubrics,
have exercised considerable influence on interpretation of
the structure of the poem. Yet they are almost certainly
scribal, and at times go against what L himself seems con-

cerned to say (e.g. a man cannot be content with less than his best). Charts give a complete list of passus headings and explicits from all B MSS.

53.   Patterson, Lee
'The Logic of Textual Criticism and the Way of Genius: The Kane–Donaldson *Piers Plowman* in Historical Perspective', in McGann (1985) 55–91. Reprinted in Patterson, Lee, NEGOTIATING THE PAST: THE HISTORICAL UNDERSTANDING OF MEDIEVAL LITERATURE (Madison: University of Wisconsin Press, 1987).

The distinction traditional in textual criticism between external evidence (identification and classification of variants) as 'objective' and internal evidence (interpretation of the quality of readings) as 'subjective' needs to be questioned, and the Kane–Donaldson edition of the B text provides an opportunity to do so. In fact, even the most 'scientific' analysis of variants involves acts of subjective interpretation constantly. In abandoning recension (because of the influence of coincidental error in obscuring MS affiliations), Kane–Donaldson expose fully the subjective nature of the judgements that are made in determining the originality of readings (informed though they are by knowledge of scribal habit and authorial practice). Their edition is entirely consistent with their principles. But the premises on which they base their judgements of individual readings are themselves open to question, being inspired by essentially 'Romantic' notions of poetic genius, and of the intuition that recognises that genius; of poetic meaning as somehow graspable as a mysterious essence beyond words; of poetic style as essentially 'difficult' in its fullness of meaning. Their intuitional and idealised notion of the existence of the literary text is thus, like that of the New Criticism, radically unhistorical, and also resembles that of Lachmann, who was likewise committed to an idea of the text as transhistorically stable and permanent. All serious editing must have the same ambition; the only alternative is not editing, unless the assumptions of textual transcendence are questioned, as they might be by a deconstructionist critique.

54.   Pearsall, Derek
'Editing Medieval Texts: Some Developments and Some Problems', in McGann (1985) 92–106.

The nature of a poem like *PP* may be obscured by modern editors in their search for a definitive text. The poem was being continually revised, and the surviving MSS may well bear witness to the existence of more stages in the process of revision than the traditionally accepted three versions.

55.   Kane, George
'The "Z Version" of *Piers Plowman*', *Speculum* 60:4 (October 1985) 910–30.

A very long review of Rigg–Brewer 1983 [48]. 'What they put forward is actually not a hypothesis in any strict sense, but an assemblage of arguments, linked by iterative assertion, in support of a poorly based and admittedly subjective literary opinion' (pp. 910–11). Kane deals with these arguments in turn, dismissing first the editors' claim that the Z portion of MS Bodley 851 is unusually early, and that the language and style of material peculiar to Z is characteristically 'Langlandian'. Kane argues that variant readings of A in Z are overwhelmingly scribal in origin, and show it to belong to a poor textual tradition of A and one well down the line of transmission. Variants from non-A tradition are very frequently versions of lines or phrases in B or C, poorly remembered from bad copies. As a whole, Z is confused and makes poor sense, and the excuse that this is because it is a draft begs the question. Passages and lines unique to Z are not, despite the editors' assertion, of Langlandian quality (three passages are analysed in detail). Kane ends with a 'profile' of the Z-writer, and detailed criticisms of the text of the Z edition and of the interpretations offered in the notes.

56. Doyle, A. I.
'Remarks on Surviving Manuscripts of *Piers Plowman*', in Kratzmann and Simpson (1986) 35–48.

Perhaps twenty of the fifty-four MSS, complete and incomplete, date from the fourteenth century; they are of B and, especially, C rather than A. MSS with S.W. Midland characteristics may well have been copied in London. Discusses, in turn, MSS of A, B, C, and AC conflated, and ends with comparisons of *PP* MSS with MSS of those other works to which they bear the most resemblance.

57. Duggan, Hoyt N.
'The Authenticity of the Z-text of *Piers Plowman*: Further Notes on Metrical Evidence', *MÆ* 56:1 (1987) 25–45.

Duggan restates here the rules for alliterative verse that he has derived from analysis of 12,806 lines from fifteen alliterative poems. He finds that L and the author of *Pierce the Ploughman's Creed*, alone among alliterative poets, do not observe his fifth rule (in the b-verse, 'if two or three dips are filled, only one can have two or more syllables, but either the first or the second dip must have two or three syllables', pp. 32–3). The unusual metrical pattern allowed thereby appears in the unique lines of the Z version, offering further evidence that these lines are by L. Duggan accepts the parallel but different arguments of Schmidt 1984 [49], with some discussion.

58. Green, Richard Firth
'The Lost Exemplar of the Z-Text of *Piers Plowman* and its 20-line Pages', *MÆ* 56:2 (1987) 307–10.

Some of the unique passages in Z were explained by Kane (in Kane–Donaldson 1975 [42], cf. Kane 1985 [55]) as due to memorial reconstruction by a scribe of passages of about twenty or forty lines presumably lost from or defaced in an exemplar containing that number of lines per side or leaf. Green demonstrates that this explanation is unsatisfactory. The hypothesis of Rigg–Brewer 1983 [48] thus continues to demand serious consideration.

59.   Scase, Wendy
'Two *Piers Plowman* C-Text Interpolations: Evidence for a Second Textual Tradition', *NQ* 34 (232):4 (December 1987) 456–63.

There are passages in the Ilchester MS (see Pearsall 1981 [46]) and in HM 114 that contain unique material on false hermits and *lolleres* (usually found in C IX) and unique versions of the Ophni and Phinees episode in the C Prologue. The texts of these two passages are closely related and clearly go back to a single exemplar. They therefore give witness to a second textual tradition of C, and a further indication of the revision to which the poem continued to be subject even in its latest state.

60.   Russell, G. H.
'The Imperative of Revision in the C Version of *Piers Plowman*', in Kennedy, Waldron and Wittig (1988) 233–44.

Concentrates on the revision of the Pardon episode in C IX (especially 1–61), showing how L, though not revising the whole poem systematically, works very closely here with passages dealing with sensitive issues, and how he tries to clarify the obscurities of the scribally transmitted text of B he is using. The reviser is clearly the same person as the author of A and B, and his revisions have the stamp of authority.

61. Fisher, John H.
'*Piers Plowman* and the Chancery Tradition', in Kennedy, Waldron and Wittig (1988) 267–78.

A study of the B MSS of *PP* shows that script and spelling are increasingly adapted to the standard practice of Chancery English.

62. Kane, George
'The Text', in Alford (1988) 175–200.

An account of early study of the text; of the evidence for the existence of three versions of the poem, and of their manuscript traditions; of the nature of scribal activity in the MSS; of the textual problem; and of the character of textual criticism. There is a list of the fifty-two MSS, pp. 178–80.

63. Clopper, Lawrence M.
'Langland's Markings for the Structure of *Piers Plowman*', *MP* 85:3 (February 1988) 245–55.

Argues from the MSS of A, AC and C (cf. Adams 1985 [52], on B) that L intended a quadripartite division for his poem (*Visio*, and *Vita* of Dowel, Dobet and Dobest), and that the consecutive passus numbering system is scribal, having been introduced by the scribes of B.

Editions of portions of the poem, and of extracts

64. Skeat, Revd Walter W. (ed.)
THE VISION OF WILLIAM CONCERNING PIERS
THE PLOWMAN (Oxford: Clarendon Press, 1869;
frequently revised, the latest revision being the 10th edn,
1923, frequently reprinted).

This, as the title implies, is an edition of Prologue and Passus
I-VII only, the text taken from the edition of the complete B
text that Skeat published in the same year. Introduction,
notes and glossary took material from the EETS series of
editions as they progressed, with abridgements and additions thought suitable for the students to whom the edition
was directed. It is a work of great importance in the history
of *Piers Plowman* studies, since it shaped the perception of
the poem for generations of readers (until superseded by
Bennett 1972 [77]), particularly in fostering the view of the
poem as primarily a work of social commentary.

65. Davis, J. F. (ed.)
LANGLAND, PIERS PLOWMAN. PROLOGUE AND
PASSUS I–VII: TEXT B (The University Tutorial Series)
(London: W. B. Clive, University Tutorial Press, 1896;
2nd edn revised by E. S. Olszewska, 1928).

Uses the same MS as Skeat 1869 [14], and is deeply indebted
to Skeat for Introduction, notes and glossary. Certain indel-
icacies are silently removed, the book being 'intended primarily for university students' (p. v), and some nonsense
made, e.g. of the description of the Sins. The revision is

chiefly concerned to introduce mention of Manly's theory of multiple authorship.

66.   Cook, Albert Stanburrough (ed.)
      A LITERARY MIDDLE ENGLISH READER (Boston: Ginn & Co., 1915).

      Extracts from Skeat's text of B, portions of Prologue, III, V, and VI (pp. 334–52).

67.   Sisam, Kenneth (ed.)
      FOURTEENTH CENTURY VERSE AND PROSE (Oxford: Clarendon Press, 1921; frequently reprinted).

      Extracts, B VI (complete) and C VI 1–104, with excellent notes and glossary (the latter by J. R. R. Tolkien).

68.   Patterson, R. F. (ed.)
      SIX CENTURIES OF ENGLISH LITERATURE (London and Glasgow: Blackie, 1933).

69.   Auden, W. H. and Pearson, Norman Holmes (eds.)
      MEDIEVAL AND RENAISSANCE POETS, LANGLAND TO SPENSER (Viking Portable Poets of the English Language) (New York: Viking Press, 1950).

      Extracts reprinted from Skeat's edition: part of B Prologue and C XXI (the Harrowing of Hell), and snippets from C II, X, XIV.

70.   Mossé, Fernand
      A HANDBOOK OF MIDDLE ENGLISH, trans. Walker, James A. (Baltimore: The Johns Hopkins Press, 1952; originally published in French, 1949).

Extracts from A Prologue, B Prologue, B V and C VI, with headnote and notes.

71. Ford, Boris (ed.)
     THE AGE OF CHAUCER (Pelican Guide to English
     Literature I) (London: Penguin Books, 1954). Revised
     edn., MEDIEVAL LITERATURE, PART ONE:
     CHAUCER AND THE ALLITERATIVE TRADITION
     (The New Pelican Guide to English Literature I)
     (Harmondsworth: Penguin Books, 1982).

     Includes, in the 'Anthology of Medieval Poems' edited by
     Francis Berry, B XVIII of *PP* (pp. 334–50), copied from
     Skeat 1886 [18], with minor modernizations. The Anthology
     in the revised edition, edited by Thorlac Turville-Petre,
     includes C V 1–104 and C XX, from Pearsall 1978 [43]. [See
     also Traversi 1936 [433].]

72. Kaiser, Rolf
     MEDIEVAL ENGLISH: AN OLD ENGLISH AND
     MIDDLE ENGLISH ANTHOLOGY (Berlin: Kaiser,
     1958; translated, revised and enlarged from the original
     German edn. of 1954).

     Extracts from C VI, B Prologue, II, V, C XI, XXI, XXIII
     (pp. 305–21), with scattered extracts elsewhere, under
     'thematic' headings, from B II (p. 569) and B V (pp. 533–5).

73. Wilcockson, Colin (ed.)
     SELECTIONS FROM PIERS PLOWMAN (English
     Classics, new series) (London: Macmillan, 1965).

     Extensive extracts from B, excellently annotated and
     introduced.

74. Salter, Elizabeth and Pearsall, Derek (eds.)
PIERS PLOWMAN. Selections from the C-text (York
Medieval Texts) (London: Edward Arnold, 1967).

An edition of selections from the C text, in all over a third of
the poem, based on MS HM 143 (see Chambers 1935, 1936
[25, 26]), with select variants from two MSS, linking commentary, full annotation and a glossary. The important
Introduction (by Salter) is long (pp. 1–58), and deals particularly well with the allegorical procedures of the poem,
especially the 'figural' approach (see Salter 1968 [391]), and
with its form and structure. It is, all in all, the best introduction to the poem for the student and general reader.

75. Haskell, Ann S. (ed.)
A MIDDLE ENGLISH ANTHOLOGY (Garden City:
Anchor Books, 1969).

76. Sisam, Celia and Kenneth (eds.)
THE OXFORD BOOK OF MEDIEVAL ENGLISH
VERSE (Oxford: Clarendon Press, 1970).

Extracts, with some regularisation and modernisation of
spelling, and page-glosses: A Prologue 1–109, C I 165–215,
C VI 1–104, C VII 350–97, C X 71–95, C XX 168–215. A is
edited from Trinity College, Cambridge MS R.3.14, and C
from the 1936 facsimile of Huntington Library MS HM 143.

77. Bennett, J. A. W. (ed.)
LANGLAND, PIERS PLOWMAN. PROLOGUE AND
PASSUS I–VII OF THE B TEXT AS FOUND IN
BODLEIAN MS. LAUD MISC.581 (Clarendon Medieval
and Tudor Series) (Oxford: Clarendon Press, 1972).

Designed to supersede Skeat's century-old students' edition
of 1869 [64] of the same part of B, edited from the same MS,

with a select Table of Variants, brief Preface, very extensive notes, and glossary. The notes (pp. 79–226) are in the best tradition of Bennett's scholarship, alert to every allusion and backed by a comprehensive knowledge of every aspect of the poem's background.

78.   Dunn, Charles W. and Byrnes, Edward T. (eds.)
MIDDLE ENGLISH LITERATURE (New York: Harcourt Brace, 1973).

Text from Skeat of B Prologue, I, V, VII, XVIII.228–431, XIX, with side-glosses. A passus is referred to as a canto throughout.

79.   Brook, Stella (ed.)
LANGLAND, PIERS PLOWMAN. SELECTIONS FROM THE B-TEXT (Manchester Medieval Classics) (Manchester: Manchester UP; New York: Barnes & Noble, 1975).

Extracts from MS Laud misc.581 of B (the MS used by Skeat), in four sections, consisting of parts of: (A) Prologue, I, II (B) V (C) XIII–XV (D) XVIII–XX. Modern prose translation on facing page. Brief, serviceable Introduction, and notes.

80.   Burrow, J. (ed.)
ENGLISH VERSE 1300–1500 (London: Longman, 1977).

Text of B VI and XVIII edited from Bodleian MS Laud misc.581, with page-glosses and excellent brief notes and Introduction (pp. 105–45).

81.   Garbáty, Thomas J. (ed.)
MEDIEVAL ENGLISH LITERATURE (Lexington and
Toronto: D. C. Heath, 1984).

Extensive extracts from Skeat's edition of the *Visio*: B
Prologue and II, C, VI (apologia), B V, C VIII–IX and end
of X.

Translations

82. Converse, Florence
LONG WILL (Everyman's Library No. 328) (London: J.
M. Dent, 1908; first published Boston: Houghton-Mifflin,
1903).

William Langland is an important character in this historical
romance, and several lines from his poem are quoted in
verse translation (pp. 7–8, 55, 86, 88, 122, etc.).

83. Skeat, The Revd Professor (trans.)
THE VISION OF PIERS THE PLOWMAN BY
WILLIAM LANGLAND DONE INTO MODERN
ENGLISH (The King's Classics, ed. Professor Gollancz)
(London: Alexander Moring, The De La Mare Press,
1905).

Tactful modernisation of B Prologue and I–VII, following
the verse-form, with the minimum of change. Brief Introduction and notes. Skeat's view of translation, as well as of
the poem generally, is interestingly alluded to in the final
sentence of the Introduction: 'I believe it will be found that,
even in the poverty of its modern dress, the poem is of
considerable interest as a historical document, as a comment
on the times, and, perhaps, to some extent, as a literary
work' (p. xxv).

84. Burrell, Arthur (trans.)
PIERS PLOWMAN. THE VISION OF A PEOPLE'S

CHRIST, BY WILLIAM LANGLAND. A VERSION
FOR THE MODERN READER (Everyman's Library
No. 571) (London: J. M. Dent; New York: E. P. Dutton,
1912; reprinted 1931).

Simplified, quite free verse translation, with half-lines dis-
tinctly separated, of B, conflated with material from C. The
Visio (Prologue and I–VII) is fully represented, but thereafter only occasional passages are translated, except for B
XVIII, which is there in full. The brief Introduction and
concluding 'Comment', as well as the translator's subtitle,
represent very clearly the view of the poem held in the early
years of the century, influenced by Jusserand 1894 [505] and,
more generally, by William Morris. It is the poem of the
'ordinary man, PIERS PLOWMAN, the people's man, the
people's Christ, poor humanity adorned with love, hard-
working humanity armed with indignation' (p. x); it
preaches 'the gospel of true work for self and others, for
home and country . . . . England for England is his cry' (p.
xii); it is a protest against all oppression, injustice, corruption and hypocrisy by a man who was 'a reformer of Church
and State and a defender of the poor' (p. 187). The 'Comment' merges the poem, or at least the *Visio*, into a lively
picture of Langland's times, and also offers contemporary
instances, as of able-bodied beggars in 1911, to show that
Langland's message is still relevant.

85. Neilson, W. A. and Webster, K. G. T. (eds.)
CHIEF BRITISH POETS OF THE FOURTEENTH
AND FIFTEENTH CENTURIES: SELECTED POEMS
(London: Harrap; Cambridge, Mass.: Riverside Press,
1916).

Close verse modernisation of the A *Visio* (Prologue and I–
VIII), pp. 48–78.

86.   Attwater, Donald (trans.)
A VERSION OF THE VISION OF WILLIAM
CONCERNING PIERS THE PLOWMAN (London:
Cassell, 1930).

This verse translation of the B *Visio* (Prologue and I–VII) is
based on Skeat's B text, and is complete, close to the
original, clear, sensible and unfussy. The Introduction
marks the change that had come about since Burrell 1912
[84] in the attitude to the poem: 'Those who have never read
the book commonly suppose it to be an attack on the
iniquities of those in places of power and advantage, especially of spiritual authority: that the author was a morning-
star of the Reformation and a forerunner of what is called
modern democracy. This is a complete misunderstanding.
Langland was a faithful son of the medieval Church, and his
politics were anything but "radical" . . . .' The emphasis is
on the moral meaning of the poem, and the search for the
Good Life.

87.   Wells, Henry W. (trans.)
WILLIAM LANGLAND, THE VISION OF PIERS
PLOWMAN, NEWLY RENDERED INTO MODERN
ENGLISH. With an Introduction by Nevill Coghill
(London and New York: Sheed & Ward, 1935).

Careful verse translation, somewhat 'literary', not as close as
Attwater 1930 [86], of the whole of B, with good bits from A
and C inserted here and there. In his Introduction, Coghill
alludes to some of his favourite themes (cf. Coghill 1933
[511]), in relation to the allegory of the poem, its poetic
range and its meaning ('an enquiry into the nature of the
Good Life', p. xviii).

88.   Loomis, Roger Sherman and Willard, Rudolph (trans.)
MEDIEVAL ENGLISH VERSE AND PROSE, IN

MODERNIZED VERSIONS (New York: Appleton-Century-Crofts, 1948).

Extracts (pp. 294–313) from B Prologue and I, C VI, B V–VI and XVIII, in good modern English verse translation, with attempt to preserve alliteration and rhyme.

89. Coghill, Nevill (trans.)
VISIONS FROM PIERS PLOWMAN, TAKEN FROM THE POEM OF WILLIAM LANGLAND (London: Phoenix House, 1949).

Vivacious and idiosyncratic verse translation of well-chosen extracts from B, with some good bits from C. Four illustrations, from Samuel Palmer and William Blake. An appendix gives as good a brief account of the form and meaning of the poem and its allegory (cf. Wells 1935 [87]) as one could wish. There is also a note on metre.

90. Attwater, Donald and Rachel (trans.); Attwater, Rachel (ed.)
WILLIAM LANGLAND, THE BOOK CONCERNING PIERS THE PLOWMAN (Everyman's Library No. 571) (London: J. M. Dent; New York: E. P. Dutton, 1957).

The 1930 [86] translation of the *Visio* by Donald Attwater, completed by Rachel Attwater, with the addition of Passus VIII–XX, likewise based on Skeat's text of B. The whole translation was then issued in Everyman's Library to supersede Burrell 1912 [84].

91. Goodridge, J. F. (trans.)
WILLIAM LANGLAND, PIERS THE PLOUGHMAN (Harmondsworth: Penguin Books, 1959; revised edn., 1966).

An excellent translation into vigorous modern English prose of the whole of B, with two appendices containing translation of passages unique to C. Exceptionally acute short general introduction, and substantial notes and commentary.

92.   Lawlor, John
'Two Scenes from *The Vision of Piers Plowman*', in Lawlor, John and Auden, W. H. (eds.), TO NEVILL COGHILL, FROM FRIENDS (London: Faber & Faber, 1966) 43–63.

Two excerpts from an adaptation of *PP* for modern theatre-audiences: very free verse rendering of material from the episode in which Meed appears before the King, and from the beginning and ending of the penultimate passus. Much of the dramatic action is suggested in lengthy stage directions.

93.   Williams, Margaret, R. S. C. J. (trans.)
PIERS THE PLOWMAN, BY WILLIAM LANGLAND (New York: Random House, 1971).

Lengthy introduction, most notable for its attempt to relate the mood of the poem (desire for change, fearless criticism, vision of ideal order) and its concerns ('salvation for all men, peace between peoples, the war on poverty', p. 4) to those of the modern age; for the diagrammatic plan of the structure of the poem (p. 21); and for a series of reference tables that give the 'keys to the allegory' (p. 49). The translation is into a plain and unpretentious kind of verse, with some attempt to preserve the alliteration and rhyme of the original.

94.   Trapp, J. B. (trans.)
'Medieval English Literature', in Kermode, Frank and Hollander, John (eds.), THE OXFORD ANTHOLOGY

OF ENGLISH LITERATURE (London: OUP, 1973) 1–500.

Trapp gives the Prologue and Passus I from B in modern verse, with some attempt to keep rhythm and alliteration. In his brief Introduction (pp. 348–51) he comments on the use of allegory and dream, and describes the poem as learned and didactic, and 'strongly and carefully structured'. Strangely, he thinks the authorship question still unsettled and 'Langland' a convenient fiction.

95. Abrams, M. H. *et al.* (eds.)
THE NORTON ANTHOLOGY OF ENGLISH LITERATURE (New York: W. W. Norton, 1962, 1968, 1974, 1979, 1986).

Extracts from B Prologue and the whole of B XVIII are given in the third edition (1974) in a lively translation by E. Talbot Donaldson, the senior medieval editor of this widely used college reader. In the fifth edition (1986), where Donaldson provides a new translation, the confessions of Envy and Gluttony from B V are added.

Brook 1975 [79] has facing-page translation of the extracts provided.

96. Tiller, Terence (trans.)
THE VISION OF PIERS PLOWMAN, BY WILLIAM LANGLAND (London: British Broadcasting Corporation, 1981).

Translation into modern English verse, as originally designed for radio performance, with some smoothing and simplification. Brief Introduction and notes.

97.   Donaldson, E. Talbot
'A Vision of Will', *Speculum* 56:4 (October 1981) 707–9.

A poem in pseudo-Langlandian modern alliterative verse: it provides, oddly enough, one of the best glimpses one could have of the essential L.

98.   Kane, George
'Poetry and Lexicography in the Translation of *Piers Plowman*', *Medieval and Renaissance Studies* 9 (1982) 33–54 [Proceedings of the Southeastern Institute of Medieval and Renaissance Studies, Summer 1978].

Translation of anything but utilitarian prose is bound to represent its original very imperfectly, and translation into Modern English of a great poem in Middle English is particularly difficult. Kane gives examples of the losses endured in Modern English prose translation – losses of concision and poetic energy, of emotional power in figurative language, of witty and ironic incongruity and word-play, of tone of voice. But translation, though 'a melancholy event' (p. 50), has a value, if only in making clear what is lost and in representing at least the abstractable prose content of the poem.

99.   Donaldson, E. Talbot
'Long Will's Apology: A Translation', in Kratzmann and Simpson (1986) 30–4.

A verse translation of C V 1–104, with brief Introduction.

The authorship controversy; the author; his dialect

100. Jack, A. S.
'The Autobiographical Elements in Piers the Plowman',
JEGP 3:4 (October 1901) 393–414.

Questions the value of autobiographical elements for constructing a biography of the poet. The references which
purport to relate to the life of the poet are not consistent
chronologically, and are to be taken not literally but as part
of the conventional literary framework. However, the poem
does record the true history of the poet's inner life.

101. Manly, John Matthews
'The Lost Leaf of Piers the Plowman', *MP* 3:3 (January
1906) 359–66. Reprinted in EETS, OS 135B (1908), with
Manly 1908.

There are so many differences, in vocabulary, style, versification and poetic ability, between the versions that they
must be by different authors. The so-called 'autobiographical' references (mostly in C) are fictitious attributes of the
dreamer. An awkward transition at A V 235–6, where Sloth
suddenly starts to talk about restitution, can best be explained in terms of a lost leaf: the lost leaf would have
contained the missing material, as well as the confession of
Wrath unaccountably missing from A. That B did not recognise the loss, but tried to patch it, proves that B was by a
different author. There are five authors in all, responsible
for A *Visio*, A *Vita*, A XII (John But), B, and C. The A *Visio*

is clear, unified, consistent, vivid, one of the finest poems of the fourteenth century; B by contrast is incapable of consecutive thought, full of digressions, vague, lacking in imagination. With this brief essay, with its one piece of 'evidence' and its many assertions of what was to be fully demonstrated in a forthcoming book, Manly unleashed a half-century of more or less pointless controversy about the authorship of *PP*.

102.   Bradley, Henry
'The Misplaced Leaf of *Piers the Plowman*', *Athenaeum* 4095 (21 April 1906) 483. Reprinted in EETS, OS 135B (1908) with Manly 1908.

Manly's theory of a lost bifolium of A which would have contained the confession of Wrath and the link from Sloth to Robert the Robber still leaves the latter out of place. Argues instead for a misplaced leaf, which produced disorder in the sequence of material. The conclusion would still be that the author of B, not recognising the accidental transposition, was not the author of A.

103.   Manly, John Matthews
'Piers Plowman and its Sequence', Chapter I in THE CAMBRIDGE HISTORY OF ENGLISH LITERATURE, vol. II: THE END OF THE MIDDLE AGES (Cambridge: CUP, 1908) 1–42. Reprinted as EETS, OS 135B (1908).

A fuller statement of the argument of Manly 1906 [101]. Manly announces his theory of multiple authorship at the beginning of this essay, which stands as the first chapter in a volume of the then-standard history of English literature. He claims that the failure to recognise that there are five authors involved in 'the poems' of *PP* has resulted in misunderstanding of their nature. He analyses first the *Visio* of A in such a way as to bring out its incisive clarity, vividness and structural excellence; Passus IX–XII of A are by contrast vague and rambling, and surely by a different author. The B revision is marked by different political attitudes, but chiefly by a general incapacity for organised or consecutive thinking; in the later-added passus the argument defies rational presentation (Manly uses inadequate summary to enforce this point). The B-reviser had 'no skill in composition, no control of his materials or thought' (p. 28), though he has sincerity and emotional power. The C-reviser is briefly dismissed as 'a man of much learning, of true piety and of genuine interest in the welfare of the nation, but unimaginative, cautious and a very pronounced pedant' (p. 31); his revisions are mostly tinkering. Manly draws attention to further differences, not already brought out in summary of the versions, between the four authors (five with John But, author of A XI 57ff) in terms of handling of metre and faculty of visual imagination, and to 'mistakes' made by the B-reviser (including the missing of the 'lost leaf' at A V 235–6; see Manly 1906 [101]) and 'spoiling' of B by C. There are dialectal differences too. Manly concludes by asserting that the so-called autobiographical references are merely conventional, and the Langland tradition largely a myth. Furnivall reprinted Manly's chapter as a special volume for the EETS (OS, Extra Volume 135B, 1908), with enthusiastic Forewords by himself ('the best thing done in my time in Early English', p. iii), to which he appended reprints of Manly 1906 [101] and Bradley 1906 [102].

104.   Hall, Theophilus D.
'Was Langland the Author of the C-text of *The Vision of Piers Plowman?*' *MLR* 4:1 (October 1908) 1–13.

B is a good poem, whatever its relation to A, but C is a debasement of the B-author's work, inept alike in its omissions, additions (e.g. the 'palpable hypocrisy' of the autobiographical passage in C VI) and alterations, and evidently the work of a schoolman and moralist with little imaginative sensibility.

105.   Jusserand, J. J.
       '*Piers Plowman*, the Work of One or Five', *MP* 6:3
       (January 1909) 271–329. Reprinted as EETS, OS 139B
       (1910).

The opening has a classic statement of the late nineteenth century view of L as a man 'deeply concerned with the grave problems confronting his countrymen' (p. 273), and alone in giving us 'a true impression of the grandeur of the internal reform that had been going on in England during the century: the establishment on a firm basis of that institution, unique then and destined to be imitated throughout the world, in both hemispheres five hundred years later, the Westminster Parliament' (p. 272). Jusserand accepts Bradley's version of Manly's 'lost leaf' hypothesis (i.e. the leaf was misplaced and Robert the Robber should go with Covetousness), but says that the confusion could be otherwise explained (e.g. the complex processes of revision and copying, with added bits of vellum getting disarranged) than by multiplying authors. Manly exaggerates the difference between the versions: this sometimes leads Jusserand into the rather ridiculous situation where he has to assert that A is 'worse' than Manly says so that B can appear 'better'. But in any case differences are to be expected, and are not to be interpreted as failures of understanding on the part of different authors. The autobiographical references confirm common authorship, and how unlikely it is that there should have been four different authors (John But should be excluded) involved in the same poem. Jusserand's work is courteous and full of goodwill but sometimes savours of desperation. Furnivall, excited by the furore caused by Manly, followed up the special volume of EETS (OS 135B), in which he had reprinted Manly 1908 [103], with a volume added to the issue of OS 139 in which he reprinted Jusserand

1909 [105], Manly 1909 [109], Jusserand 1910 [111], Chambers 1910 [113] and, initially as a separate offprint, Bradley 1910 [114]. [See also Chambers and Grattan 1909 [19], which has an important bearing on the question of authorship].

106. Brown, C. E.
'The "Lost Leaf" of *Piers the Plowman*'. *Nation* 88 (25 March 1909) 298–9.

Comes independently to the same conclusion about the displaced leaf as Hall 1910 [112]. A V 236–41 are indeed out of place, as Bradley 1906 [102] argued. But a simpler explanation will suffice: they should follow A V 253. But still, the author of B failed to notice the mistake that the scribe of A had made.

107. Bradley, Henry
'The "Lost Leaf" of *Piers the Plowman*', *Nation* 88 (29 April 1909) 436–7.

Reasserts his opinion of 1906 [102] against Brown 1909 [106].

108. Knott, Thomas A.
'The "Lost Leaf" of Piers the Plowman', *Nation* 88 (13 May 1909) 482–3.

Supports Manly 1906 [101] against Brown 1909 [106] and Bradley 1906, 1909 [102, 107].

109. Manly, John Matthews
'The Authorship of Piers Plowman', *MP* 7:1 (July 1909) 83–144. Reprinted as EETS, OS 139C (1910).

Tedious reply to Jusserand 1909 [105], answering his objections point by point, but merely going over old ground: this is not the full and detailed statement of his position that Manly had promised.

110.   Deakin, Mary
'The Alliteration of *Piers Plowman*', *MLR* 4:4 (July 1909) 478–83.

Comparison of alliteration argues for single authorship.

111.   Jusserand, J. J.
'Piers Plowman: The Work of One or Five: A Reply', *MP* 7:3 (January 1910) 289–326. Reprinted as EETS, OS 139D (1910).

A reply to the reply of Manly 1909 [109], rather scrappily put together. The courtesy of the initial exchanges grows increasingly strained.

112.   Hall, Theophilus D.
'The Misplaced Lines, *Piers Plowman* (A) V, 236–41', *MP* 7:3 (January 1910) 327–8.

Takes issue with the dismissal by Manly 1909 [109] of the argument of Hall 1908 [104] that lines 236–41 belong to Robert the Robber.

113.   Chambers, R. W.
'The Authorship of *Piers Plowman*', *MLR* 5:1 (January 1910) 1–32. Reprinted as EETS, OS 139E (1910).

The hypothesis of the misplaced leaf is not necessary (in accepting it, Jusserand 1909 [105] concedes the case of

Manly 1906 [101]): within the context of L's poem, the sequence of thought at this point is not specially incoherent. Nor is the placement of Robert the Robber at the end of the confession of Sloth unquestionably non-authorial (Bradley 1906 [102]), nor the 'dislocation' in the account of Piers' testament (Manly 1906 [101]). 'It should be enough if the MS order has been shown to be possible: it is unreasonable to call upon an author, under pain of being divided into five, to prove that his arrangement of his matter cannot be improved' (p. 11). So-called misunderstanding of A in B may be simply the misreadings of faulty texts. Dialect suggests single authorship. There is no substantial difference of style or views between A and B, and 'Will' is constantly referred to in both as poet-dreamer.

114.　Bradley, Henry
'The Authorship of *Piers the Plowman*', *MLR* 5:2 (April 1910) 202–7. Reprinted as EETS, OS 139F (1910).

Reiterates his argument (against Chambers 1910 [113]) that Robert the Robber would go better with Covetousness (as in C), and that the omission of the confession of Wrath in A is oddly dealt with by B. Also, John But, at the end of A, says that 'Will' is dead; his lines furthermore were added to a MS which contained only Dowel, the reference to Will's 'other works' being to the rest of A.

115.　Macaulay, G. C.
'The Name of the Author of *Piers Plowman*', *MLR* 5:2 (April 1910) 195–6.

Argues, against the view established by Skeat 1867 [13] (etc.), that the author's name was Robert not William Langland.

116.   Mensendieck, O.
'The Authorship of *Piers Plowman*', *JEGP* 9:3 (July 1910) 404–20.

The Dowel passus in B show clear continuity from the Dowel passus in A in the development of the autobiographical theme and chronology, and this argues for single authorship. The visions of Dowel contain the experiences of the author, the different events of his life represented allegorically in the order in which they followed each other.

117.   Dobson, M.
'An Examination of the Vocabulary of the "A-Text" of "Piers the Plowman" ', *Anglia* 33:3 (1910) 391–6.

There are no differences of vocabulary within A which need a theory of dual authorship to explain them.

118.   Chambers, R. W.
'The Original Form of the A-Text of *Piers Plowman*', *MLR* 6:3 (July 1911) 302–23.

The evidence of John But's addition to A is misconstrued by Bradley 1910 [114]. A did not circulate in instalments; the MSS show that it was regarded as an integrated whole, to one MS only of which But added his remarks. The 'other works' he refers to can still be the B additions.

119.   Coulton, G. G.
'Piers Plowman, One or Five', *MLR* 7:1 (January 1912) 372–3.

Does not think Manly's evidence sufficient to overthrow the traditional view of single authorship; adds that B's description of Wrath, supposedly a weak attempt to fill the gap in A, is actually quite powerful, and very appropriately located among the religious; and that the association in A of Sloth with failure of restitution is likewise traditional.

120. Bradley, Henry
'Who was John But?', *MLR* 8:1 (January 1913) 88–9.

John But, who names himself as author of part of A XII, was perhaps the King's messenger of that name documented as having died in 1387. If so, the 'Will' he declares to be dead could not have written C.

121. Rickert, Edith
'John But, Messenger and Maker', *MP* 11:1 (July 1913) 107–16.

Same identification as Bradley 1913 [120]. But's testimony is reliable and supports the multiple authorship theory.

122. Moore, Samuel
'Studies in Piers the Plowman: I. The Burden of Proof: Antecedent Probability and Tradition', *MP* 11:2 (October 1913) 177–93; 'II, The Burden of Proof: The Testimony of the Manuscripts; The Name of the Author', *MP* 12:1 (May 1914) 19–50.

The argument for single authorship is based on antecedent probability, 'tradition', manuscript testimony and the name of the author. The first two are equivocal at best, the third serves only to link A *Vita* and B. As to the name of the author there is a degree of confusion (e.g. between William and Robert as his first name), which argues against single authorship. 'We have not found a single piece of evidence in favor of single authorship of all the texts' (p. 49).

123.   Manly, John Matthews
       'The Authorship of *Piers the Plowman*', *MP* 14:5
       (September 1916) 315–16.

       The idea of multiple authorship was entertained long ago by
       G. P. Marsh.

124.   Knott, Thomas A.
       'Observations on the Authorship of *Piers the Plowman*',
       MP 14:9 (January 1917) 531–58; *MP* 15:1 (May 1917) 23–
       41.

       A long and intemperate reply to Chambers 1910 [113] and
       his objections to Manly 1906 [101], especially those that
       imply the attribution of 'incoherence' in A to L himself.

125.   Chambers, R. W.
       'The Three Texts of *Piers Plowman* and Their
       Grammatical Forms', *MLR* 14:2 (April 1919) 129–51.

       Recapitulates the arguments against multiple authorship,
       and adds evidence based on the learning displayed in the
       three texts, especially the nature and frequency of biblical
       quotation, and on certain dialectal grammatical forms (*ben*
       and *arn*, *she* and *heo*, *church* and *kirk*). None of this evi-
       dence supports a theory of multiple authorship.

126.   Bannister, Arthur T.
       'William Langland's Birthplace', *TLS* (7 September 1922)
       569.

       L's birthplace was a place called Langlands (Longlands) on
       the western slope of the Malvern Hills, now just some fields
       and a few cottages, but with the name recorded as early as
       1719. The surrounding landscape is what L describes at the
       opening of *PP*.

127. Day, Mabel
'The Alliteration of the Versions of *Piers Plowman* in Its Bearing on Their Authorship', *MLR* 17:4 (October 1922) 403–9.

The study of alliteration (cf. Deakin 1909 [110]) argues for at least five authors, and maybe more: there are marked differences in alliterative practice between the rewritten A text of B and the B continuation.

128. Day, Mabel
'The Revisions of *Piers Plowman*', *MLR* 23:1 (January 1928) 1–27.

The differences in the methods of revision, the cases where the C-author misunderstands B, as well as using a different MS of A, and the changes in the presentation of Piers, all argue for multiple authorship.

129. Bright, Allan H.
NEW LIGHT ON 'PIERS PLOWMAN'. With a preface by R. W. Chambers (London: OUP, 1928).

The 'Cleobury' of tradition is really Ledbury, eight miles from the Malvern Hills. Between Ledbury and the Malverns is a farm called Longland(s), from which the poet took his name (instead of that of his father, the Eustace de Rokayle of the record in Trinity College, Dublin MS D.4.1, since he was illegitimate). He was educated at Malvern Priory. At the foot of the Malverns is a little brook called Primeswell, lying on the banks of which the poet would see Herefordshire Beacon towering above and the dungeon of an old castle in the dale at his feet. Between is a space of flat ground, the scene of the 'fair field full of folk'. Bright also identifies the Knight and the Waster of A VII. Chambers' Preface argues again the case for single authorship, and for the propriety of

using evidence from within the poem in constructing a biography of the poet. [Bright's detective work has a romantic appeal, but it mixes together relevant and irrelevant facts with naïve speculation.]
[See also Chambers and Grattan 1931 [23] which has an important bearing on the question of authorship.]

130. James, Stanley B.

'The Mad Poet of Malvern: William Langland', *Month* 159 (February 1932) 221–7.

L possibly became unhinged because of what he saw of civilisation collapsing around him, though he would also be encouraged to represent himself as a mad wandering prophet in order to give force to his apocalyptic vision.

131. Cargill, O.
'The Langland Myth', *PMLA* 50:1 (March 1935) 36–56.

Argues, against Bright 1928 [129], that the evidence of Langland's life in the Dublin MS is unreliable (see Kane 1965 [143]); traces the origins and growth of the tradition that L wrote the poem; puts forward his own (unlikely) candidate, William de la Rokele.

132. Chambers, R. W.
'Incoherencies in the A- and B-Texts of *Piers Plowman* and their Bearing on the Authorship', *LMS* 1:1 (1948, for 1937) 27–39.

The Psalter text that Piers quotes after tearing the Pardon is an assertion, when it is understood in the light of the *Glossa Ordinaria*, of where salvation truly lies, and leads naturally into the search for Dowel that follows. A breaks off, and B takes up the quest, the poet now some fifteen years older. Wit and Reason, it is recognised, are insufficient: Imagination, however, proves a more capable guide, concluding with the lines from the Psalter quoted earlier. B follows on naturally from and *explains* A, and could not be by a different person. A is a careful artist; but so is B. There are no inexplicable incoherences, and the arguments of Manly (1906 [101], 1908 [103]) in relation to the Sins can be readily answered. The C text, meanwhile, can be accepted to be by someone else.

133. Chambers, R. W.
'Robert or William Langland?' *LMS* 1:3 (1948, for 1939) 430–62.

A survey of the evidence in MSS and literary tradition for the two names, with particular attention to the argument that 'Will' represents a purely imaginary personage. Chambers concludes that such an argument is based on unhistorical assumptions about the separation of author and narrator, and gives many parallels from medieval writings. The autobiographical references likewise may be generally taken to be non-fictitious, even if not all literally 'true'. Chambers shows the consistency of such references through A, B and C; he is of course arguing throughout the case against multiple authorship.

134. Mitchell, A. G.
'Notes on the C-Text of *Piers Plowman*', *LMS* 1:3 (1948, for 1939) 483–92.

C's changes of B are explicable and intelligent, and are made by someone intimate with the thought-processes and way of writing of B.

135. Bloomfield, Morton W.
'Was William Langland a Benedictine Monk?' *MLQ* 4:1
(March 1943) 57–61.

Accepts the identification of L made by Bright 1928 [129]
with the William of Colwall ordained at Bromyard in 1348;
suggests that a William Colvill recorded as a monk of Whitby
in 1366 is the same person. If L had been a Benedictine
Monk, this would help explain his generally good opinion of
monks, his support for the monk Uhtred de Boldon in his
dispute with the friars (Marcett 1938 [153]) and the Augustinian bias of his philosophical position. This is all highly
speculative.

136. Huppé, Bernard F.
'The Authorship of the A and B Texts of *Piers Plowman*',
Speculum 22:4 (October 1947) 578–620.

The *Visio* and *Vita* in A are closely linked, the search for
Dowel growing naturally from the Pardon episode. The
changes made in B do not misunderstand A: on the contrary,
there is clear reason for all of them. Nor is the A *Vita*
complete: it breaks off, and B continues naturally with a
repudiation of the intellectual presumption revealed earlier.
A and B are by the same author.

137. Hulbert, J. R.
'*Piers the Plowman* after Forty Years', *MP* 45:4 (May
1948) 215–25.

A survey of arguments for and against single authorship. A
prejudice in favour of single authorship must be recognised,
influenced by tradition, Skeat's edition, the desire for economy in hypotheses and the (unhistorical) modern sense that
non-authorial revision of the kind suggested is unlikely. The
impression of homogeneity in ideas and style may be partly
due to unfamiliarity. On the other hand, differences be-

tween A, B and C, and the 'spoiling' of A in B, or of B in C, do not necessarily imply multiple authorship: an author might forget, change his mind, change his poetic priorities. The arguments from the continuity of the 'autobiographical' references (Chambers 1924 [481], 1931 [23]) are not, however, strong, since such references are likely to be fictitious.
[Meroney 1950 [523] has a novel view of the authorship question.]

138.   Fowler, D. C.
      'The Relationship of the Three Texts of *Piers the Plowman*, *MP* 50:1 (August 1952) 5–22.

Many errors and attempts at correction in individual MSS of A are clearly the work of scribes; in B and C the same kind of scribal corruption exists in nearly all MSS and must go back to their archetypes; the failure of B to recognise scribal error in A, and the more serious failure of C with B (where the MS available to the C-reviser was superior to any now surviving), argue that the author of C was not the same person as the author of B, nor (probably) the author of B the same person as the author of A, unless the putative single author was so careless as to make any close criticism of his work pointless. [See also Knott–Fowler 1952 [34].]

139.   Mitchell, A. G. and Russell, G. H.
      'The Three Texts of "Piers the Plowman" ', *JEGP* 52:4 (October 1953) 445–56.

Fowler 1952 [138] argues that the C-author fails to recognise scribal corruption in his text of B, and cannot therefore be the same person as the author of B; so with B and A. Seven passages are here analysed to show that the differences between the texts are not signs of failure to recognise scribal corruption but evidence of intelligent revision by the same author.

140.   Donaldson, E. T.
'The Texts of *Piers Plowman*: Scribes and Poets', *MP* 50:4
(May 1953) 269–73.

A reply to Fowler 1952 [138]. We do not know for certain
what the A-author wrote, so that the identification of scribal
'error' is not as clear-cut a matter, even with A, as Fowler
makes out. The relationship of B to A, as of C to B, is thus
much more difficult to talk about with the kind of certainty
that gives conviction to assertions that they are by different
authors. Also, 'errors' may indeed be the responsibility of
the poet, if he were copying his own work, and the poem
generally is not of the kind that disallows local incoherences.
Donaldson ends with a noble plea for attention to the poem
as a poem (even if it is 'the work of a committee of poets', or
'somehow or other the product of the collective mind of
many godly men in deeply troubled, late-medieval England', p. 273), as 'something for humanity to be proud of',
and not as a collection of cruxes for arguing about
authorship.

141.   Fowler, David C.
PIERS THE PLOWMAN: LITERARY RELATIONS
OF THE A AND B TEXTS (Seattle: University of
Washington Press, 1961).

The continuation of the *Vita* in B must have been completed
at least in draft before the B-continuator began to revise A.
Though Fowler does not accept that A and B are by the same
author, he claims that this does not affect the validity of his
analysis of their relationship, which places important emphasis on differences in the use of literary tradition. The A
Vita is a separate poem, textually, from the *Visio*, but closely
related: it grows out of Piers' impatience with paper pardons, but also a more generalised dissatisfaction with the
priest's power of using reason to impugn the pardon. The

purpose of the A *Vita* is 'to *prove* that Learning is *not* the way to salvation' (p. 16). The B continuation is a different kind of poem, deeply immersed in the Scriptures and Scriptural commentary, based on a chronology from Creation (B XI–XV), through Fall and Redemption (B XVI–XVIII), to the Apostolic Age and Apocalypse (B XIX–XX), and working within the traditions of vernacular treatments of biblical narrative (e.g. *Cursor Mundi*, the mystery plays) and of romance (it is a kind of grail-quest, or 'Estoire de Piers', p. 54). Its purposes are to modify the hostility to learning in A, and to make the friars more a focus of attack. The role of the dreamer, as 'God's fool', is now quite different; the author emerges more and more as a secular cleric. The B revision of A shows a tendency to differ sharply from A, and to move towards attitudes and criticisms characteristic of the B continuation (e.g. sharper criticism of bishops) as well as to reveal more clearly that the reviser is a cleric. A final chapter identifies the author of B – learned, a secular cleric, a relentless opponent of corruption within the Church and of the friars – as John Trevisa, vicar of Berkeley and translator of Higden's *Polychronicon* and much else, including perhaps the Bible. Many parallels are drawn. [Though there is much that is illuminating in Fowler's account of the poem, there is the constant sense that his interpretations are liable to be distorted by his rather eccentric views on the authorship question.]

Reviews: M. W. Bloomfield, *Speculum* 37:1 (January 1962) 120–3.
S. S. Hussey, *RES*, NS 14:54 (April 1963) 177–9.
G. Kane, *MÆ* 33:3 (1964) 230–1.
R. E. Kaske, *JEGP* 62:1 (January 1963) 208–13.

142. Samuels, M. L.
'Some Applications of Middle English Dialectology', *ES* 44:2 (April 1963) 81–94.

A brief announcement of some of the findings of the new techniques of dialectological analysis developed by Samuels and Angus McIntosh in Edinburgh. On p. 94 it is noted that C texts of *PP* circulated mostly in L's own native area of the Malvern Hills. B texts were more cosmopolitan, but tend to concentrate in the London and Worcester areas, while A texts are more scattered – though few come from the more central areas where B and C texts were written.

143. Kane, George
PIERS PLOWMAN: THE EVIDENCE FOR
AUTHORSHIP (University of London: The Athlone
Press, 1965).

A thorough and scrupulous examination of all the evidence, both internal and external, relating to the authorship of *PP*, and of the rationale for the interpretation of that evidence. The conclusion is that the three versions of the poem were all the work of one man, William Langland, and that the theory of multiple authorship has no foundation whatsoever. Kane's book, inspired by his work on the Athlone Press edition of *PP*, and prompted by Fowler 1961 [141], marks the effective end of the authorship controversy. It also contains an important and illuminating discussion of the nature of the relationship between dreamer, narrator and poet in other medieval vision poems as well as *PP*, and the extent to which events, though fictitious, may yet be 'true'.

Reviews: D. C. Fowler, *ELN* 3:4 (June 1966) 295–300.
R. E. Kaske, *JEGP* 65:3 (July 1966) 583–6.
P. M. Kean, *RES* NS 17:67 (July 1966) 303–4.
T. A. Stroud, *MP* 65:4 (May 1968) 366–7.

144. Donaldson, E. Talbot
' "Piers Plowman": Textual Comparison and the Question of Authorship', in Esch, Arno (ed.), CHAUCER UND SEINE ZEIT: SYMPOSION FÜR WALTER F.

SCHIRMER (Tübingen: Max Niemeyer Verlag, 1968) 241–7.

The authorship controversy was always really based on literary-critical judgement (B 'spoils' A, etc.) masquerading as objective analysis; it tended to substitute poets, of whom we know nothing, for texts, which are all we have. Textual comparison cannot clarify questions of authorship; editors must work with assumptions based on evidence from other sources.

145. Covella, Francis D.
'Grammatical Evidence of Multiple Authorship in *Piers Plowman*', *Language and Style* 9:1 (Winter 1976) 3–16.

Analysis of the frequency of repetition of certain grammatical patterns (e.g. the part of speech of the word at the beginning of the half-line) shows sharp distinctions between the practice of A and B (and between AB and C, too, though the comparatively small number of new lines in C makes the analysis less effective). If grammatical patterning of this kind is to be associated with individual style, the statistics here, the author argues, must reopen the question of multiple authorship. [The statistics look impressive, but there are many questions of text and content, and their impact on grammatical patterns, that are not answered in this brief study.]

146. Burrow, John
'Langland *Nel Mezzo del Cammin*', in Bennett (1981) 21–41.

Langland's references to Will's encroaching age at B XII 3, lacking as they do any clear consequence in the strategy of the poem, are indeed actual references to the poet's own life, and his sense of guilt at having left his great work in abeyance for so long.

147. DiMarco, Vincent
'Eighteenth-Century Suspicions regarding the Authorship of *Piers Plowman*', *Anglia* 100:1/2 (1982) 124–9.

Both Thomas Hearne (1725) and Joseph Ritson (1782) recognised that *PP* existed in different forms, and had doubts that they were by the same author.

148. Samuels, M. L.
'Langland's Dialect', *MÆ* 54:2 (1985) 232–47.

Evidence from alliterative practice indicates south-west Worcestershire. Surviving MSS of A are too mixed for identification of the dialect of the archetype to be possible; C MSS, however, nearly all belong to a dialectally cohesive south-west Midland group (suggesting that L returned there in later life), with the best MSS (X,U,Y,I) located in the Malvern area. Furthermore, two MSS of B (the rest are too mixed to be helpful) are unmistakably from the same area. L's dialect is well represented by MS X.

149. Samuels, M. L.
'Dialect and Grammar', in Alford (1988) 201–21.

A brief introduction to Middle English dialects and the means by which an author's own dialect may be recovered from scribal copies of his work; identification of L's dialect (as in Samuels 1985 [148]); and brief account of L's phonology and grammar.

Date

150. Cargill, Oscar
'The Date of the A-Text of Piers Ploughman', *PMLA* 47:2
(June 1932) 354–62.

Dates A Prol. and I–IV to 1376 on the basis of some (very
unlikely) allusions to historical events and personages of that
year.

151. Kellogg, Eleanor H.
'Bishop Brunton and the Fable of the Rats', *PMLA* 50:1
(March 1935) 57–68.

The sermon by Thomas Brunton, Bishop of Rochester,
containing the rat-fable that influenced L (Owst 1925 [272]),
was delivered on 18 May 1376, which is therefore a significant date for the revision of the Prologue. A note by Sister
Mary Aquinas Devlin, *PMLA* 51:1 (March 1936) 300–2,
disputes some of Kellogg's dating.

152. Coghill, Nevill
'Two Notes on *Piers Plowman*: I. The Abbot of Abingdon
and the Date of the C text; II. Chaucer's Debt to
Langland'. *MÆ* 4:2 (June 1935) 83–94.

Interpretation of prophetic passage, B X 317–30. The mention of the Abbot of Abingdon is merely alliterative in B, but
its absence in C indicates a date after 1393. Chaucer's debt to
L is very clear, especially in the description of the Monk and
Plowman in the General Prologue.

153.   Marcett, Mildred Elizabeth
UHTRED DE BOLDON, FRIAR WILLIAM JORDAN,
AND PIERS PLOWMAN. Ph.D. dissertation, New York
University (New York: published by the author, 1938).

Identifies the fat Doctor of B XIII with the Dominican
William Jordan (see B XIII 83), who had attacked the
antimendicant writings of the Durham monk Uhtred de
Boldon, which L may have admired. Jordan left England in
1378, suggesting a date before then for B. [See Gwynn 1943
[156], Russell 1966 [485].]

154.   Huppé, Bernard F.
'The A-Text of *Piers Plowman* and the Norman Wars',
PMLA 54:1 (March 1939) 37–64.

The references to the Norman wars are not to those that
ended with the Treaty of Bretigny in 1360 (Skeat's argument
for a date in the early 1360s), but to the campaign of 1373.
The influence of Alice Perrers on the portrayal of Lady
Meed, and the representation of the King as in decline,
suggest a date well after 1370.

155.   Huppé, Bernard F.
'The Date of the B-Text of *Piers Plowman*', *SP* 38:1
(January 1941) 34–44.

The Prologue must have been written after the Good Parliament of 1376, to which it refers, and probably after February
1377. The references to the papal wars in B XIX are to
Clement VII and would indicate a date for that part of the
poem late in 1378.

156.   Gwynn, A. S. J.
'The Date of the B-Text of *Piers Plowman*', *RES* 19:73
(January 1943) 1–24.

Allusion to Friar William Jordan supposed to be introduced at B XIII 83 (Marcett 1938 [153]) suggests a date before he died (before 1374). Further allusions are adduced to suggest a date 1370–2 for the composition of B XIII–XX (the revision of the A *Visio* and *Vita*, it is accepted, came later).

157. Bennett, J. A. W.
'The Date of the A-Text of *Piers Plowman*', *PMLA* 58:2 (June 1943) 566–72.

If Lady Meed is Alice Perrers (Huppé 1939 [154]), then A III 191 is a reference to the death of Queen Philippa (1369); 'Rome-renners' (A IV 110) would be appropriate between 1367 and 1370, when the Pope was not at Avignon. There is no evidence for a date later than 1370.

158. Bennett, J. A. W.
'The Date of the B-Text of *Piers Plowman*', *MÆ* 12 (1943) 55–64.

Nine pieces of evidence indicating that L was working on this recension between 1377 and 1379.

159. Huppé, Bernard F.
'*Piers Plowman*: The Date of the B-Text Reconsidered', *SP* 46:1 (January 1949) 6–13.

Discusses and dismisses the arguments of Gwynn 1943 [156] and repeats the arguments of Huppé 1941 [155] for 1377–9.

160. Fowler, David C.
'A Pointed Personal Allusion in *Piers the Plowman*', *MP* 77:2 (November 1979) 158–9.

The identification of an allusion to Simon Sudbury, Archbishop of Canterbury, in B XV 556 argues for a later date for B than is usually thought, for the status of disputed MSS R and F as a revised form of B and for a connection between B and Trevisa. [See Fowler 1961 [141].]

161.   Selzer, John L.
'Topical Allegory in *Piers Plowman*: Lady Meed's B Text Debate with Conscience', *PQ* 59:3 (Summer 1980) 257–67.

Supporting evidence for the view that the portrayal of Lady Meed alludes to Alice Perrers. Conscience, however, is patterned after not John of Gaunt (see Huppé 1939 [154]), but Edmund Mortimer, Earl of March, who was active in support of the Commons against the Court Party at the Good Parliament of 1376. Meed's references to a disastrous winter campaign in France are to Mortimer's expedition of 1374–5.

Metre

162. Saintsbury, George
A HISTORY OF ENGLISH PROSODY FROM THE
TWELFTH CENTURY TO THE PRESENT DAY, 2
vols. (London: Macmillan, 1906).

There is increased regularity in the handling of the alliterative line in *PP* (pp. 179–86), compared with Old English poetry and Layamon, and some tendency to be sucked into the metrical. But L is a master of the alliterative line: 'There *is* music in this *un*metre; and what is more, the music is neither unpleasant nor monotonous' (pp. 185–6).

163. Saintsbury, George
HISTORICAL MANUAL OF ENGLISH PROSODY
(London: Macmillan, 1910).

L does the best than can be expected with verse that is essentially non-metrical, and separated from prose only by alliteration, accent and a strong middle pause. There are, however, occasional metrical accidents (p. 49) and 'a sort of anapaestic underhum' (p. 153).

164. Schipper, Jakob
HISTORY OF ENGLISH VERSIFICATION (Oxford: Clarendon Press, 1910). Translated from the abridged version, published in 1895, of the author's ENGLISCHE METRIK IN HISTORISCHER UND SYSTEMATISCHER ENTWICKELUNG DARGESTELLT, 2 vols. (Bonn, 1881).

Accepts the traditional 'five types' (A,B,C,D,E) of Old English as continuing to provide the staple line of Middle English alliterative verse, including *PP*. But the versification of *PP* (pp. 93–5) is often irregular, with long sequences of syllables between the stresses of the normally four-beat line where there may be an added secondary stress.

165.   Leonard, William Ellery
'The Scansion of Middle English Alliterative Verse', University of Wisconsin Studies in Language and Literature, No. 11: Studies by members of the Department of English, Series Number 2 (Madison, 1920) 58–104.

Extends his 'four accent' reading of earlier Germanic poetry to Middle English alliterative verse, including *PP*. The long line in *PP* has two half-lines of four and three accents respectively: lines from *PP* and *The Tale of Gamelyn* are set side by side (pp. 72–4, 77–80) to demonstrate (the occasional plausibility of) this argument.

166.   Stewart, George R., jun.
'The Meter of *Piers Plowman*', *PMLA* 42:1 (March 1927) 113–28.

The alliterative line is usually read with four stresses, but some (e.g. Leonard 1920 [165]) read with seven. The analogy of popular verse resolves the contradiction: it is a line of four dipodic feet, each foot containing a primary and a secondary stress, of which the latter may be represented by a pause before caesura or line-end. Stress does not necessarily coincide with alliteration.

167.   Hulbert, J. R.
'Quatrains in Middle English Alliterative Poems', *MP* 48:2 (November 1950) 73–81.

Thinks that *PP*, like *Patience* and *Cleanness* and other alliterative poems, may have been (originally) composed in quatrains; quotes A Prologue, so divided, to demonstrate the point (unsuccessfully).

168. Sapora, Robert William, jun.
A THEORY OF MIDDLE ENGLISH ALLITERATIVE METER, WITH CRITICAL APPLICATIONS.
Mediaeval Academy of America, Speculum Anniversary Monographs 1 (Cambridge, Mass 1977).

Considers that previous accounts of alliterative metre have been descriptive rather than explanatory. The present theory is designed to explain all the phenomena, and to be predictive. It does not posit a norm, but accepts a wide range of metrical 'variants' as part of the norm, on the basis that linguistic stress cannot be violated by metrical stress. It accepts that there may be four or five stressed syllables in the line, of which at least two must bear alliteration (see the chart of line-types at pp. 26–7); the half-line structure of Old English is no longer important. The theory, which presents an orthodox account of Middle English alliterative metre in an elaborately technical and theoretical manner, is applied to *PP* A, pp. 59–62, and is seen, inevitably, to work.

169. Kane, George
'Music "Neither Unpleasant nor Monotonous" ', in Bennett (1981) 43–63.

An admirably full and clear statement of the perception that 'alliteration can have a substantive phonetic existence independent of the metrical accents of a line' (p. 47). L is skilful in modulating between stress and alliteration; his handling of the alliterative line is different from that of all other poets.

170.   Beckwith, Marc A.
'The Alliterative Meter of *Piers Plowman*', *Comitatus* 12
(1981) 31–9.

Survey of interpretations of L's metre in Skeat 1885 [17],
Oakden 1930 [274], Sapora 1977 [168], etc. An elementary
guide, but there are pointed criticisms of some of the assumptions about L's metre in Kane–Donaldson 1975 [42],
especially of the difficulties of allowing stress on alliterating
'little' words.
[Schmidt 1984 [49] and Duggan 1987 [57] use metrical evidence in the determination of the authenticity of the Z text.]

171.   Duggan, Hoyt N.
'The Shape of the B-Verse in Middle English Alliterative
Poetry', *Speculum* 61:3 (July 1986) 564–92.

Establishes the presence in the 'classical corpus' of Middle
English alliterative poetry of a rule for the distribution of
syllables in the second half-line (no poet allowed two or
more syllables in both the initial and medial dip). L, almost
alone, does not observe this rule, perhaps because he was
more 'literate', working further removed from the oral-aural
tradition (pp. 577–8). Duggan adumbrates this argument in
'Alliterative Patterning as a Basis for Emendation in Middle
English Alliterative Poetry', *SAC* 8 (1986) 73–105 (at p. 79).

172.   Duggan, Hoyt N.
'Notes toward a Theory of Langland's Meter', *YLS* 1
(1987) 41–70.

In earlier essays, Duggan (1986 [171]) had regarded *PP* as an
exception to the metrical rules he had formulated. He now
considers that L observed the same rules, but the fact that he
did so has been obscured by editors who did not understand
the rules. Specifically, L observed Metrical Rule V concern-

ing rhythmic patterning in the b-verse (of the two dips before the lifts one must, but both may not, have two or more syllables). Analysis of the anomalous verses in the editions of B by Kane–Donaldson and Schmidt shows that all are scribal. In other respects, L works individual variations on the alliterative line, though within the rules: in particular, he allows alliteration to fall more frequently on words of low stress. This does not, however, raise the stress of such words: they remain 'mute staves' (the term coined by Schmidt [1978] [44]), and furthermore occur only in the b-verse. Lines of the form *aa:ax* and *aaa:xx* are suspect.

[There is an important discussion of metre in Schmidt 1987 [603] (see also Schmidt 1978 [44]).]

173. Cable, Thomas
'Middle English Meter and its Theoretical Implications', *YLS* 2 (1988) 47–69.

Agrees with Duggan 1986 [171], 1987 [172] on the hitherto unrecognised rhythmical patterning of the b-line, but considers this to be part of a larger pattern relating to distinctions between a- and b-lines; he also considers that final -e was commonly sounded in Middle English alliterative verse. He offers detailed critique of Duggan's methods and principles. L's procedures are significantly different from those of other alliterative poets, but much of the syntactical detail in the texts of *PP*, and the metrical patterns that can be deduced therefrom, remain 'unassignable between scribe and author' (p. 67).

174. Lawton, David A.
'Alliterative Style', in Alford (1988) 223–49.

Chiefly a discussion of metre, and of the relation of metre to syntax, choice of words and use of collocations, with sample analysis of B Prol.58–67, and some discussion of the affiliations of L's metrical usage.

Sources

Identification of specific sources for particular
passages (usually in the form of short notes)

175. Bradley, Henry
'Some Cruces in "Piers Plowman" ', *MLR* 5:3 (July 1910)
340–2.

Offers some valuable hints for the interpretation of B XIII
150–1 (*'ex vi transicionis'*) (see Kaske 1963 [437], Middleton
1972 [443]), and the enigmatic prophecy at B VI 328–9.

176. Baum, Paull Franklin
'The Fable of Belling the Cat', *MLN* 35:8 (December
1919) 462–70.

Traces the early origins of the fable; suggests that L may
have got the fable orally or from the Latin *Fabulae* of Odo of
Cheriton (c. 1220).

177. Cornelius, Roberta D.
THE FIGURATIVE CASTLE. A STUDY IN THE
MEDIAEVAL ALLEGORY OF THE EDIFICE WITH
ESPECIAL REFERENCE TO RELIGIOUS
WRITINGS. Ph.D. dissertation, Bryn Mawr College
(Bryn Mawr, 1930).

An account (pp. 26–36) of the Latin and vernacular tradition
that lies behind L's Castle of Kynde (A X), especially the

tradition of the Wardens of the Soul; patristic origins for the personifications of Anima, Inwit, etc.

178. Gaffney, Wilbur
'The Allegory of the Christ-Knight in *Piers Plowman*',
PMLA 46:1 (March 1931) 155–68.

Traces the image of Christ jousting in a medieval tournament (B XVI, XVIII) in medieval lyric, in a French poem by Bozon, in Latin sermons and in the *Ancrene Riwle*. Bozon is closest to *PP*.

179. Cornelius, Roberta D.
'*Piers Plowman* and the *Roman de Fauvel*', *PMLA* 47:2 (June 1932) 363–7.

Argues that L knew this early fourteenth-century French poem: he uses Favel (A II 6, etc.), otherwise unexplained, as the name for an abettor of Falsehood, and the allegorical marriage of Meed shows some similarities to the French poem.

180. Burton, Dorothy Jean
'The Compact with the Devil in the Middle-English *Vision of Piers the Plowman*, B. II', *California Folklore Quarterly* 5:2 (April 1946) 179–84.

The motif of the compact with the devil appears in every recorded folk-literature. It appears in L in the allegory of the wedding of Lady Meed to Falsehood, though handled with much originality, especially in the development of the idea of the marriage-contract.

181. Kellogg, Alfred L.
'Satan, Langland, and the North', *Speculum* 24:3 (July
1949) 413–14. Reprinted in Kellogg (1972) 29–31.

Traces a supposedly 'inaccurate' biblical quotation at C II
113 to Augustine's paraphrase of the Bible.

182. Kaske, R. E.
'*Gigas* the Giant in *Piers Plowman*', *JEGP* 56:2 (April
1957) 177–85.

Gigas in B XVIII 250 clearly refers to Christ: the allusion is
to Psalm 18:6 and commentaries thereon, which emphasise
Christ's indomitability as well as his dual nature (like the
giants of Genesis 6) as both God and man. The *gynne* in the
latter part of line 250 would then refer to the trick played on
the devil at the Incarnation. Allusions to commentary on
Psalm 18 seem to run through the whole passage.

183. Kaske, R. E.
'Langland and the *Paradisus Claustralis*', *MLN* 72:7
(November 1957) 481–3.

L's praise of the 'hevene on erthe' which is the life of the
cloister is very probably derived from Benvenuto da Imola's
commentary on Dante. It is a common topos, and is not
evidence of personal experience.

184. Kellogg, Alfred L.
'Langland and Two Scriptural Texts', *Traditio* 14 (1958)
385–98. Reprinted in Kellogg (1972) 32–50.

Traces the Latin quotation after C II 111 to Augustine's
commentary on Psalms, and the 'longe carte' of B II 181 to
biblical commentary on the chariots of Pharaoh in Exodus

and on other passages. L was familiar with a wide range of biblical interpretation and allusion, and knew how to recombine such materials in an artistically effective way.

185.   Kaske, R. E.
'The Speech of "Book" in *Piers Plowman*', *Anglia* 77:2 (1959) 117–44.

A different reading of the syntax of B XVIII 252–7 (taking *but* in 252 as a co-ordinating conjunction, and with *wil* understood before *rise*) associates Book's remarks with a Trinitarian theory of history expounded by Joachim of Flora: Book looks forward to the third age or *status mundi*, the age of the Holy Ghost, when the Scriptures will be superseded by the Eternal Gospel. [Kaske's syntax is questioned by Hoffman 1964 [189] and Donaldson 1966 [191].]

186.   Kaske, R. E.
'Langland's Walnut-Simile', *JEGP* 58:4 (October 1959) 650–4.

The simile (in B XI 247–57) draws on biblical exegesis of Canticles 6:10 and Numbers 17:8, where the hardships and consolations (especially the sweetness of Christ) of the virtuous are similarly related to nuts. The allusion shows the purposefulness of L's poem, and the ordered complexity of its structure of metaphysical allusion.

187.   Kellogg, Alfred, L.
'Langland and the "Canes Muti" ', in Kirk, Rudolf and Main, C. F. (eds.), ESSAYS IN LITERARY HISTORY PRESENTED TO J. MILTON FRENCH (New Brunswick, NJ: Rutgers UP, 1960) 25–35. Reprinted in Kellogg (1972) 51–8 as 'Langland's "Canes Muti": The Paradox of Reform'.

The 'doumbe houndes' of B X 287 are from Isaiah, but the image is also widely used by Dominican (Bromyard) and Lollard alike in their attacks on the indolence of the secular clergy. The difference is that L genuinely seeks reform.

188.   Smith, Ben H., jun.
'Patience's Riddle, *Piers Plowman* B,XIII', *MLN* 76:8 (December 1961) 675–82.

In B XIII 150–5, the phrase '*ex vi transicionis*' refers to grammatical transitivity, and the 'half a laumpe lyne' is to be construed as a half-verse (of Psalm 4:7). The general reference is to the communication of God's love in the Incarnation. The cryptic lines that follow (152–5) refer to the Passion and Resurrection.

189.   Hoffman, Richard L.
'The Burning of "Boke" in *Piers Plowman*', *MLQ* 25:1 (March 1964) 57–65.

Argues that the reading of B XVIII 252–7 in Kaske 1959 [185] is syntactically impossible, but proposes another version of the sentence, with '[I, Book, will]' understood before the '*be lost*' of 257. In this way the certainty of the future conversion of the Jews is emphasised. [But see Donaldson 1966 [191].]

190.   Wilkes, Gerald L.
'The Castle of Unite in *Piers Plowman*', *MS* 27 (1965) 334–6.

Direct source for Castle of Unite of B XXII in the *Ancrene Riwle*.

191. Donaldson, E. Talbot
'The Grammar of Book's Speech in *Piers Plowman*', in
Brahmer (1966) 103–9. Reprinted in Blanch (1969) 264–
70.

Analyses the misreading of the syntax of B XVIII 252–7 in
Kaske 1959 [185] and Hoffman 1964 [189]. [But see Wittig
1986 [214].]

192. Saint-Jacques, Raymond
'Langland's Christ-Knight and the Liturgy', *Revue de
l'Université d'Ottawa* 37:1 (January–March 1967) 146–58.

The liturgy, with the commentary and homilies that accrued
to it, is a rich and important influence in *PP*. Finds many
sources for the warrior-knight (he is not, *pace* Gaffney 1931
[178], a lover-knight in L) of B XVI, XVIII, in the liturgy,
especially that for Easter.

193. Saint-Jacques, Raymond
'The Liturgical Associations of Langland's Samaritan',
Traditio 25 (1969) 217–30.

The liturgy for the thirteenth Sunday after Trinity provides
the essential associations (closer than those from patristic
sources) that make sense of the structure of B XVI–XVII,
especially the link between the Priest and the Levite of the
parable and the figures of Abraham-Faith and Moses–Hope,
between the Samaritan and Christ, in his Incarnation and
Passion, and between the remedies for the wounded man
and the sacraments.

194. Saint-Jacques, Raymond
'Conscience's Final Pilgrimage in *Piers Plowman* and the
Cyclical Structure of the Liturgy', *Revue de l'Université
d'Ottawa* 40:2 (April–June 1970) 210–23.

L's handling of man's recurring relapses, his constant need to undertake a new spiritual pilgrimage, as in B XIX, XX, is much influenced by the liturgy for Pentecost and Advent, where we find the urgent call for renewal, as well as particular things like the use of military and farming imagery, the theme of *redde quod debes*, the figure of Antichrist. Like the liturgy, L's poem comes full circle.

195.   Orsten, Elisabeth M.
' "Heaven on Earth" – Langland's Vision of Life within the Cloister', *ABR* 21:4 (December 1970) 526–34.

Monks are severely attacked in B X, but their life is also portrayed in a curiously idyllic way, as 'hevene on erthe'. L seems to be echoing a popular saying about the life of the cloister to which Bishop Brinton also refers in one of his sermons. The rather sentimental idealisation of the monastic life may arise from memory of his youthful education in a Worcestershire monastery, but may be due to limited experience of what monasteries were really like.

196.   Taitt, Peter
'In Defence of Lot', *NQ* 18 (216):8 (August 1971) 284–5.

L accuses Lot of committing incest with his daughters (C II 25–8), rather unfairly it may seem, since Lot was drunk and incapable at the time, and the whole idea was his daughters'. L's source is not the Bible but the biblical history of Comestor.

197.   Lunz, Elisabeth
'The Valley of Jehoshaphat in *Piers Plowman*', *Tulane Studies in English* 20 (1972) 1–10.

L's allusion to the promise of Christ's love being finally

rendered in the Vale of Jehoshaphat shows his extraordinary emphasis on the doctrine of love and the independence of his poetic vision. He goes far beyond, even rejects traditional exegesis (so often cited as the means to understanding L's poetry), where the significance of the Vale is as a place of merciless judgement rather than overflowing love.

198. Hill, Thomas D.
'The Light that Blew the Saints to Heaven: *Piers Plowman* B,V.495–503', *RES*, NS 24:95 (October 1973) 444–9.

B V 502–3 seems confused, but it is in fact a highly disciplined and learned allusion to the theology of the generation of the Son by the Father, and of insufflation by the Holy Spirit.

199. Alford, John A.
'Haukyn's Coat: Some Observations on *Piers Plowman* B.XIV.22–7', *MÆ* 43:2 (1974) 133–8.

The account of Haukyn's coat needs explaining from the exegetical tradition relating to the Sermon on the Mount.

200. Hill, Thomas D.
'Two Notes on Exegetical Allusion in Langland. "Piers Plowman" B,XI,161–7, and B,I,115–124', *NM* 75:1 (March 1974) 92–7.

Biblical exegesis elucidates a reference to the 'neutral' angels in B I, who acquiesced in Lucifer's action but did not fall as far as hell; and to the finger of God writing as a metaphor for the Holy Spirit (an allusion that cleverly links the old law of the Mosaic tablets, on which God wrote, and the new law of love announced by Trajan in B XI).

201. Hill, Thomas D.
'A Liturgical Allusion in "Piers Plowman" B.XVI.88:
Filius, bi the Fader wille. and frenesse of Spiritus Sancti',
NQ 22 (220):12 (December 1975) 531–2.

The reference to the Incarnation as an act in which all
members of the Trinity participated fully is made more fully
resonant by the echo of a communion prayer. Hill also has a
note on the poetic aptness of the word *jouke* in B XVI 92.

202. Hill, Thomas D.
'Davidic Typology and the Characterization of Christ:
"Piers Plowman" B.XIX.95–103', *NQ* 23 (221):7 (July
1976) 291–4.

The identification of Christ as conqueror is an allusion to
David, especially to his struggle to establish himself as King
of Israel (a Messianic type): David's tactics as a guerrilla
leader adumbrate Christ's preaching. Hill comments on the
imaginative quality of the typological association, and on L's
skill in exploiting it in his poetry.

203. Saint-Jacques, Raymond
'Langland's Bells of the Resurrection and the Easter
Liturgy', *English Studies in Canada* 3:2 (Summer 1977)
129–35.

B XVIII 424–31 contain allusions to some of the most
moving Easter liturgical ceremonies that evoke the mystery
of the Resurrection – the bells, creeping to the cross, the
jewelled cross. Like these ceremonies, Will's waking is both
the confirmation of and the call to celebrate the reality of
Christ's sacrifices.

204. Saint-Jacques, Raymond
'Langland's "Spes" the Spy and the Book of Numbers',
NQ 24 (222):6 (December 1977) 483–5.

Hope is called a 'Spy' in B XVII 1 and his search for Christ is
a kind of spying mission, in allusion to the spies sent out by
Moses in Numbers 13:26, and to the commentary on that
passage, where the link is made with the Law and a suggestion made of a possible association (as in L) with the Levite
of the Parable of the Good Samaritan.

205. Hill, Thomas D.
'Christ's "Thre Clothes": "Piers Plowman" C.XI.193',
NQ 25 (223):3 (June 1978) 200–3.

The allusion is to a patristic tradition of three garments,
scarlet, purple and white, worn by Christ before the Crucifixion. Hill comments on the precision and coherence of L's
use of the 'language' of exegesis.

206. Tavormina, M. Teresa
'Kindly Similitude: Langland's Matrimonial Trinity', *MP*
80:2 (November 1982) 117–28.

Abraham's comparison of the Trinity to marriage in C XVIII
211–39 has a respectable patristic tradition behind it, and
performs important thematic and structural functions within
the poem (e.g. to reinforce the general analogy of man to
God as *imago Dei*, and remind us of L's good opinion of
marriage), as well as being a fine piece of discursive rhetoric.

207. Schmidt, A. V. C.
'Langland's "Book of Conscience" and Alanus de Insulis',
NQ 29 (227):6 (December 1982) 482–4.

L's reference to Conscience as a book that was sufficient for
early Christian ascetics to read in (B XV 534) is generally
indebted to patristic commentary on Daniel 7:10, but more
particularly to a passage in the *Summa de Arte Praedicatoria*
of Alanus. Schmidt also argues more generally for L's
knowledge of the works of Alanus.

208.   Schmidt, A. V. C.
'Langland, Chrysostom and Bernard: A Complex Echo',
NQ 30 (228):2 (April 1983) 108–10.

The precise wording of L's image in B I 188–9 suggests a
direct debt to Bernard's Epistle 42, though L may also be
echoing a passage in a homily attributed to Chrysostom,
whose works (as translated into Latin) he may well have
known.

209.   Biggs, Frederick M.
' "Aungeles Peeris": *Piers Plowman*, B 16.67–72 and C
18.85–100', *Anglia* 102:3/4 (1984) 426–36.

Patristic sources for L's references to virgins as the equals of
angels, to fruit and the pun on peers/pears, and to the state of
virginity in which Adam and Eve lived before the Fall and to
which redeemed man will return.

210.   Schmidt, A. V. C.
' "A Covenant more than Courtesy": A Langlandian
Phrase in its Context', *NQ* 31 (229):2 (June 1984) 153–6.

Revision of the enigmatic B XII 288–91 in C XIV 214–16
introduces an allusion to the Parable of the Vineyard to
emphasise that God's love and promise of salvation goes
beyond the Law, and extends to pagans as to the late arrivals
of the parable. Schmidt points to the influence of the passage
on *St Erkenwald* (another London poem), and to association

too with *Pearl* (which may be by the same poet as *St Erkenwald*).

211. Heffernan, Carol F.
'*Piers Plowman* B.I.153–158', *ELN* 22:2 (December 1984) 1–5.

Sees the power of the figurative language in this famous passage as deriving partly from the allusion to images in two well-known Latin hymns, *Rorate Celi* and *Crux Fidelis*.

212. Goldsmith, Margaret E.
'Piers' Apples: Some Bernardine Echoes in *Piers Plowman*'. in Collins, Price and Hamer (1985), *LSE* NS 16 (1985) 309–25.

Parallels between L and St Bernard, particularly Sermon 51 on the Canticles, where he has an apple-tree allegory (cf. Tree of Charity).

213. Szittya, Penn R.
'The Trinity in Langland and Abelard', in Groos (1986) 207–16.

Association of the Trinity with the triad of *myght*, *wit* and *blisse* (*Potentia*, *Sapientia*, *Benignitas*) in B XVI 184–93 may well be drawn directly from Abelard. His influence helps to explain the enigmatic line 192, and also the allusion to a lord's need of parchment to write a letter (alluding to the enabling agency of the Son in relation to the creative power of the Father) in B IX 39–41.

214. Wittig, Joseph S.
'The Middle English "Absolute Infinitive" and "The Speech of Book" ', in Groos (1986) 217–40.

Interpretation of B XVIII 255–60 depends partly on the question of the 'absolute infinitive' construction. Donaldson 1966 [191] argued against the reading of *but* in 255, put forward by Kaske 1959 [185], as adversative conjunction (rather than 'unless') but had to presume the existence of an absolute infinitive in 258. Wittig demonstrates in an extensive analysis of such constructions that this is not one of them. He suggests that *lyue* in 255 is infinitive and the rest of the infinitives are parallel with it. (He thus basically supports Donaldson's reading.)

215. Simpson, James
' "Et vidit deus cogitaciones eorum": A Parallel Instance and Possible Source for Langland's Use of a Biblical Formula at *Piers Plowman* B.XV.200a', *NQ* 33 (231):1 (March 1986) 9–13.

Literary procedures change, with the cognitive development of the dreamer, from analytic to 'poetic'. An important passage in the definition of Charity at B XV 151–3 uses rhetorical *aenigma* to communicate an enigmatic concept ('enigmatic allegory . . . is proposed . . . as a provisional way of knowing in itself', p. 12) of the nature of the image of God in man, in precisely the way analysed by Augustine in the *De Trinitate*. The suggestion of a power of perception beyond mere words, which L incorporates into the figure of Piers, is also indebted to Augustine.

216. Middleton, Anne
'The Passion of Seint Averoys [B.13.91]: "Deuynyng" and Divinity in the Banquet Scene', *YLS* 1 (1987) 31–40.

Seint Averoys is an outrageous coinage referring to the Arabic philosopher Averroes, here being used as a representative of 'the natural supernaturalism of much contemporary higher learning' (p. 33), of that speculative and materialistic natural philosophy which forms the basis of the fat Doctor's wisdom. The accusation, that natural science had ousted divinity in the teaching of the friars, had long been familiar. The library of John Erghome, Austin friar of York, is a good example of such learning.

217. Wirtjes, Hanneke
'*Piers Plowman* B.XVIII.371: "right ripe must" ', in Stokes and Burton (1987) 133–43.

Must means wine of the new vintage, produced here with miraculous speed. Association of wine and vintage with the Resurrection was traditional in Scripture and liturgy, but it is to the exegetes that L has gone to get the particular association between *must* and the vinegar (wine gone bad) drunk by Christ on the Cross.

218. Tavormina, M. Teresa
'Piers Plowman and the Liturgy of St. Lawrence: Composition and Revision in Langland's Poetry', *SP* 84:3 (Summer 1987) 245–71.

Two passages introduced in C (II 127–36, XVII 64–71) cite St Lawrence as a counter-example to certain degenerate churchmen of L's day. The legend of the saint and the passages in the liturgy where he is mentioned are very apt, in the first, to Theology's attack on the corruption of the ecclesiastical courts, and to the general question of proper and improper rewards; and in the second, to the discussion of the proper and improper ways for the clergy to receive and administer alms. 'Lawrence's life and death illustrate an ideal directly opposed to the clerical corruption, simony and greed so hated by Langland' (p. 266). The Lawrentian passages also contribute to some important general themes – emphasis on the duties of the clergy, concern about the right use of money and about the nature of heavenly reward.

219.   Galloway, Andrew
'Two Notes on Langland's Cato: *Piers Plowman* B.I.88–9;
IV.20–23', *ELN* 25 (December 1987) 9–12.

L shows a keen interest in Cato, especially in his position (as
a pagan writer) in a Christian moral hierarchy. He cites him
at an important moment in Holy Church's discourse (B I 90–
1; cf. Vasta 1965 [545]), and it is Cato who helps Reason by
saddling his horse (B IV 17).

Sources and use of Latin quotations; general use of scriptural exegesis and patristic writing

220.   Adams, M. Ray
'The Use of the Vulgate in *Piers Plowman*', *SP* 24:4
(October 1927) 556–66.

Relative frequency and source of biblical quotations in the
three texts argues against multiple authorship. L's learning
mainly scriptural and patristic, such as would have been
appropriate to a humble priest in lower orders. Quotations
are mostly from the Psalter and the Gospels, and mostly of
those passages found in the Breviary and the Missal.

221.   Sullivan, Sister Carmeline
THE LATIN INSERTIONS AND THE MACARONIC
VERSE IN PIERS PLOWMAN. Ph.D. dissertation,
Catholic University of America (Washington: Catholic
University of America Press, 1932).

PP is exceptional in the number of Latin scriptural quotations, patristic *excerpta* and aphorisms that are introduced
into the text. Some of these, especially scriptural quotations,
are extraneous to the text, acting as authoritative footnotes;
others are syntactically articulated with the text. There are
no great differences in practice between the three versions.

The purpose of the quotations seems always to be didactic rather than artistic, and they are introduced in a stereotyped way; they argue some familiarity with the original sources, not merely with *florilegia*. There are also, more interestingly, macaronic lines in which Latin words and phrases, usually scriptural, are worked into the English lines of the poem, often incorporated into the alliteration. [See also Hort 1938 [276].]

222. Donna, Sister Rose Bernard
      DESPAIR AND HOPE: A STUDY IN LANGLAND
      AND AUGUSTINE. Ph.D. dissertation, Catholic
      University of America (Washington: Catholic University
      of America Press, 1948).

      Investigates the meanings of hope and *wanhope* as they are used in *PP* and as they are to be understood against an Augustinian background. L's conception of both is primarily theological. Despair, being the vice directly opposed to the theological virtue of hope, is one of the sins against the Holy Ghost: it is freely chosen. It is treated by L on several occasions, and shown to be closely associated with presumption (in the account of Recklessness) and directly connected with sloth. The mentions of hope in the poem are similarly itemised. The motives for hope are in the promise of Redemption (e.g. in the Pardon episode) and its fulfilment (in Christ's Passion), and in the fruits of the Incarnation (Christ as physician, worker of miracles, fount of baptism and source of forgiveness). *PP* 'is not a poem of despair' (p. 176), despite what critics have said about its ending. Donna offers an elementary theological background to the poem, with very extensive quotation from it.

223. Robertson, D. W., jun. and Huppé, Bernard F.
      PIERS PLOWMAN AND SCRIPTURAL TRADITION
      (Princeton: Princeton UP, 1951). Excerpts (1–16, 234–48)
      reprinted in Vasta (1968) 190–216.

The scriptural quotations in the poem are the key to its allegorical meaning. The authors' method is to work from the quotations to the larger biblical context from which they are drawn, from there to patristic commentary ('in many respects . . . history's most significant intellectual achievement', p. 235) and from the commentary back to the allegorical meaning of the poem. They assume that L was working, if not with the authorities they cite, yet within the tradition they represent, including the tradition of fourfold exegesis of scripture (literal, moral or tropological, allegorical, anagogical). Where there are no scriptural quotations, the authors deduce their implied existence from allusions to key words and images (e.g. of food, clothing, money) in biblical concordances. The particular theme of the poem is the restoration, through Piers, of the true prelatical life, God's ministry on earth, which has been usurped by the friars (the attack on the friars is given a very important place in the poem, and much material is drawn from the antimendicant controversy, e.g. on poverty). More generally, like all medieval literature, the poet promotes *caritas* (love of God and one's neighbour) against *cupiditas* (love of oneself and the world). The analysis proceeds sequentially: the tower and the dungeon of the Prologue represent, allegorically, the Jerusalem and Babylon of scriptural tradition, Lady Meed the Whore of Babylon of the Apocalypse, and Piers the prelate whose tilling of the field is the preparation of the human heart through good works for the building of the tabernacle (Hunger is the false fear of temporal harm, though also spiritual hunger and the threat of excommunication). The interpretation of Dowel, etc. follows generally the scheme of Wells 1929 [508]. The book is important in drawing attention to levels of meaning that the modern reader, less versed in the Bible, may miss, and illuminating on certain parts and aspects of the poem where L is clearly working within the tradition of scriptural commentary (e.g. the Good Samaritan). But the denial of the literal meaning of the narrative, the extraction of the poem from its history (except that of the antimendicant controversy), the schematic rigidity with which methods of interpretation evolved for the purposes of Bible study are applied to a vernacular poem, the extrapolation from the poem of themes so general that their absence or presence could hardly be a matter of remark, are commonly recognised weaknesses of the book. [See e.g. Donaldson 1960 [224], Aers 1975 [399], 1986 [409].]

Reviews: M. W. Bloomfield, *Speculum* 27:2 (April 1952) 245–9.
T. P. Dunning, *MÆ* 24:1 (1955) 23–9.
R. W. Frank, *MLN* 68:3 (March 1953) 194–6.
S. Neuijen, *ES* 34:2 (April 1953) 79–83.
R. Quirk, *JEGP* 52:2 (April 1953) 253–5.

224. Donaldson, E. Talbot
'Patristic Exegesis in the Criticism of Medieval Literature: The Opposition', in Bethurum (1960) 1–26. Reprinted in Donaldson, SPEAKING OF CHAUCER (University of London: The Athlone Press, 1970) 134–53.

Witty attack on the excesses of the 'exegetical' method, pp. 5–16 taking issue with the interpretation of *PP* in Robertson and Huppé 1951 [223], and the authors' habit of constantly 'contorting the text to find the message they want to find' (p. 15). [See Kaske 1960 [225].]

225. Kaske, R. E.
'Patristic Exegesis in the Criticism of Medieval Literature: The Defense', in Bethurum (1960) 27–60. Reprinted in Vasta (1968) 319–38.

Shows the value, in relation to *PP* (pp. 32–48), of interpretation based on analysis of 'small and clear-cut uses of exegetical imagery' (p. 34), as opposed to the large claims of Robertson–Huppé 1951 [223]. [See Donaldson 1960 [222].]

226.   Fuller, Anne Havens
'Scripture in "Piers Plowman" B', *MS* 23 (1961) 352–62.

Listing of scriptural quotations and references to supersede
and correct that of Skeat 1877 [16].

227.   Smith, Ben H., jun.
TRADITIONAL IMAGERY OF CHARITY IN *PIERS
PLOWMAN* (Studies in English Literature XXI) (The
Hague: Mouton, 1966).

Uses medieval biblical exegesis (cf. Robertson and Huppé
1951 [223]) as the key to the meaning and function of certain
images of charity in *PP*; mounts a careful defence (pp. 7–16)
of the use of exegetical writing in literary investigation, as
well as of his own choice of the thirteenth-century biblical
commentary of Hugh of St Cher and the fifteenth-century
commentary of Denis the Carthusian to explicate the writings of a fourteenth-century poet. The passages examined,
using both L's own Latin quotations and also implied references to the Scriptures (identified from medieval concordances), are B I 146–62 (love as 'triacle of hevene'), B XIII
135–56 (Patience's definition of Dowel, etc.), B XVI (the
Tree of Charity) and B XVII (the Good Samaritan). Smith
chooses his ground effectively, and gives welcome emphasis
to the poetic reworking of traditional materials.

228.   Ames, Ruth M.
THE FULFILLMENT OF THE SCRIPTURES:
ABRAHAM, MOSES, AND PIERS (Evanston:
Northwestern UP, 1970).

Christian doctrine and history fulfil the Old Testament
promises of redemption, and thus reveal the unity of the
divine plan, the eternality of the temporal, and the Judaism

of Christianity. L writes within the context of this doctrine of fulfilment, as is shown particularly in his handling of the Messianic prophecies in B III, of Abraham (Faith), Moses (Hope) and the Good Samaritan (Charity) in B XVI–XVII and of Piers, as the embodiment of the New Law which fulfils the Old, in B VII and XVIII. (An extensive background to these ideas is given from patristic and Middle English writings.) But there was inevitably ambiguity in the medieval attitude to the Jews – reverence for their law and lawgivers, hostility to them for their rejection of Jesus. L unfortunately inherits these prejudices, though he shows a more than usual concern for the conversion of the Jews, both in the immediate and the apocalyptic future. This book is useful as a commentary on B XVI–XVII, but the rest is peripheral: a lot of attention is given to the comparatively minor theme of L's attitude to the Jews.

229. Barney, Stephen A.
'The Plowshare of the Tongue: The Progress of a Symbol from the Bible to *Piers Plowman*', *MS* 35 (1973) 261–93.

An important essay, which analyses in detail the symbolism of agricultural imagery in biblical, patristic and related writings, and shows how L makes use of this symbolism, particularly the close relationship traditionally established between ploughing and preaching (the tilling of the human soul and the planting of good works by the clergy). Related images are those of the word of God as seed, the soul as field and penitential activity as the cultivation of the soul. It is because of the existence of this body of imagery that L makes Piers a ploughman, and there are many evidences that he is using the traditional symbolism that related agricultural and ecclesiastical work (e.g. C VI, C XI 199, C XXII 252–336). The symbolism is, however, natural, and does not mean that Piers lacks a literal level – at the same time, he is not an 'ordinary plowman'. He is potentially allegorical from the start, as is shown in detailed analysis of C VIII–IX, and it is this that gives him the power to be developed later as a more comprehensively significant spiritual figure.

230. Alford, John A.
'Some Unidentified Quotations in *Piers Plowman*', *MP* 72–4 (May 1975) 390–9.

Sources for thirty-nine Latin quotations, traced chiefly to proverbial, legal, liturgical and patristic sources.

231. Benson, C. David
'An Augustinian Irony in "Piers Plowman" ', *NQ* 23 (221):2 (February 1976) 51–4.

The dreamer's attack on learning in B X 450–64, with his recommendation of the simple prayers of the unlearned, has vigour and dramatic plausibility, but is undermined by the quotation of the passage from St Augustine that purports to support it. In context, the passage is clearly a recommendation of learning, properly used, not a rejection of it.

232. Adams, Robert
'Langland and the Liturgy Revisited', *SP* 73:3 (July 1976) 266–84.

Generalisations about the liturgical structure of *PP* have been based on assumptions about L's knowledge of the Breviary drawn from the lists of Latin quotations in Hort 1938 [276]. But Hort's attributions are unreliable: in particular, L, though clearly familiar with parts of the Bible and with the Missal, shows little knowledge of the Breviary. Any extended structural debt to the liturgy is thus difficult to demonstrate. On the other hand, B XVI–XX, where quotations from the liturgy are much more frequent, do have a more liturgical structure – appropriately enough, since they celebrate, like the annual cycle of the liturgy, the gift of Christ's sacrificial love.

233. Lindemann, Erika C. D.
'Analogues for Latin Quotations in Langland's *Piers Plowman*', *NM* 78:4 (1977) 359–61.

Thirteen Latin quotations from non-biblical sources are used to point to the possible range of L's reading in exegetical, rhetorical and homiletic traditions.

234. Alford, John A.
'The Role of the Quotations in *Piers Plowman*', *Speculum* 52:1 (January 1977) 80–99.

The large number of Latin quotations is a striking feature of the poem: they are intrinsic to the poem's structure and meaning. They operate as a 'verbal concordance', following the well-established practice of homiletic and exegetical writers, associating biblical words, phrases and texts so as to demonstrate their unifying doctrinal significance and to pump out further meaning from them. The quotations act as an index to the larger contexts from which they are drawn and to which they return the reader. Alford claims that this was L's method of composition and that 'any passage will do' (p. 86) to illustrate the fact. The one he chooses is B XIV 1–96 (Haukyn's coat, Patience's explanation), where he shows how the Latin quotations are 'the matrix out of which the poetry developed' (p. 96). L's poem is thus carefully structured, the apparent roughness deriving from our failure to recognise the sub-textual processes of argument. The picture of the poet we should have is not of the inspired but untutored genius but of the typical medieval scholar 'poring over a variety of commentaries and preachers' aids' (p. 99). [Alford's article is an important one, and the passage he analyses works well to illustrate his argument, but his larger claim for his method ('any passage will do') will not do.]

235. Bennett, J. A. W.
'Langland's Samaritan', *Poetica* 12 (1981: for Autumn
1979) 10–27.

An analysis of patristic commentary on the biblical parable
of the Samaritan, and on the iconography of the Samaritan
in visual representation, as a context for a reading (essentially in the form of a detailed commentary) of L's treatment
of the episode as a paradigm of the Fall and restoration of
man.

236. Goldsmith, Margaret E.
THE FIGURE OF PIERS PLOWMAN: THE IMAGE
ON THE COIN (Piers Plowman Studies II) (Cambridge:
D. S. Brewer, 1981).

Uses the four Fathers of the Church (Augustine, Ambrose,
Gregory and Jerome) to open out themes and texts inter-
woven into the poem, especially those relating to Piers and
his transformations; assumes that L knew these writers,
directly or indirectly, and was fluent in Latin. The analysis
proceeds sequentially, with passages from the Fathers used
to illustrate Piers as 'pattern of righteousness' (Augustine),
something that dwells within us; as the image of God in man
(stamped in the coin of his soul); as Peter, or Moses, or
homo carnalis (e.g. in his recommendation of work on the
half-acre, which Goldsmith says is not equivalent to the
journey to Truth); as Patience; as the 'sinner' who shakes the
fruit from the tree (like Augustine in the *Confessions*) in the
Tree of Charity episode; as the Samaritan and Christ, Truth
clothed in flesh; and as the ploughman, using Gregory's
ploughing imagery. [Goldsmith manipulates an arbitrarily
chosen range of patristic authorities to produce parallels of
varied relevance, sometimes cues for misreading. The picture of Piers that emerges is confused rather than complex or
enigmatic, and the central idea, that the progressive revelations of Piers are like the burnishing of a coin so that the

King's image is more readily discernible, is simply not supported by the text of the poem (it is from Augustine's commentary on Psalm 4:7). The objections to the deliberate (p. 4) ignoring of contemporary theological writing (see Coleman 1981 [304]) must be considerable.]

Reviews: R. Adams, *SAC* 5 (1983) 144–6.
J. A. Alford, *Speculum* 59:1 (January 1984) 146–9.

237. Allen, Judson Boyce
THE ETHICAL POETIC OF THE LATER MIDDLE AGES: A DECORUM OF CONVENIENT DISTINCTION (Toronto: University of Toronto Press, 1982).

The book generally argues that reading medieval commentaries on classical writers is the best way of understanding the way medieval poetry works. *PP* is alluded to quite frequently. Allen follows Alford 1977 [234] and Adams 1978 [497] (and also the view of Bloomfield 1961 [283], p. 32, that reading *PP* is like 'reading a commentary on an unknown text') in arguing that 'the text of the poem obeys no logic of its own, but occurs as commentary on a development of an array of themes already defined elsewhere as an ordered set – usually by the Bible' (p. 275). He analyses B Prol. on the assumption that L 'begins by thinking about an array of Bible passages treating some common theme, and therefore, under medieval definitions, a concordance or a distinction. In the light of this array, he will develop examples, illustrations, or explanations, whose coherence as an assembled text derives from and depends simultaneously on the Bible passages under consideration, and the human situation which L feels those passages instruct' (p. 276). The relevant verses may not be actually quoted. To understand the text, the critic follows the process of amplification backwards. Analysis of *distinctiones* suggests that 'speech' and 'bonds or chains' are the major themes of the Prologue, whose message is that truth is to be found in proper use of language and the acceptance of right law. The question of salvation in the singular is answered, as often in L, in the plural, in terms of a Christian society (p. 278), though the arrival at the answer is specifically an individual one – it is an 'experiencing text' (p. 281). It is a poem essentially related, as commentary, to a world beyond itself: there is no textuality of poem as poem: what it does is what it is about (the *forma tractandi* and the *forma tractatus* are the same, p. 198). [Allen's remarks on *PP* are suggestive, but it will be seen that his machinery is more impressive that what it produces.]

238.   Donaldson, E. Talbot
'Langland and some Scriptural Quotations', in Benson and Wenzel (1982) 67–72.

L's use of scriptural quotation is often witty and playful, twisting the syntax to produce unexpected results, or applying familiar texts in unusual ways. His adaptation of the Pauline text in B XVIII 396 is particularly daring in relation to the promise of salvation for the unbaptised.

239.   Alford, John A.
'More Unidentified Quotations in *Piers Plowman*', *MP* 81:3 (February 1984) 278–85.

Sources of a further eleven quotations, mostly Latin. See also Alford 1975 [230].

240.   Allen, Judson Boyce
'Langland's Reading and Writing: *Detractor* and the Pardon Passus', *Speculum* 59:2 (April 1984) 342–62.

Many of the Latin quotations in A, especially the Pardon

passus, are found in the Psalter commentary of Hugh of St Cher, which L came across after doing his first draft (in Z). L characteristically worked, as Alford 1977 [234] argues, with such compilations, and with concordances and lists of *distinctiones* (tracing the meaning of a word in different biblical passages), building up his text from the rich apparatus of suggestion he found there. Quotations from commentaries like that of Hugh would carry with them the force of their context, and in this case, especially in the Pardon passus, the theme of the context is the *detractor*. L's response to criticism of Z was to build into his version, with help from Hugh, a condemnation of those who, like the priest who impugns the pardon, attempt to deny the value of the simple faith of those who do their duty well in the spiritual pilgrimage to truth. This way of reading L's poem accepts that one reads it '*already knowing* the answer' (p. 358) to the problems it presents, since the Latin authorities quoted constantly reinforce that knowledge. This is how allegory works, and we have to repeat L's way of reading. The strength of the poem is that L demands that his reading describe himself and his England correctly. [There is much that is suggestive, in this wildly vigorous essay, about L's reading and his way of writing, but the bearing that it has on the interpretation of the poem is difficult to see.]

241. Gray, Nick
'Langland's Quotations from the Penitential Tradition', *MP* 84:1 (August 1986) 53–60.

A group of Latin quotations in *PP* (eight are discussed), usually assumed to be from canon law, *auctoritates* or modified versions of Scripture, are taken from the Latin penitential tradition, that is, from the confessional manuals for parish priests and the penitential sections of the scholastic *summae*. L often employs them in contexts recalling their use by such writers.

242.   Barr, Helen
'The Use of Latin Quotations in *Piers Plowman*, with
Special Reference to Passus XVIII of the "B" Text', *NQ*
33 (231):4 (December 1986) 440–8.

Latin quotations are extensively used throughout *PP* to
support arguments and to teach. (There are also several
passages that show how such use of authorities can be
misused.) Commonly such quotations stand apart from the
surrounding syntax of the English verse lines, though there
are examples of syntactical integration. In B XVIII,
however, more of the quotations are absorbed into the
surrounding syntax than anywhere else; also, many more are
drawn from the church services, and give a more intense
sense of drama and a greater emotional power. The move
from instruction to action, from words to redemptive grace,
is thus reinforced.

243.   Goldsmith, Margaret E.
'Will's Pilgrimage in *Piers Plowman* B', in Stokes and
Burton (1987) 119–32.

In Scripture (especially the Epistle of James) and exegesis
(especially Augustine and Bernard) can be found the origins
of L's portrayal of Will as one who gradually comes to
recognise his own 'face in the mirror' (see B XV 162)
through his journey of self-discovery.

244.   Davlin, Sister Mary Clemente, OP
'*Piers Plowman* and the Books of Wisdom', *YLS* 2 (1988)
23–33.

L frequently quotes from the five Wisdom books of the
Bible, which constitute an 'intertext' for *PP*, informing
many of its apparent discontinuities and providing a model

for its generic variety, its theme of the search of the individual within the community for a knowledge of God and its often punning, riddling style.

Analysis of personifications, especially of the faculties (commonly with reference to origins in scholastic theology)

(*See* also [387]–[415] (Allegory).)

245. Jones, H. S. V.
'Imaginatif in Piers Plowman'. *JEGP* 13:4 (October 1914) 583–8.

Ymaginatif, as he is represented by L (a spokesman of Reason, entitled to speak of the spiritual uses to which knowledge of the physical world may be put), is derived from medieval faculty psychology, as represented in the *Benjamin Minor* of Richard of St Victor. Here, imagination is that power that conducts man from the plane in which the affections are in the service of God to the plane where the mind is put to that service. It was not just the power of recording, collating and recalling sense-impressions, but essential to the 'noetic soul'.

246. Sanderlin, George
'The Character "Liberum Arbitrium" in the C-Text of *Piers Plowman*', *MLN* 56:6 (June 1941) 449–53.

Cites patristic authorities to explain L's extension of the power of Liberum Arbitrium in C, where free choice becomes a universal power of the soul, capable of choosing good over evil in accord with its final goal of rectitude. The learning and theological subtlety of the C-reviser is thus further demonstrated.

247.   Quirk, Randolph
'Langland's Use of *Kind Wit* and *Inwit*', *JEGP* 52:2 (April 1953) 182–8. Reprinted in Quirk (1968) 20–6.

Kind Wit is the natural and inborn power of reason in all creatures. *Inwit* for the most part signifies the intellect (the *agens* aspect of *intellectus* in Thomist terms) which, with its power of distinguishing between good and evil, comes close to conscience. But L does not use it to mean conscience: his usage is 'precise and technical to a degree hard to parallel in Middle English' (p. 187).

248.   Quirk, Randolph
' "Vis Imaginativa" ', *JEGP* 53:1 (January 1954) 81–3. Reprinted in Quirk (1968) 27–9.

L's use of the term is rare in Middle English. Usually it refers to the reproductive imagination, a kind of memory bank of sense data. L uses it to mean the productive imagination, acting in a creative way upon the totality of images and with access to things spiritual.

249.   Schmidt, A. V. C.
'A note on the Phrase "Free Wit" in the C-Text of "Piers Plowman" (Passus XI.51)', *NQ* 15 (213):5 (May 1968) 168–9.

The introduction of 'fre wit' in C parallels the change of Anima to Liberum Arbitrium in C XVII in stressing the cognitive as well as the affective element in the activity of the will. The change is 'yet another instance . . . of his close acquaintance with the terminology and thought of scholastic theologians' (p. 169).

250. Schmidt, A. V. C.
'A Note on Langland's Conception of "Anima" and "Inwit" ', *NQ* 15 (213):5 (October 1968) 363–4.

The reference to Anima and Inwit in A X 43–54 are directly indebted to the *De Anima* of Cassiodorus and the *De Spiritu et Anima* attributed to Alcher of Clairvaux, memories of which are fused together in a characteristic Langlandian way.

251. Orsten, Elisabeth M.
'*Patientia* in the B-Text of "Piers Plowman" ', *MS* 31 (1969) 317–33.

L's idea of patience as an active virtue, not a merely passive one, is related to patristic writing, especially Augustine. It is traced through an analysis of Patience's role in B XIII–XIV, with special stress on the necessary relation of patience and poverty. Will's own growth in patience is the key to his spiritual progress.

252. Schmidt, A. V. C.
'Langland and Scholastic Philosophy', *MÆ* 38:2 (1969) 134–56.

L's personifications of the 'noetic' ('knowing') faculties of the mind are still often puzzling. The change from Anima in B to Liberum Arbitrium in C is intended to give the faculty a more universal significance: Schmidt traces this conception of *liberum arbitrium* as the 'essence' of human nature, the most significant of man's faculties, to a contemporary theologian, Ayguani. He also discusses theological origins of the new definition of *liberum arbitrium* in C, and of the idea that animals have free will (B VIII 52–6).

253.   Schroeder (Carruthers), Mary C.
'The Character of Conscience in *Piers Plowman*', *SP* 67:1
(January 1970) 13–30.

Personifications are not fixed in meaning but may shift and
develop in the narrative context. This is especially true of
Conscience, representing a complex and shifting theological
concept, who develops and is educated through his encounters in the poem. In the debate with Lady Meed, he is shown
as that aspect of moral discernment which seeks a reasonable
solution to things. But he lacks the illumination of grace; he
is also far too courteous to Meed. In B XIII he is again too
polite (to the Doctor), though he recognises now the limitations of rational knowledge and is prepared to learn from
Patience. In B XIX his mode of understanding, though still
human, is informed by grace. In the last passus, deserted by
grace, his human weakness is again revealed, and his (con-
scientious) courtesy towards the friars brings about disaster.

254.   Harwood, Britton J. and Smith, Ruth F.
'Inwit and the Castle of *Caro* in *Piers Plowman*', *NM* 71:4
(December 1970) 648–54.

Inwit is the faculty known as synderesis in Dominican theology, the cognitive attachment to the sovereign good – man's
direct knowledge of God – which informs conscience in its
active role.

255.   Whitworth, Charles W.
'Changes in the Roles of Reason and Conscience in the
Revisions of "Piers Plowman" ', *NQ* 19 (217):1 (January
1972) 4–7.

In scholastic terminology Conscience is that activity of
reason which is directed towards the ethics of conduct,
whether governed by the speculative reason or by synderesis

(the innate propensity to good). L's changes in the roles assigned to Reason and Conscience, from A to B, and from B to C, show him becoming more fully aware of this distinction, while the absence of Reason in C XXIII is a mark of the precariousness of Conscience guided by the innate habit of good alone.

256. Trower, Katherine B.
'The Figure of Hunger in *Piers Plowman*', *ABR* 24:2 (June 1973) 238–60.

Hunger in B VI has the literal meaning of famine, but also signifies spiritual hunger and, further, the hunger of the folk for Christ and of Christ for man's soul. Wasters offer no sustenance to this hunger, and the penitential life must be restored through a period of privation. This is Hunger's 'leechcraft', which is dramatised further in the episode of the Good Samaritan and in the false friar of B XX. That Hunger grows hungry again at B VI 278 is a sign of the unending hunger of Christ (with whom Piers is increasingly identified) for man's soul.

257. Harwood, Britton J.
'*Liberum-Arbitrium* in the C-Text of *Piers Plowman*', *PQ* 52:4 (October 1973) 680–95.

Liberum Arbitrium is not simply all the powers of the soul lumped together, but a specific faculty defined in scholastic terms as the power of will informed by reason. The choice that the will best makes (viz. Christ) is outlined in the discourse on Charity. The episode of the Tree of Charity puts the discourse into practice: the three props are a trinitarian metaphor for the activity of memory, intellect and will through which Liberum Arbitrium marshals his best understanding to a good act.

258.   Harwood, Britton J.
'Imaginative in *Piers Plowman*', *MÆ* 44:3 (1975) 249–63.

Reviews previous interpretations, which often assign Ymaginatif a high place among the mental faculties instructing the dreamer, and concludes that L uses Ymaginatif to personify the mind's power of making similitudes, of using natural phenomena as similitudes of spiritual truth. This was the usual medieval understanding of the term, and it is not a very lofty one. It gives no direct or intuitive knowledge of God, and leaves the dreamer none the wiser.

259.   Harwood, Britton J.
'Langland's *Kynde Wit*', *JEGP* 75:3 (July 1976) 330–6.

Cf. Quirk 1953 [247]. *Kynde wit*, the *vis cogitativa*, is man's power of knowing what is good for him *as a whole*, and refers basically to material benefit. It is not opposed to *clergye*, but is inferior to it, and in other respects limited.

260.   Clutterbuck, Charlotte
'Hope and Good Works: *Leaute* in the C-Text of *Piers Plowman*', *RES*, NS 28:110 (April 1977) 129–40.

Argues that *leaute*, though it does mean 'justice' (Kean 1964 [543], 1969 [553]), also has a theological meaning: it implies the virtue of hope. Hope of salvation is the source of good deeds. Instances of the use of the word (but more of the adjective *leel*) are cited to demonstrate this. The appearance of the allegorical figure *Leaute* at C XII is a turning-point, signalling the reawakening of hope in Will.

261.   Kaulbach, Ernest N.
'*Piers Plowman* B.IX: Further Refinements of *Inwitte*', in Jazayery, Mohammad, Polomé, Edgar C. and Winter,

Werner (eds.), LINGUISTIC AND LITERARY
STUDIES IN HONOR OF ARCHIBALD A. HILL, IV:
LINGUISTICS AND LITERATURE/
SOCIOLINGUISTICS AND APPLIED LINGUISTICS
(Trends in Linguistics, Studies and Monographs 10) (The
Hague: Mouton, 1979) 103–10.

Inwit in B IX, as defined by Quirk 1953 [247], needs to be
further refined, with the help of Augustine and John of
Salisbury, as that power of *ratio* which takes counsel of God
in its capacity as 'watchman' over the senses, determining
between good and bad. It 'is indeed a highly technical term'
(p. 108).

262. Minnis, Alastair J.
'Langland's Ymaginatif and Late-Medieval Theories of
Imagination', *Comparative Criticism: A Year Book* 3
(1981) 71–103.

Traces scholastic theories of the function of the *virtus imaginativa*, showing that its role, in calling up images of absent
things and using them to 'invent' new schemes or hypotheses, was not a humble one. But it needed the control of
reason to prevent it becoming mere fantasy. L's Ymaginatif
offers answers of a practical and readily understandable kind
to the intellectual questions raised in B VIII-XI – the relative
functions of faith and reason, the problem of predestination
and the fate of the righteous heathen. Ymaginatif gives help
in guiding the dreamer to reason through the use of images
and *exempla* – not 'the truth' but the means to understand it.
The passus also contains an important discussion and defence of the use of images, derived from imagination, in
poetry and other writing. L is not writing for scholars, and
the approach made through Ymaginatif is appropriate to 'an
audience of parish priests and literate laymen' (p. 91). An
appendix comments on the relationship between prophetic
dream vision and the faculty of the imagination.

263. Kaulbach, Ernest N.
'The "Vis Imaginativa" and the Reasoning Powers of
Ymaginatif in the B-Text of *Piers Plowman*', *JEGP* 84:1
(January 1985) 16–29.

Ymaginatif is a reliable spokesman for Reason, untainted by
sensuality. This allocation to Ymaginatif of a power of
reasoning from the senses is derived from Avicenna via
Vincent of Beauvais. It is animal sense reasoning, superior
to the human sense reasoning (with its vulnerability to
concupiscence) given to Thought earlier.

264. Morgan, Gerald
'The Meaning of Kind Wit, Conscience, and Reason in
the First Vision of *Piers Plowman*', *MP* 84:4 (May 1987)
351–8.

L's fictions and personifications are as usual clear and based
on precise theological distinctions. Kind Wit is the natural
understanding of the first principles of the speculative as well
as the practical intellect, something wider than the synderesis of Aquinas. Conscience is the fallible application of
this knowledge to act. Reason is the intellectual virtue of
prudence or practical wisdom, determining the means and
commanding the act.

265. Kaulbach, Ernest N.
'The "Vis Imaginativa secundum Avicennam" and the
Naturally Prophetic Powers of Ymaginatif in the B-text of
Piers Plowman', *JEGP* 86:4 (October 1987) 496–514.

Ymaginatif prophesies to Will in such a way as to blur
distinctions between natural and supernatural knowledge.
This power of transforming the data of human sensory
experience into the matter of revelation is the faculty attributed to the *vis imaginativa* by Avicenna (*Liber De*

Anima), who associates it specifically with the insight conferred on the natural prophet. This is the power associated with Ymaginatif in his interpretation of *vix salvabitur iustus*, in his many sensory discernments concerning supernatural truths, and in his power of interpreting Will's inner dream, his innate and natural prophetic intuition, which transcends that of *vis cogitativa*, being based on the Reson of Kynde rather than the Reson of Thought.

266. Morgan, Gerald
'Langland's Conception of Favel, Guile, Liar, and False in the First Vision of *Piers Plowman*', *Neophiloogus* 71:4 (October 1987) 626–33.

Favel represents cunning, not necessarily in itself duplicitous, Guile the power through which Favel's schemes are executed, Liar the falsification of the significance of things, and False the resultant deceit. These analyses are supported from Aquinas. Morgan notes a tendency towards clarification in B and C, but the figures are never as vague and confused as they have often been supposed to be.

267. Alford, John A.
'The Idea of Reason in *Piers Plowman*', in Kennedy, Waldron and Wittig (1988) 199–215.

L's idea of Reason is basically that of Latin *ratio* ('the poet thought in one language and wrote in another', p. 200). One context is legal, where law is an embodiment of divine reason, not of a social or human will: as a manifestation of the supreme truth, law reveals itself primarily to reason (*lex est ratio*), that power of the intellect which perceives God's transcendental order. Reason in *PP*, in three major appearances (the trial of Lady Meed, preaching to the people, instructing Will in the Vision of Middle Earth), functions thus in the poem as a moral absolute, a representative of divine order and divine justice. The Vision of Middle Earth shows particularly clearly that Will can have no power of reason of his own, only that in which he participates in the divine.

268.   Kaske, R. E.
'The Character Hunger in *Piers Plowman*', in Kennedy, Waldron and Wittig (1988) 187–97.

The character Hunger in B VI, though basically to do with physical hunger, has an added spiritual significance as that 'hunger and thirst after justice' of the fourth Beatitude, which, as the biblical exegetes show, is the particular enemy of idleness (so prevalent among the wasters of B VI, and indeed, as *acedia*, the root sin of *PP*), and particularly concerned with the rendering of what is due, *redde quod debes*, to God, one's neighbour and one's self.

Literary relationships

Relationships with literary traditions, and with (near-contemporary) religious and theological writing

269. Traver, Hope
THE FOUR DAUGHTERS OF GOD: A STUDY OF THE VERSIONS OF THIS ALLEGORY, WITH ESPECIAL REFERENCE TO THOSE IN LATIN, FRENCH, AND ENGLISH. Ph.D. dissertation, Bryn Mawr College (Philadelphia: John C. Winston, 1907).

A survey of the use of the allegory, with brief comment on the version in B XVIII, specifically on the peculiarity of placing the debate immediately before the Harrowing of Hell, and on the freedom and originality with which L handles the tradition.

270. Tucker, Samuel Marion
VERSE SATIRE IN ENGLAND BEFORE THE RENAISSANCE. (Columbia University Studies in English, Series II, Vol. III, No. 2) (New York: Columbia UP, 1908).

Satire is destructive, its weapons ridicule, contempt, exaggeration, its aim reform. *PP* (discussed pp. 70–9) is a satire 'in the broadest possible sense' (p. 70), but more a didactic poem. Concentrates on the 'satire against classes' and the portrayal of the Sins, thinks the poem graphic but lacking in humour, treats only the *Visio*, the rest being 'rather a tedious piece of work' (p. 79).

111

271.   Owen, Dorothy L.
PIERS PLOWMAN: A COMPARISON WITH SOME
EARLIER AND CONTEMPORARY FRENCH
ALLEGORIES (London: University of London Press,
1912; reprinted in Folcroft Library Editions, 1971).

Compares *PP* with *Li Romans de Carité*, by Barthélemy,
Renclus de Moillens; *Le Songe d'Enfer* and *La Voie de
Paradis*, by Raoul de Houdenc; the part of *Le Roman de la
Rose* by Jean de Meun; *Le Tournoiement d'Antéchrist*, by
Huon de Méri; *La Voie de Paradis*, by Rutebeuf; and *Le
Pélerinage de Vie Humaine*, by Deguileville. Compares their
use of allegory in general, of dream-setting, of personification, of allegorical action (e.g. quest or pilgrimage, joust,
battle or siege, marriage) and of allegorical devices (e.g.
clothing, armour, horses, the body as castle, food, medicine,
cleansing, documents, mirrors, trees). It is possible that L
knew some of these works, though much of the material is
from common stock. Owen attempts to relate the resemblances to the French poems in the different versions of
PP to the authorship debate then raging.

272.   Owst, G. R.
'The "Angel" and the "Goliardeys" of Langland's
Prologue', *MLR* 20:3 (July 1925) 270–9.

Owst's first statement of his view that the medieval sermon is
'the one complete clue to L's own thought and method of
treatment' (p. 270). *PP* is 'the fine product of English
medieval preaching' (p. 271) and it is only dilettanti like W.
P. Ker who do not recognise the fact. As an example, he
points to the close links between L's rat-fable and the
sermon preached by Bishop Brunton of Rochester after the
Good Parliament of 1376. The 'angel' is Brunton, and the
'goliardeys' is Sir Peter de la Mare, Speaker of the Commons. L and Brunton are both courageous and outspoken
critics of the political abuses of the time. [see Orsten 1961
[365].]

273. Owst, G. R.
PREACHING IN MEDIEVAL ENGLAND: AN
INTRODUCTION TO SERMON MANUSCRIPTS OF
THE PERIOD c. 1350–1450. (Cambridge Studies in
Medieval Life and Thought) (Cambridge: CUP, 1926).

Frequent mention of *PP*, and how, in its use of satirical
portraits and *exempla*, its citation of Latin authorities, its
knowledge of legal and commercial misdoing, its passion for
reform combined with conservative attitudes towards authority, its praise for the labouring poor, 'it represents
nothing more nor less than the quintessence of English
medieval preaching gathered up into a single metrical piece
of unusual charm and vivacity' (p. 295).

274. Oakden, J. P.
ALLITERATIVE POETRY IN MIDDLE ENGLISH,
vol. I: THE DIALECTAL AND METRICAL SURVEY;
vol. II: A SURVEY OF THE TRADITIONS.
Publications of the University of Manchester, Nos. CCV,
CCXXXVI (English Series, Nos. XVIII, XXII)
(Manchester UP, 1930, 1935).

In this, long the standard survey of Middle English alliterative verse, Oakden defers to Chambers on the dialect of *PP*,
accepts single authorship on the basis of metrical evidence (I
61) and includes *PP* (I 186–7) in the metrical survey, in which
he generally sees marked continuity from Old English. In
Volume II there is a brief account of *PP* (pp. 55–8) in the
chapter on 'The Poems as Literature', emphasising its debt
to *Winner and Waster* and its relationship to other alliterative poems of satire and allegory, its concern for social
issues, its realism, its idiosyncratic yet powerfully dynamic
structure, its spiritual intensity. In later chapters, *PP* appears, as one amongst many sources of statistical data in
Oakden's endless lists, in discussions of vocabulary, alliterative phrases and style.

275.   Owst, G. R.
LITERATURE AND PULPIT IN MEDIEVAL
ENGLAND (Cambridge: CUP, 1933; 2nd edn,
revised, Oxford, 1961). Pp. 548–75 reprinted in Vasta
(1968) 22–53.

Frequent illustrations from *PP*, throughout this important
and still unsuperseded study, of Owst's proposition that *PP*
is the prime example of a literary work that draws its
materials and language from the vernacular medieval sermon, e.g. realistic portrayal of the Sins, satire and complaint
against the abuses of the time, the political ideal of the
commonwealth, championship of justice for the oppressed,
respect for institutions and indignant rebuke of those who
corrupt them, stress upon good deeds, the gospel of hard
work.

276.   Hort, Greta
PIERS PLOWMAN AND CONTEMPORARY
RELIGIOUS THOUGHT (London: SPCK; New York:
Macmillan, 1938).

The Latin quotations are numerous, and are used in a way
that shows familiarity with the use of authorities in theological argument (probably gained from L's teachers). L knows
the Breviary and the Missal well, but shows no direct acquaintance with learned theological works. His understanding of contemporary theology underlies the *Visio*, the
faculties ascribed to man by scholastic theologians (e.g.
synderesis) helping him in his striving towards truth and
salvation. The *Vita* similarly draws on scholastic concepts,
e.g. Thought is *intellectus agens*, and Inwit *sensus communis*.
The debate about faith and good works, free will and grace
and predestination, uses the theologians' techniques of argument, as does the legal justification of the Atonement. L
moves between different authorities in a scholastic way, e.g.

in his discussion of penance, where different views are canvassed on the necessity of oral confession. It is the sort of poem that shows theological learning spreading down to parish priests and also to pious laymen, in a manner that foreshadows the Reformation. Hort's book is a valuable one, though much of it is superseded, and her attention to 'contemporary' religious thought hardly extends beyond Aquinas; her view of the state of L's learning has much to recommend it, though most would say now that it is understated. There are useful appendices showing the sources in the Breviary of L's Latin quotations.

277. Gwynn, Aubrey, SJ
THE ENGLISH AUSTIN FRIARS IN THE TIME OF WYCLIF (London: OUP, 1940).

Places L's attack on the greed and worldliness of the friars in the context of antimendicant writing, especially that of FitzRalph (pp. 221–4). Finds a specific allusion in B X 323 to the petition to Parliament in 1370 by two Austin friars to have the possessioners expropriated (for the friars' advantage, it was suspected).

278. Bloomfield, Morton W.
THE SEVEN DEADLY SINS: AN INTRODUCTION TO THE HISTORY OF A RELIGIOUS CONCEPT, WITH SPECIAL REFERENCE TO MEDIEVAL ENGLISH LITERATURE (East Lansing: Michigan State UP, 1952).

Briefly notes the personification of the Sins as characters rather than abstractions, their shifting identities, and the unusual framework of confession (pp. 196–8). L's is 'probably the greatest treatment of the cardinal sins in English literature' (p. 196). [There is a follow-up to Bloomfield's general treatment of the topic in Siegfried Wenzel, 'The

Seven Deadly Sins: Some Problems of Research', *Speculum* 43:1 (January 1968) 1–22.]

279.   Peter, John
COMPLAINT AND SATIRE IN EARLY ENGLISH
LITERATURE (Oxford: Clarendon Press, 1956).

Compares Chaucer's Monk and L's Sloth (pp. 4–9), contrasting L's directness and lack of ambiguity with Chaucer's lifelike vividness and subtlety. Sloth is a caricature, not a person, 'an incarnate abstract of the vices of a whole class or group' (p. 7). 'The poem seems hardly to have a personal author at all . . . he seems no more than an inspired spokesman for the commonplaces of medieval religion' (pp. 8–9). These are odd views, and seem to be the product of Peter's desire to make L represent the medieval genre of 'Complaint' (conceptual or allegorical, impersonal, systematic and mechanical, corrective, universal) as against Chaucerian or Renaissance 'Satire' (particular, personal, varied and flexible, enjoyably scornful, specific). It was sixteenth-century editors who made *PP* into a 'satyr' (p. 109).

280.   Erzgräber, Willi
WILLIAM LANGLAND'S 'PIERS PLOWMAN': EINE
INTERPRETATION DES C-TEXTES (Frankfurter
Arbeiter aus dem Gebiete der Anglistik und der Amerika-
Studien 3) (Heidelberg: Carl Winter, 1957).

The *Visio* is concerned with the problem of creating the just society, seeing the power of man to do so resting on natural reason (*ratio naturalis*) and obedience to the law of God as represented in the Old Testament. The Hunger episode and the Pardon scene show that this natural morality is insufficient to bring about an ordered human society. Man's sinfulness reveals to Piers that he places too much reliance on man's natural ability to do well. In the *Vita*, Dowel emphasises that the attempt to order man and society must rest on divine law and begin in humility and poverty. Dobet expands on this theme of patient poverty while moving towards the full demonstration of Christian law in the law of love, as it is manifested in man through his free will and in Christ through his Incarnation. Dobest comes back to the world, to establish there the love of Christ through the foundation of the Church. Erzgräber's book is a passus-by-passus account of the poem, using principally Aquinas and Duns Scotus as the sources for a commentary on L's theological meanings. It is as a theological work that the poem is chiefly regarded, and there is little attention to its form or structure or to its poetry.

Reviews: M. W. Bloomfield, *Anglia* 76:4 (1958) 550–4.
          S. Neuijen, *ES* 42:4 (August 1961) 244–8.

281.   Bowers, R. H.
'*Piers Plowman* and the Literary Historians', *CE* 21:1 (October 1959) 1–4.

Traditional characterisation of *PP* as a satire is very misleading: it is more in the genre of *consolation*, where a bewildered and unhappy narrator is instructed and comforted, especially through dialogue with an allegorical figure of authority, as in Boethius. Nor is the poem sprawling and lacking in design: the sense of confused direction is accurate to the experience of being educated.

282.   Wenzel, Siegfried
THE SIN OF SLOTH: *ACEDIA* IN MEDIEVAL THOUGHT AND LITERATURE (Chapel Hill: University of North Carolina Press, 1960).

A study of the history of the concept of the sin of sloth from early Christian times to the end of the Middle Ages, mostly drawn from theological and religious writings, but with a chapter on 'The Poets' that includes a section on L (pp. 135–47). Sloth figures in four passages as one of the Seven Deadly Sins. L's concept of sloth is most akin to the popular image of the sin, and bears a strong social or secular emphasis (having as much to do with neglect of worldly responsibilities as with spiritual neglect), though he does emphasise the link between sloth and despair. L does not seem to have inherited fully the scholastic definition of the vice, nor to have worked out his own ideas completely. Wenzel incidentally demolishes the old argument of Manly 1906 [101] that the sequence of events at the end of the confession of Sloth (B V 462–3) argues for a lost leaf and consequently for multiple authorship.

283.   Bloomfield, Morton W.
PIERS PLOWMAN AS A FOURTEENTH-CENTURY
APOCALYPSE (New Brunswick, NJ: Rutgers UP, N.D.
[1961]).

Aims to relate *PP*, in both form and content, to its fourteenth-century intellectual milieu, and especially to two traditions, the monastic tradition of perfection, and the Joachite tradition of apocalyptic history. Basically, the subject-matter of the poem is Christian perfection, which is a broader term than salvation and includes it. It is the creation of the monastic tradition, and the older and more social Christian world view (also related to Judaeo-Christian tradition), which sees the Kingdom of God not as a conglomeration of individually saved souls, but as a society of the just united in Christ. The poem is about social regeneration not individual salvation. 'It is oriented towards the Kingdom of God and eschatology. It finds its natural expression in the apocalyptic frame of mind and in corresponding literary forms' (p. vii). After discussing the form of the poem (apart from its relation to the doubtful genre of 'apocalypse') as being based on three literary genres (allegorical dream-narrative; dialogue, *consolatio*, or debate; encyclopaedic or

Menippean satire) and influenced by three religious genres (complaint, commentary and sermon), Bloomfield traces the development of the Christian monastic tradition of perfection, especially in its apocalyptic and eschatological aspects. Monasticism is the anticipation in this world of the Kingdom of God, and is concerned, in Joachim of Flora especially, with the realisation of that kingdom in history. The threat to this tradition offered by the friars, the pattern of all Christian and especially ecclesiastical corruption, is why the reform of the friars is such a crucial issue for L. L was well acquainted with monastic philosophy, including that of the fourteenth century (e.g. Uthred of Boldon, Thomas Wimbledon), showed sympathy towards the monastic orders, and shares their hostility to the friars. He also shares their apocalyptic sense of history: there are numerous prophetic passages in the poem, warning of imminent disaster (e.g. in the Prologue, the Meed episode, the Ploughing, frequently in Dowel, after the Harrowing), and an extensive analysis is offered of Dobest (B XXI—XX), where the deep immersion of *PP* in the apocalyptic vision of the world and its history is made fully explicit. Appendices deal with the knowledge of Joachim in fourteenth-century England, with L's knowledge of scholasticism, with the problem of interpreting Ymaginatif and with the place of the apocalyptic view of history in the late Middle Ages. Not everyone will agree on the presence or importance of Bloomfield's two traditions in *PP*, but this book remains a mine of information on religious and political thought in the fourteenth century, and his emphasis on L's historical consciousness and philosophically endorsed social commitment is important.

Reviews: T. P. Dunning, *RES*, NS 16:62 (April 1965) 188–90.
D. C. Fowler, *MLQ* 24:4 (December 1963) 410–13.
S. B. Greenfield, *CL* 15:4 (Fall 1963) 374–6.
R. E. Kaske, *JEGP* 62:1 (January 1963) 202–8.
R. E. Sullivan, *Speculum* 39:1 (January 1964) 121–4.

284. Bloomfield, Morton W.
'*Piers Plowman* as a Fourteenth-Century Apocalypse',
The Centennial Review of Arts and Sciences 5:3 (Summer
1961) 281–95).

Emphasises the importance of understanding the power of
apocalyptic vision in shaping the sense of history. *PP* is
primarily an apocalyptic poem, concerned not with the
individual's search for God, but with the quest for perfection
and the setting up of the Kingdom of God on earth. It is a
monastic ideal, to which the friars pose the greatest threat.

285. Yunck, John A.
THE LINEAGE OF LADY MEED: THE
DEVELOPMENT OF MEDIEVAL VENALITY
SATIRE (University of Notre Dame Publications in
Mediaeval Studies XVII) (Notre Dame: University of
Notre Dame Press, 1963).

An account of the growth of the tradition of venality satire in
medieval Latin and vernacular writing. Provides an important background for the Lady Meed episode (B II–IV) and
for L's 'vivid allegorical dramatization of the power of
money, of the secret and insidious effects of "graft" and
venality in blunting justice, oppressing the poor, the weak,
and the peaceful, undermining piety, concealing and supporting commercial fraud and all the sins of the senses,
gaining high position for the unworthy in the State and
especially in the Church' (p. 6). Yunck comments particularly (pp. 10, 290, 294ff) on the ambiguous way in which
Lady Meed is presented, as both attractive and reprehensible, and the way this reflects the perplexity caused to
moralists by money and the money economy. He thinks of
venality and the power of wealth as perhaps the fundamental
social problem for L, and one not confined to the Lady Meed
episode.

286. Spearing, A. C.
'The Art of Preaching and *Piers Plowman*', in Spearing,
A. C., CRITICISM AND MEDIEVAL POETRY
(London: Edward Arnold, 1964; 2nd edn, revised, 1972)
68–95 (107–34 in revised edn). Reprinted in Newstead
(1968) 255–82.

The course of events seems enigmatic, even phan-
tasmagoric, if *PP* is thought of as a story: but it is close to the
medieval sermon in many of its procedures, particularly its
readiness to digress on profitable matters (something came
up 'that seemed to need preaching about', p. 125), to come
back to points made earlier, to make apparently abrupt
transitions, to use verbal repetition. Good background on
the *artes praedicandi*.

287. Hussey, S. S.
'Langland's Reading of Alliterative Poetry', *MLR* 60:2
(April 1965) 163–70.

Surveys the field of alliterative verse and concludes that L
probably knew *Winner and Waster*, possibly *The Parliament
of the Three Ages*, *Wiliam of Palerne* and *Somer Soneday*,
but that he was not much indebted to any of them.

288. Salter, Elizabeth
'*Piers Plowman* and *The Simonie*', *Archiv* 203:4 (January
1967) 241–54.

L's literary antecedents are to be found not in full-scale
alliterative poems but in the loose semi-alliterative predomi-
nantly six-stress couplet of a poem like *The Simonie* ('On the
Evil Times of Edward II'), where there are common themes
of estates satire and the abuses of the time as well as metrical
and stylistic similarities. It is through such associations that
he would be acceptable to a more general audience, and to a
London one.

289.   Wesling, Donald
'Eschatology and the Language of Satire in "Piers
Plowman" ', *Criticism* 10:4 (Fall 1968) 277–89.

The eschatological view of a world on the verge of destruction seizes on satire as a weapon to give urgency to the vision
of the corrupt state of the world. Satire is dominant in the
Lady Meed episodes ('dialectic satire', the exposure of false
rhetoric and argument), in the Ploughing scene and the
banquet of B XIII ('invective satire', explosive abuse directed against wasters, fat scholars, etc.), and in B XIX–XX
('apocalyptic satire', specific examples of the decay of the
world and man's alienation from God). Satire is thematically
normative: it works to clarify language and understanding.

290.   Fowler, David C.
'Poetry and the Liberal Arts: The Oxford Background of
Piers the Plowman', in *Artes libéraux et philosophie au
moyen âge*. Actes du quatrième congrès international de
philosophie médiévale, Université de Montréal, 1967
(Montreal: Institut d'études médiévales, 1969) 715–19.

Regards L as a supporter of the secular against the regular
clergy, and of the tradition of the liberal arts against the new
scholasticism of the friars; in particular, sees the Barn of
Unity as representing Oxford University under attack by
Antichrist and the friars, with perhaps specific reference to
events of 1382.

291.   Knight, S. T.
'Satire in *Piers Plowman*', in Hussey (1969) 279–309.

Satire, understood as that realistic mode of writing which
aims at the correction of human behaviour in terms of the
conduct of life in the world, is present throughout the poem,
and is not superseded by the theological investigations that
grow out of and never entirely lose contact with it.

292. Shepherd, Geoffrey
'The Nature of Alliterative Poetry in Late Medieval
England' (The Sir Israel Gollancz Memorial Lecture,
British Academy, 1970), *PBA* 56 (1970) 57–76.

Considers the 'mnemonic cast' of alliterative poetry (its
fondness for lists, for instance, and other mnemotechnic
devices), its ultimate dependence upon memory, as related
to a generally traditional and backward-looking quality in
that poetry, a seriousness and ancient wisdom, a desire to
seek out the truth, a view of the poet as a kind of oracle.
Above all, in *PP*, memory is that which works on the
material of vision, attempting to render it memorable. L's
poem, like Julian's *Revelations*, may originally have taken its
inspiration from a series of actual, inexplicable visions (a
pardon being torn, a propped-up tree in an orchard). He did
not know, and had to work out, what they meant, in a series
of explorations.

293. Burrow, J. A.
RICARDIAN POETRY: CHAUCER, GOWER,
LANGLAND AND THE *GAWAIN* POET (London:
Routledge & Kegan Paul, 1971).

Associates *PP* with other 'Ricardian' poetry in its use of a
homely, 'unpoetic', loose-woven, open style (note especially
the ironic use of the traditional diction of alliterative
poetry), its use of fictional framed narrators, its use of the
'drastic' (p. 134) simile, its predilection for the literal even in
the midst of allegory and its generally unheroic view of
human life. Reference to *PP* throughout.

294. Harwood, Britton, J.
'*Piers Plowman*: Fourteenth-Century Skepticism and the
Theology of Suffering', *Bucknell Review* 19:3 (Winter
1971) 119–36.

The power of the poem is in the sense it conveys of being 'a processive and self-correcting work' (p. 120) rather than the orderly exposition of a system. The dynamic of the process is the search for that inward knowledge of God which leads man to Christ. Fourteenth-century nominalism had made this knowledge more problematic: God is not to be known by the rational faculty, but only through intuition. L's 'kynde knowyng' is an attempt to establish this knowledge as an activity of the dreamer's consciousness, rather than an abstraction, and it is associated closely with Conscience. The development of the poem is epistemological, as it tests out various ways of knowing, concluding upon Conscience as the recognition of divine suffering and of man's suffering in his recognition of the inadequacy of his response to the divine offer of grace.

295.   Means, Michael H.
THE CONSOLATIO GENRE IN MEDIEVAL ENGLISH LITERATURE (University of Florida Humanities Monograph 36) (Gainesville: University of Florida Press, 1972).

PP (pp. 66–90), principally to be thought of as a quest for perfection, is a fragmented *consolatio*, participating in the genre in that 'the subject of the poem is the education or enlightenment of the narrator, in this case concerning the nature of perfection and the necessity (both for the individual and society) of seeking perfection'; and in that 'the narrator's instructors teach what is appropriate to their allegorical nature; that is, the authority and bias of each instructor is limited by his nature, the mental faculty or the social or cosmological status he personifies' (p. 68). These propositions are best exemplified in the *Vita de Dowel*.

296.   Medcalf, Stephen
' "Piers Plowman" and the Ricardian Age in Literature', Chapter 19 in Daiches, David and Thorlby, Anthony

(eds.), THE MEDIEVAL WORLD (Literature and
Western Civilization 2) (London: Aldus Books, 1973)
643–96.

A full and lively account of the Prologue, with many comparisons with contemporary literature (pp. 643–54), and
some cursory remarks on the rest of the poem (pp. 684–8).

297. Krochalis, Jeanne and Peters, Edward (eds. and trans.)
THE WORLD OF *PIERS PLOWMAN* (University of
Pennsylvania Press, 1975).

A collection of primary sources, either in Middle English or
in English translation, to illustrate the intellectual and social
context of *PP*. Seven sections cover cosmology and geo-
graphy, social and anticlerical complaint, Brinton and Wyclif, moral *exempla* and saints' lives, practical instruction and
regulation of conduct, modes of allegorical interpretation
and, finally, death, punishment and the after-life. The editors try to choose works that would have been widely known,
and some that occur in conjunction with *PP* in manuscripts.

298. Lawton, David
'English Poetry and English Society: 1370–1400', in
Knight, Stephen and Wilding, Michael (eds.), THE
RADICAL READER (Sydney: Wild & Woolley, 1977)
145–68.

L represents the social upheavals of his day (Lollardy, the
Peasants' Revolt) far more powerfully than Chaucer. He
shares certain reforming tendencies with the Lollards (anticlericalism, attitude to clerkly learning), and his references
to *lollares* in C suggest at least a tense awareness on his part
of his relation to Lollard ideas. (Cf. Gradon 1980 [303],
Lawton 1981 [306]). He is sympathetic to the grievances of
the peasants.

299.   Turville-Petre, Thorlac
THE ALLITERATIVE REVIVAL (Cambridge: D. S.
Brewer; Totowa, NJ: Rowman & Littlefield, 1977).

PP in the context of other alliterative poems (more MSS,
more widely read, less specialised in diction, more flexible in
metre), comparatively briefly treated (chiefly pp. 31–2, 45–
7, 59–60). Note on its later reputation (pp. 125–8).

300.   Middleton, Anne
'The Idea of Public Poetry in the Reign of Richard II',
Speculum 53:1 (January 1978) 94–114.

The character of this poetry (Usk, Gower, Langland) is in
the 'constant relation of speaker to audience within an
ideally conceived worldly community' (p. 95). This manifests itself in serious public concerns, agreement on the
object of those concerns (the public good), plain style,
avoidance of exclusiveness, and the attempt to be comprehensive. There is also discussion of the role of the poet in
the activity of the world: L occupies a place somewhere
between minstrelsy and 'clergye', and for him the social role
of the poet is firmly grounded in experience, which is what he
speaks from, not clerical authority. It is not necessarily
personal experience, but 'a rhetorical embodiment of their
audience's best and most actively responsible selves as members of the human community' (p. 109).

301.   Salter, Elizabeth
'Alliterative Modes and Affiliations in the Fourteenth
Century', *NM* 79:1 (January 1978) 25–35.

The idea of an 'alliterative revival' and the associated idea of
a common inherited poetic tradition in fourteenth-century
alliterative verse rest upon very little real evidence. The
diversity, in origin and nature, of this verse needs to be

stressed, and particularly its association with forms of writing not usually classed as 'verse', e.g. rhythmically alliterative prose writing. One of these pieces of writing, Gaytryge's *Treatise*, shows particularly close resemblance to *PP* in metre and phrasing; so too do certain semi-alliterative sermons in British Library MS Add.41321. These and other such works are the raw materials from which L refined his poetic techniques.

302. Salter, Elizabeth
'Langland and the Contexts of "Piers Plowman"', *E&S*, NS 32 (1979) 19–25.

The contexts are not in other alliterative poetry, but in religious writing generally, particularly encyclopaedic compilations. L is in many ways more of a *compilator* than a poet, having a limited opinion both of his own role as a poet and of the value of what he does except as communication of truth. Yet of course he is far more than a compiler, particularly in the imaginative power he displays in the creation of a figure like Piers.

303. Gradon, Pamela
'Langland and the Ideology of Dissent', Sir Israel Gollancz Memorial Lecture, British Academy, 1980, *PBA* 66 (1980) 179–205.

L had ample opportunity, historically, to absorb and be influenced by Wyclif and Wycliffite ideas, but whether he was much influenced is doubtful. His criticism of the clergy is traditional, as is the attack on their temporalities; recommendations of clerical poverty have a long history, as have denunciations of fighting clerics and attacks on relic-mongering. L's use of *loller* probably has nothing to do, specifically, with Lollards. Piers Plowman himself is not to be identified in any way with the poor priest idealised by the

Lollards, and L's attitude to the Church is quite different from that of Wyclif and his followers. At most, *PP* may reflect contemporary controversy surrounding the Lollards, and some of his characters may, for purposes of demonstration, adopt ideas and ways of speaking that were or came to be associated with the Lollards.

304.   Coleman, Janet
PIERS PLOWMAN AND THE *MODERNI* (Letture di Pensiero e d'Arte) (Rome: Edizioni di Storia e Letteratura, 1981).

L is fully conversant with contemporary philosophical, theological and legal debate, and his vision of society and its reform is throughout informed by his knowledge. Much of *PP* is a vernacular version of what was going on in the schools. The concern of the *moderni* (William of Ockham and his followers), once they had distinguished between the sphere of faith (of God's *potentia absoluta*) and the sphere of moral reason (of God's *potentia ordinata*, or power deliberately made contingent), was with the great questions of salvation, of foreknowledge, predestination and free will, of merit, reward and justification – as well as the role that language plays in the demonstration of truth. The quest for salvation, which is also the search for the meaning of justice, is to learn what you owe, and how the rendering of what you owe (*redde quod debes*) will win salvation. This is the organising principle of *PP*, and relates L to the *moderni* and their belief that God's grace is granted to him who 'does what is in him' (p. 39). The *Visio* is much occupied with these questions of reward, good and bad, in relation to divine and human law, as is illustrated in extended analysis. These are moral questions, where Conscience is the guide. The problem with the Pardon is that it works according to the *potentia ordinata* but impinges upon the *potentia absoluta*. The discussion of the salvation of the righteous heathen in B X–XV is likewise much indebted to contemporary scholastic debate

(Trajan is saved by 'doing what is in him'), though C modifies the position, emphasising *sola fides*, thus reflecting a late fourteenth-century reaction against the *moderni*. Coleman also deals, with similarly persuasive authority, with non-scholastic Latin writing of the period (e.g. Holcot) which may have acted as a channel through which university theological and other debate passed to L, and also with the means by which such debate filtered down through education to the non-ecclesiastical layman (e.g. the grammatical metaphors in *PP*). [See also Coleman 1981 [374].]

305. Emmerson, Richard Kenneth
ANTICHRIST IN THE MIDDLE AGES: A STUDY OF MEDIEVAL APOCALYPTICISM, ART, AND LITERATURE (Seattle: University of Washington Press, 1981).

Analyses (pp. 193–203) Antichrist's attack on the Church of Unity in B XX, the climax of the poem, in the context of the popular medieval Antichrist tradition. The poem as a whole, through its numerous prophecies, develops a sense of apocalyptic expectation, in which the hopes of a *renovatio mundi* expressed in the *Visio* seem unlikely to be fulfilled. In Dobest, there are two attacks on the Church, one in B XIX, in the past, by a type of Antichrist, allegorically Pride, which is withstood, the other in B XX, in the present, to which the corrupted Church succumbs. The latter is conducted by Antichrist himself, portrayed as a historical character and in other respects (e.g. the image of the uprooted tree whose roots are made to bloom, B XX 53–5) in accordance with the tradition of the eschatological figure who precedes the Second Coming. The conclusion shows humankind unable to stand against Antichrist's attack, and presages not the millennial social transformation but the Coming of Christ (in the person of Piers, whom at the end Conscience goes out to seek).

306.　Lawton, David A.
'Lollardy and the "Piers Plowman" Tradition', *MLR* 76:4
(October 1981) 780–93.

Brief reference to *PP* itself (pp. 792–3) suggests that the
issue is not so much whether L had Lollard sympathies, as
that 'Lollards had Langlandian sympathies' (p. 793).

307.　Braswell, Mary Flowers
THE MEDIEVAL SINNER: CHARACTERIZATION
AND CONFESSION IN THE LITERATURE OF THE
ENGLISH MIDDLE AGES (London and Toronto:
Associated UPs, 1983).

PP is discussed, pp. 72–81. Confession of Sins (B V) is
directly influenced by confessional manuals such as John
Mirk's *Instructions for Parish Priests*. Presentation through
monologue is very similar to that in the fourteenth-century
penitential manual *The Clensyng of Mannes Soule*. The
penitential tradition is also active in the false 'confession' of
Lady Meed, and in the process of reform in Haukyn and
Long Will.

308.　Salter, Elizabeth
FOURTEENTH-CENTURY ENGLISH POETRY:
CONTEXTS AND READINGS (Oxford: Clarendon
Press, 1983).

Argues (pp. 86–116) that *PP* cannot usefully be seen as part
of any 'school' of alliterative writing. It is better seen in the
context of moral satire (e.g. Gower) or of late fourteenth-
century spiritual writers like Hilton. It is a powerful response, full of disturbance and conflict, in structure, style
and allegory as well as content, to the intellectual and social
crisis of the late fourteenth century, yet characterised by the
strength of L's inner vision.

309. Lawton, David A.
'The Unity of Middle English Alliterative Poetry',
Speculum 58:1 (January 1983) 72–94.

The unity of a central body of alliterative poetry is in issues
raised most importantly and influentially in *PP* – 'penance
and the role of vernacular writing in inducing it' (p. 74).
'Penance, both on the individual and social level, is Langland's primary concern in *Piers Plowman*' (p. 77). He means
to disturb his audience into awareness of the need for it: this
is how the vernacular poet justifies his existence. 'After *Piers
Plowman*, for an English vernacular poet to write alliterative
poetry is to do well' (p. 80).

310. Emmerson, Richard Kenneth
'The Prophetic, the Apocalyptic, and the Study of
Medieval Literature', in Wojcik, Jan and Frontain,
Raymond-Jean (eds.), POETIC PROPHECY IN
WESTERN LITERATURE (London and Toronto:
Associated UPs, 1984) 40–54.

(*PP* occupies pp. 49–54 of this valuable survey.) The *Visio*
focuses upon the contemporary world, the concern of the
prophet. It is a vision of the future as it will be unless certain
reforms are made, and as it may be if they are. The shift from
social concerns to the quest for individual salvation after the
Pardon scene brings in an increasingly apocalyptic view of
the contemporary scene, concluding in the portrayal of a
world suffering from the evils of the last days, an apocalyptic
vision of the imminent future – the attack of Antichrist upon
Unity. There is no hope, except of a divine intervention.

311. Adams, Robert
'Some Versions of Apocalypse: Learned and Popular
Eschatology in *Piers Plowman*', in Heffernan, Thomas J.
(ed.), THE POPULAR LITERATURE OF MEDIEVAL

ENGLAND (Tennessee Studies in Literature 28)
(Knoxville: University of Tennessee Press, 1985) 194–236.

Attempts to distinguish the kinds of apocalyptic tradition
that are important for understanding *PP*; rejects the influence of Joachim (see Bloomfield 1961 [283]), and argues that
Langland's apocalypticism is in a conservative tradition
going back ultimately to St Augustine.

312.   Dolan, T. P.
'*Passus* in FitzRalph and Langland', *ELN* 23:1
(September 1985) 5–7.

The use of the term *passus* is found before L in a sermon
delivered by Richard FitzRalph in London in 1356, where
the Latin version of the sermon has the text divided into
sections called *passus*.

313.   Schless, Howard H.
'Fourteenth Century *Imitatio* and *Piers Plowman*', in
Boitani, Piero and Torti, Anna (eds.),
INTELLECTUALS AND WRITERS IN
FOURTEENTH-CENTURY EUROPE. The J. A. W.
Bennett Memorial Lectures, Perugia, 1984 (Tübingen:
Gunter Narr Verlag; Cambridge: D. S. Brewer, 1986)
164–77.

One source of sanctity is the patterning of one's life to some
holy model (e.g. the *imitatio Christi*). There are many
resemblances between the early *devotio moderna* of the
fourteenth-century (originating with Gerard Groote) and
PP, particularly the idea that through *imitation* one may rise
to *identification*. The poem consists of a series of upliftings:
Piers becomes identified with the perfect life of man in
Christ, while Will, through imitation of Piers, especially in B
XV–XVII, comes to recognise the God within.

314. Szittya, Penn R.
THE ANTIFRATERNAL TRADITION IN
MEDIEVAL LITERATURE (Princeton: Princeton UP,
1986).

A comprehensive history of the literary tradition and language of antifraternal writing in France and England in the
thirteenth and fourteenth centuries (especially William of St
Amour, Richard FitzRalph and Wyclif), showing how fully
L draws upon this tradition, especially for his figure of *Sire
Penetrans-domos*, the friar of B XX, in whom we are to
recognise the friar of apocalyptic and prophetic antifraternal
writing, whose appearance at the door of the Church presages the coming of Antichrist. Chapter 7 deals specifically
with *PP*, showing how insistently throughout the poem L
recurs to the friars as the most potent forces working for the
corruption and downfall of the Church. L is different from
Chaucer in his emphasis on the symbolic and eschatological
role of the friars as the agents of Antichrist. He also associates them, in a poetically powerful way, with other groups
who pervert God's law – wanderers, minstrels and beggars –
and indeed with Will himself. The last passus shows us Will
in the final stages of physical decay, subject to the specious
arguments of Need (who speaks like a friar), conscious only
of the desire to hang on to life, and in the same state of
spiritual torpor as a Church annexed by the friars. In the
latter half of the passus, the friars, penetrating the Church
and driving out Conscience, are the omen of the approach-
ing end of the world. If the problem set by the friars is not
solved the Church is doomed.

315. Dolan, T. P.
'Langland and FitzRalph: Two Solutions to the Mendicant
Problem', *YLS* 2 (1988) 35–45.

L's concern that friars should have a 'fyndynge', or regular
income, is directed specifically at the Franciscans, who were

most absolute in their insistence on poverty. They were also the order of friars who in their (would-be) uncompromising imitation of Christ came closest to L's ideal of the religious life. He wants to save them. By contrast, FitzRalph, whose attacks on the Franciscans seem superficially similar, wants to destroy them.

316. Von Nolcken, Christina
'*Piers Plowman*, the Wycliffites, and *Pierce the Plowman's Creed*', *YLS* 2 (1988) 71–102.

Enthusiasm to associate L with the Wycliffites has its roots in the Reformation, but L probably knew little of their writings. His poem is never associated with them in manuscript, nor with heresy in contemporary opinion. He has little to say about the major articles of their belief. His uncertainty about knowledge and the processes of our understanding within our temporal existence, like that of the nominalists, contrasts with Wyclif's 'realism', his certainty that the archetypal can be perceived in the temporal. *Pierce the Plowman's Creed*, by contrast, is thoroughly representative of the views of the Wycliffites, and its allegory is clear and certain. It has acted as a false bridge between L and the Wycliffites.

317. Wenzel, Siegfried
'Medieval Sermons', in Alford (1988) 155–72.

L's debt to contemporary preaching.

318. Yunck, John A.
'Satire', in Alford (1988) 135–54.

PP seen in the context of medieval traditions of satire.

Direct comparisons with Dante and with contemporary English writers

319. Zeeman (Salter), Elizabeth
'Piers Plowman and the Pilgrimage to Truth', *E&S* NS 11 (1958) 1–16. Reprinted in Vasta (1965) 195–215, and in Blanch (1969) 117–31.

Pioneering article that discusses the parallels between *PP* and the writings of the fourteenth-century English mystics (especially Hilton's *Scale of Perfection*), particularly the idea of the 'indwelling' of Christ in the soul (B V 615), and the search for Truth directed by Love, guided by Piers, in whom man partakes in the divine.

320. Muscatine, Charles
'Locus of Action in Medieval Narrative', *RP* 17:1 (August 1963) 115–22.

The action of Dante's *Divine Comedy* is set in a world that is ordered and intelligible, corresponding to the equilibrium of high Gothic and scholasticism. In L (pp. 120–2), by contrast, the spatial environment is restlessly shifting, even surrealistic, creating a sense of instability that figures the disintegration of Gothic and the world view that sustained it.

321. Bennett, J. A. W.
'Chaucer's Contemporary', in Hussey (1969) 310–24. Reprinted in Boitani, Piero (ed.), J. A. W. BENNETT: THE HUMANE MEDIEVALIST, AND OTHER ESSAYS IN ENGLISH LITERATURE AND LEARNING, FROM CHAUCER TO ELIOT (Lettura di Pensiero e d'Arte) (Rome: Edizioni di Storia e Letteratura, 1982) 13–29.

Chaucer and L have more in common than is usually recognised: their 'Englishness', their abrupt juxtaposition of high and low, their observation of the estates of society in their Prologues. Chaucer must have known *PP*, if not L, and his ultimate concerns and deeper sympathies are not so very different.

322.   Calí, Pietro
       ALLEGORY AND VISION IN DANTE AND
       LANGLAND (Cork UP, 1971).

There are great differences: L's poem is less systematically structured, has more sense of the problems of the ordinary Christian, is more insistent on the basic simplicities of poverty and love. But L and Dante have much in common in their vivid representation and human reality and their undogmatic handling of dream-allegory. There is a similar vastness of moral landscape and closeness of detail of sinful humanity in B II–IV as in the *Inferno*, as well as similar roles for interpreters (Holy Church, Virgil). The theme of Repentance is pursued in *PP* as in the *Purgatorio*, with that sense in the Dowel passus of the dreamer, like Dante, progressing painfully in spiritual understanding. In Dobet and Dobest, Piers plays a part similar to that of Beatrice as the transfigured agent of the protagonist's growth in spiritual insight and love. As poets, Dante and L have a similar power of endowing abstract concepts with reality and vitality, of incarnating vision in flesh. 'If Dante's living characters precipitate, as it were, the moral and spiritual meaning of their symbolical function, Langland's personifications from a conventional abstractness attain to an equally valid incarnation of human truth' (p. 186).

323.   Mann, Jill
       CHAUCER AND MEDIEVAL ESTATES SATIRE
       (Cambridge: Cambridge UP, 1973).

Valuable comparison throughout of L's portrayal of the estates of society with Chaucer's. In a more specific comparison (pp. 208–12), L is shown to be closer to Chaucer than is usually recognised – in his manipulation of narrative point of view, richness of observation, sense of different viewpoints, of the world at work. L surely influenced Chaucer.

324. Taitt, Peter S.
'Incubus and Ideal: Ecclesiastical Figures in Chaucer and Langland', in Hogg, James (ed.), ELIZABETHAN AND RENAISSANCE STUDIES (Salzburg Studies in English Literature vol. 44) (Salzburg: Universität Salzburg, Institut für Englische Sprache, 1975).

Detailed analysis of L's portrayal of friars, summoners, clerks, pardoners, the monastic orders, parsons and parish priests (pp. 84–157) compared with Chaucer's treatment (pp. 158–98). Chaucer has more psychological depth and interest in characterisation, where L places figures in the context of a fuller and more overt pattern of instruction and polemic; in L there is less irony, the imagery is simpler, though often forceful, the word-play has more of a thematic function; L aims to involve the reader spiritually, in an urgent way, rather than dramatically.

325. Kirk, Elizabeth D.
' "Who Suffreth More than God": Narrative Redefinition of Patience in *Patience* and *Piers Plowman*', in Schifforst, Gerald J. (ed.), THE TRIUMPH OF PATIENCE (Orlando: UPs of Florida, 1978) 88–104.

Both poems show a movement from a negative and passive to a positive view of patience, in which it becomes a very active kind of *imitatio dei*.

326. Schmidt, A. V. C.
'Langland and the Mystical Tradition', in Glasscoe (1980) 17–38.

The usual contrast of L and Julian of Norwich (e.g. in social commitment) misses their unanimity in asserting the power of the will of good in man (represented in Conscience in *PP*). Comparison of Julian's parable of the servant and the lord with L's Tree of Charity shows in both a power to give concrete expression to mysterious spiritual truths through the creative imagination, through art. The Tree is a genuinely mystical 'showing'.

327. Windeatt, B. A.
'The Art of Mystical Loving: Julian of Norwich', in Glasscoe (1980) 55–71.

Interesting comparison (pp. 57–9) of the literary questing role of the dreamer in *PP* and the similar role, explicitly autobiographical, of Julian; the sense of structure given by exploration; the existence of both works in the form of a core of vision successively worked upon and revised.

328. Kane, George
'Langland and Chaucer: An Obligatory Conjunction', in Rose, Donald M. (ed.), NEW PERSPECTIVES IN CHAUCER CRITICISM (Norman: Pilgrim Books, 1981) 5–19.

Much is to be gained from the comparison of two poets so apparently different: common ground in vernacular tradition, in the teaching of Latin grammar and rhetoric, in their consciousness of themselves as poets. But Chaucer is confident about his poetic vocation, where L is obsessively concerned with his: his apologia in C, like the conversation with Ymaginatif in B, reveals a cruel depth of insight into the

problems of the artist who writes on moral and spiritual
themes beside which Chaucer's Retractions seem serene.

329. Holloway, Julia Bolton
'Medieval Liturgical Drama, the *Commedia*, *Piers
Plowman* and *The Canterbury Tales*', *ABR* 32:2 (June
1981) 114–21.

The liturgical play of the journey to Emmaus is behind many
of the dreamer's appearances and epiphanies in *PP* (including his first appearance as a *peregrinus*, in a sheepskin), and
echoed too in his air of self-satisfaction, while the vision of
the risen Christ in B XIX echoes the *Visitatio Sepulchri*.

330. Schmidt, A. V. C.
'The Treatment of the Crucifixion in *Piers Plowman* and
in Rolle's *Meditations on the Passion*', in Hogg, James
(ed.), SPIRITUALITÄT HEUTE UND GESTERN
(Analecta Cartusiana, 35, Band 2) (Salzburg: Universität
Salzburg, Institut für Anglistik und Amerikanistik, 1983)
174–96.

Shows how, in their use of imagery, both Rolle and L make
an effort to distil and concentrate 'the essential features of a
long and rich tradition made up of both learned and vernacular elements' (p. 176). Concentrates on the imagery of the
poisoned drink and the love-drink (B XVIII 364–72), of the
blinding of the sun at the moment of Christ's death (V 592–3,
XVIII 60) and of the poverty of Christ on the Cross (XX 40–
50).

331. Baker, Denise N.
'Dialectic Form in *Pearl* and *Piers Plowman*', *Viator* 15
(1984) 263–73.

The poems use medieval dialectic, the purpose of which is to affirm the integrity and unity of the Church's teachings by demonstrating that contradictions are only apparent, being based for instance on misunderstanding of key words. The dreamer's questions about predestination, salvation by faith or works, the necessity of baptism for salvation, are typical of the procedures of dialectic. The apparent assertion that Trajan is saved by works is superseded in the dialectic process, and Ymaginatif confirms that baptism is necessary. [But see Whatley 1984 [490].]

332. Baldwin, Anna P.
'The Tripartite Reformation of the Soul in *The Scale of Perfection*, *Pearl*, and *Piers Plowman*', in Glasscoe, Marion (ed.), THE MEDIEVAL MYSTICAL TRADITION IN ENGLAND. Papers read at Dartington Hall, July 1984 (Cambridge: D. S. Brewer, 1984) 136–49.

The restoration of God's image in man (see Raw 1969 [554], Murtaugh 1978 [572]) is conceived of as a tripartite one in some Middle English writings, including *PP* (pp. 143–7). The Trinity is important in L's analysis of the Three Lives, especially in Dobet.

333. Economou, George D.
'Self-Consciousness of Poetic Activity in Dante and Langland', in Ebin, Lois (ed.), VERNACULAR POETICS IN THE MIDDLE AGES (Studies in Medieval Culture XVI) (Western Michigan University: Medieval Institute Publications, 1984) 177–98.

L's self-consciousness of himself as a poet is acute, but different from that of Dante. It is expressed particularly in the 'apologia' and in B XII. He sees himself in the company of contemporary minstrels rather than the poets of the past, and has to create a special group of such minstrels ('God's minstrels') to associate himself with in order to justify his life and work as a poet, which in the end he does.

334. Nolan, E. Peter
'Beyond Macaronic: Embedded Latin in Dante and Langland', *Acta Conventus Neo-Latini Bononiensis* [Proceedings of the Fourth International Congress of Neo-Latin Studies, Bologna, 1979], Medieval and Renaissance Texts and Studies 37 (Binghamton, 1985) 539–48.

The Latin embedded in *PP* often serves the central literary and doctrinal purposes of the poem: the mixing of Latin and English may deliberately create a sense of conflict or disorder, or they may gloss each other, or they may stand, respectively, for the immutable and the corruptible in the account of the Incarnation. Always the effect is to give special prominence to problems of language, as is appropriate in a poem in which Meaning is the object of the quest.

335. Bishop, Ian
'Relatives at the Court of Heaven: Contrasted Treatments of an Idea in *Piers Plowman* and *Pearl*', in Stokes and Burton (1987) 111–18.

Two senses of the word *court* were available to L (court of law, king's court) and he plays upon them cleverly. He is particularly interested in the idea of having 'friends at court': it is allegorical friends and relatives who will help in gaining access to the court of heaven at the end of Piers' directions to Truth (B V). In *Pearl*, and in history, real relatives who had gone before were expected to intercede with the Prince of Heaven. Some of Piers' listeners (e.g. the *commune womman*) take his advice equally literally.

336. Cooper, Helen
'Langland's and Chaucer's Prologues', *YLS* 1 (1987)
71–81.

Chaucer knew *PP* and the version he knew was the A text.
All the passages of estates satire and social analysis that
seem to have influenced the General Prologue, including
those from the Prologue to *PP*, are there in A. Further
resemblances are to be seen in the spring-opening, the motif
of wanderings (pilgrimage), the emphasis on apparel. But
there are many differences.

337. Holloway, Julia Bolton
THE PILGRIM AND THE BOOK: A STUDY OF
DANTE, LANGLAND AND CHAUCER (American
University Studies, Series 4: English Language and
Literature, vol. 42) (New York, Berne and Frankfurt:
Peter Lang, 1987).

Chiefly interested in the writer's representation of himself as
a pilgrim, read in the context of Luke's account of the
pilgrims at Emmaus. Much on the traditional iconography of
the Emmaus story. Thus Will, Piers and Haukyn reflect the
triad of Luke, Christ and Cleophas in the Emmaus story; the
professional palmer of B V has the role of Cleophas. L
himself is a composite: a minstrel and a fool, but one who is
ever a pilgrim and wishes to know Christ.

338. Holloway, Julia Bolton
'The Pilgrim in the Poem: Dante, Langland, and
Chaucer', in Russell (1988) 109–32.

An abbreviated version of Holloway 1987 [337]. The writers
use Luke's account of the pilgrims at Emmaus as 'their
intertextual paradigm of reader response to tales within tales

within which the wise writer is present as a foolish pilgrim'
(p. 112).

Audience, reception, influence; comparisons with later writers

339. Chambers, R. W.
'Poets and their Critics: Langland and Milton'. The
Warton Lecture on English Poetry (1941), *PBA* 27 (1941)
109–54.

An attack on the 'Higher Criticism' provides the opportunity
for a further refutation of Manly's multiple authorship
theory for *PP*, which denies the unity of L's inspiration,
while an attack on the 'pseudobiographical' criticism of
Milton includes some comparisons between *PP* and *Paradise
Lost*.

340. White, Helen C.
SOCIAL CRITICISM IN POPULAR RELIGIOUS
LITERATURE OF THE SIXTEENTH CENTURY
(New York: Macmillan, 1944).

Sixteenth-century reformers appropriated medieval traditions of social-religious criticism, without respect to its
original purposes. The view of poverty in *PP*, as on the one
hand a problem for Christian justice and on the other the
solution to the world's problems, the denunciation of the
injustice of the controlling order of society, of the domi-
nance of money in social relationships, and the insistence on
the responsibility of the Church for condoning such evils, all
show L as completely orthodox. He has much in common
with contemporary preachers, and calls for no revolt but for
a return to love and law. But the sixteenth-century saw him
as a co-worker with Wyclif in a programme of much more

radical reform. Particularly they made use of Piers himself (e.g. in Crowley's edition of *PP* and in the 'Piers Plowman' complaints and treatises) in their attack on church possessions and the unequal distribution of wealth.

341.   Burrow, J. A.
'The Audience of *Piers Plowman*', *Anglia* 75:4 (1957) 373–84. Reprinted, with a new postscript, in Burrow (1984) 102–116.

Audience is different from that of alliterative poetry generally, consisting mostly of clergy, but with an increasing number of well-to-do literate laymen. It is a widespread, non-local audience, one reason for the playing-down of the traditional alliterative diction, though it is sometimes used for oblique and ironical purpose. An influential essay: the Postscript has some important updating.

342.   Hamilton, A. C.
'Spenser and Langland', *SP* 55:4 (October 1958) 533–48.

Alludes to L's influence on the *Shepheardes Calender* (use of alliterative metre, of Piers as complainant against the abuses of the world), but most of the essay is a passus-by-passus and canto-by-canto comparison of *PP* and *The Faerie Queene*, Book I.

343.   Brooke-Rose, Christine
'Ezra Pound: Piers Plowman in the Modern Waste Land', *REL* 2:2 (April 1961) 74–88.

Like Pound's *Cantos*, *PP* is 'a vast, apparently chaotic and plotless epic, constructed on several levels of apprehension and yielding the secrets of its organisation only to those who are prepared to wrestle with them' (p. 74), carrying the reader along by its vitality and occasionally magnificent poetry. Like Pound, L is fundamentally a moralist, hammering at what he believes to be the root of all evil. The keys that unlock the structure of *PP* are strangely familiar to readers of Pound: orchestration of foretastes and echoes, constant shifting of plane of (allegorical) meaning, bewildering use of the (dream as a) journey of discovery, extraordinary metamorphoses. Pound is more allusive, difficult; he spirals inwards, where L spirals outward; but both attempt to be comprehensive, both stress love.

344. Heyworth, P. L.
'*Jack Upland's Rejoinder*, a Lollard Interpolator and *Piers Plowman* B.X.249f', *MÆ* 36:3 (1967) 242–8.

The echo of *PP* in the interpolation shows the wide currency of the poem in the fifteenth century and also the desire of ordinary readers to participate in the experience it recorded and further what they saw to be its purposes.

345. Jones, Florence
'Dickens and Langland in Adjudication upon Meed', *The Victorian Newsletter* 33 (Spring 1968) 53–6.

Comparison of *Hard Times* and the *Visio* (e.g. Stephen Blackpool is like Piers), including an account of the *Visio* as told by Dickens.

346. Anderson, Judith H.
THE GROWTH OF A PERSONAL VOICE: *PIERS PLOWMAN* AND *THE FAERIE QUEENE* (New Haven and London: Yale UP, 1976).

PP is the best representative of the poetic and allegorical tradition that underlies Spenser's poem – that 'interiorizing

and more profoundly distinctive personalizing of allegory
. . . a way of organizing and conceiving experience, and a
way of exploring the self while searching for Love and Truth'
(p. 3). Both poems look like autobiography projected into
other forms, both expand and refine the personal voice of
the poet, and are much concerned with the workings of the
mind, with its play upon the world and itself. In relation to
PP specifically, Anderson shows how B Prologue and Passus
I dramatise the responses of the dreamer's mind to the world
(as well as showing that world), with its leaps, confusions,
and unexpected associations, as he engages in a search for
personal understanding. The narrator of II–VII is less personally involved in his acute perception of the world of
materialism and greed (cf. the Cave of Mammon). XII–XIV
show an expanding awareness on the part of the dreamer,
after a period (VIII–XI) of (probably real) confusion.
Ymaginatif gives a new and more mature way of looking at
experience, a new perspective. At the end of Ymaginatif's
discourse, Will is more nearly a whole person, as is shown in
his response to the gluttonous friar, or Conscience's to
Clergy, or Haukyn's to his own life. The dreamer is now
ready to catch up with Piers again, and from here to the end
of the poem, the sense of his personality (and the identification of Will with Long Will) grows stronger, and his recognition of the nearness of this personality (e.g. in its exercise of
free will, in its uniting of inner and outer worlds) to Christ's.
The acute awareness of self is returned to the world in the
last passus, with painful consequences. An intelligent book,
chiefly concerned with *The Faerie Queene*.

347.   King, John N.
'Robert Crowley's Editions of *Piers Plowman*: A Tudor
Apocalypse', *MP* 73:4 (May 1976) 342–52.

How Crowley's edition of 1550, through its preface and
marginal notes, converted L's poem into a powerful revolu-
tionary attack on monasticism and the Roman Catholic

church, and transformed it from a fourteenth-century apocalypse into a prophecy of the advent of the Protestant
millennium of the sixteenth century. *PP* is thus annexed to
the purposes of later ages, and remains vitally important to
the history of ideas and society long after it was written.

348. Mills, David
'The Dreams of Bunyan and Langland', in Newey,
Vincent (ed.), THE PILGRIM'S PROGRESS:
CRITICAL AND HISTORICAL VIEWS (Liverpool:
Liverpool UP, 1980) 154–81.

Allegory tends to curtail interpretative freedom, while the
dream-form, where the dreamer is clearly to be distinguished from the author, suggests ambiguity and uncertainty. In a series of contrasts and comparisons with Bunyan,
Mills illustrates the naturalistic dreamlike quality of *PP*, and
the rapid oscillation between the literal and the allegorical
(as in the Tree of Charity episode); the elusive and shifting
nature of Piers; the sense of inner debate and the 'objective-
subjective' existence of personification.

349. Middleton, Anne
'The Audience and Public of "Piers Plowman" ', in
Lawton (1982) 103–23.

The 'audience' is those who actually (owned and) read the
poem; the 'public' is the readers predicated within the poem.
The former is a mixed lay and clerical group concerned with
'governance' in the widest sense; the frequent presence of
historical materials in conjunction with *PP* in MSS suggests
an interest in historical analysis and reform as well as penance. Within the text, there is little definition of formal
identity or traditional didactic function, no explicit claim to
authority – in fact, the poem claims to be no more than a
work of literature, a *chanson d'aventure* as pretext for

affective and dramatic vision and dialogue, using a verse-form neither provincial nor esoteric. All this gives the poem a wider appeal (L moves beyond his 'audience'), and makes it more readable, as well as more capable of being misread.

350.   Russell, G. H.
'Some Early Responses to the C-Version of *Piers Plowman*', *Viator* 15 (1984) 275–303.

Points to the development of a non-authorial manuscript tradition for C in which certain features are picked out for emphasis (by parasigns, rubrication, marginal annotation, etc.) such as names of *personae*, of *auctores* and of biblical and patristic texts, and also certain structural features (e.g. legal documents, prophecies, striking incidents). Specifically analysed are Huntington Library HM 143, where layout and marginal comment combine to help reading and comprehension, and Bodleian Douce 104, with its marginal pictures and notes drawing attention to the poem's exploration of major themes. By contrast British Library Add. 35157 is a highly-charged commentary on the poem's religious and political meaning from a post-medieval perspective (three annotators). An appendix gives examples of marginal supply from the three manuscripts for C XI–XV.

351.   Wood, Robert A.
'A Fourteenth-Century London Owner of *Piers Plowman*', *MÆ* 53:1 (1984) 83–90.

William Palmer, a London rector (d. 1400), left a *PP* in his will. Wood comments on other known early owners and the picture of the audience of 'thoughtful clerics' that L's poem appealed to.

352. King, John N.
'Spenser's *Shepheardes Calender* and Protestant Pastoral
Satire', in Lewalski, Barbara Kiefer (ed.),
RENAISSANCE GENRES: ESSAYS ON THEORY,
HISTORY, AND INTERPRETATION (Harvard English
Studies 14) (Cambridge: Harvard UP, 1986) 369–98.

Sixteenth-century Protestant admiration of *PP* for its emphasis on individual piety, its attacks on the Roman church
and its use of the *persona* of the plain-speaking plowman as
an agent of social and religious protest (pp. 377–8).

353. Sherbo, Arthur
'Samuel Pegge, Thomas Holt White, and *Piers Plowman*',
YLS 1 (1987) 122–8.

Both these eighteenth-century writers contributed articles
on *PP* to the *Gentleman's Magazine* (in 1755 and 1787
respectively). Sherbo quotes both in full, and adds some
remarks on the circulation of *PP* in the eighteenth-century.

354. Hudson, Anne
'Epilogue: The Legacy of Piers Plowman', in Alford
(1988) 251–66.

Influence and reminiscences of *PP* in the Peasants' Revolt,
in Lollard writing and in Reformation polemic.

355. Middleton, Anne
'Making a Good End: John But as a Reader of *Piers
Plowman*', in Kennedy, Waldron and Wittig (1988)
243–66.

John But's 'ending' for A reveals much about fourteenth-century attitudes towards authorial identity. But sees Will's visions as the authentic spiritual experience of the writer, and he also wants to see that experience brought to a positive close. He alludes to Will's 'making' (one of the allusions that shows he knows either B or C well) but does not accept the doubts that L continually expresses about the spiritual value of writing poetry. For But, L's poem is itself a good work, a salvific labour, where for L the idea of salvation through works is a delusion he must constantly shock himself out of. But undertook to deliver L from the fearful logic (of man's incapacity to respond unequivocally to the offer of grace) that produces the dismaying ending of B and C. The contrast of attitudes makes it clear that A XII 99–105 are certainly, 55–98 almost certainly and 1–55 most probably not by L. What But is doing is 'to stabilise and unify the moral truth of the text that he knew circulated in the world in more than one poem' (p. 262) and in so doing to bring both poem and poet to a good end. An appendix offers further evidence that But was the King's messenger identified by Rickert 1913 [121].

Social and historical (including legal) contexts and reference

(*See* also [150]–[174] (Date).)

356. Coulton, G. G.
CHAUCER AND HIS ENGLAND (London: Methuen, 1908).

Frequent reference to *PP* and its social background, most notably in the chapter on 'The Poor': 'For glimpses of the real poor, the poor poor, we must go to "Piers Plowman" ' (p. 268).

357. Chadwick, D.
SOCIAL LIFE IN THE DAYS OF PIERS PLOWMAN (Cambridge: CUP, 1922).

Primarily 'a guide to the facts of social life recorded in *Piers Plowman*' (p. vii). Chapters are devoted to the clergy, secular government, country life, town life, wealth and poverty, the layman's religion and medieval women. The poem is specially valuable for the social historian because the lack of any carefully planned allegory allows for frequent description of real life. The author is 'a reformer who combined an enquiring spirit with a prudent regard for time-honoured distinctions and who dared to record what most men attempted to suppress' (p. 5).

358. Coghill, N. K.
'Langland, the "Naket", the "Nauzty", and the Dole', *RES* 8:31 (July 1932) 303–9.

Argues that 'nauzty' in B VI 226 does mean, as it usually
does in the sixteenth-century, 'wicked' (cf. Skeat and *OED*,
'having naught, poor' a meaning otherwise unrecorded),
and that the B revision is thus extending Hunger's recommendation of provision for the poor even to those who are
reprehensible. C retracts this generosity. [Kane–Donaldson
1975 [42] regard the line as corrupt and replace it with the
reading of A: the incident is a good example of the relation
between textual and interpretative matters.]

359. Day, Mabel
      'Piers Plowman and Poor Relief', *RES* 8:32 (October
   · 1932) 445–6.

Referring to Coghill 1932 [358], gives further examples of
C's aversion to indiscriminate charity towards the poor. This
may be due to a change of author, or to the 'increasing
conservatism of advancing years' (p. 446).

360. Kirk, Rudolf
      'References to the Law in *Piers the Plowman*', *PMLA*
      48:2 (June 1933) 322–7.

L uses proportionately more references to the law in B and C
than in A, and they become more technical.

361. Coulton, G. G.
      MEDIEVAL PANORAMA: THE ENGLISH SCENE
      FROM CONQUEST TO REFORMATION (Cambridge:
      CUP, 1938).

Uses frequent illustration from *PP*, and has a chapter on the
poem called 'The Peasant Saint' (pp. 534–54 – the term is
from Carlyle), where Piers is described as 'the working man
who gives that plain answer to the riddle of life which the

official Church and State had failed to give', as well as 'Humanity at its simplest and truest and highest' (p. 534). Coulton compares L with Carlyle and contrasts him with Chaucer; weaves an account of the poet's life out of the poem and into the social background; summarises the *Visio* and the last three passus; and speaks of L as a poet who was a true Englishman and a true Catholic, though not of the Roman variety. He was 'a worthy precursor of those Anglicans who not only accept the Creeds, but pray regularly for "the good estate of the Catholick Church" ' (p. 554).

362. Mathew, Gervase, O.P.
      'Justice and Charity in *The Vision of Piers Plowman*',
      Dominican Studies 1:4 (October 1948) 360–6.

Social problems are phrased in *PP*, in a characteristically medieval way, in terms of law. Law is the voice of justice, but it can only be preserved through charity. These generalisations are illustrated by quotation from *PP* in modern translation.

363. Eliason, Mary
      'The Peasant and the Lawyer', *SP* 48:3 (July 1951) 506–26.

Uses historical records to give a context to the portraits of poor people and lawyers in Chaucer and L.

364. Bloomfield, Morton W.
      'The Pardons of Pamplona and the Pardoner of
      Rounceval: *Piers Plowman* B XVII 252', *PQ* 35:1
      (January 1956) 60–8.

L's contemptuous reference to the pardons issued by the bishops of Pamplona is intended to cast special obloquy on the London hospital of St Mary Rounceval, closely associated with Roncesvalles and the diocese of Pamplona. The scandalous pardon-mongering of Rounceval is alluded to also by Chaucer, in connection with his Pardoner.

365.   Orsten, Elisabeth M.
'The Ambiguities in Langland's Rat Parliament', *MS* 23 (1961) 216–39.

The point of the rat-fable (there is no alternative to autocratic government) seems to be the opposite of what is usually taken to be L's opinion (he favoured constitutional limitations on the monarchy and simply thought the Good Parliament of 1376 had gone about things the wrong way). L's point is the opposite of that of Brinton in his use of the fable (Take heed of the fable and *act*). The answer is that L does not endorse the fatalistic advice of the mouse, which is an ironical version of the argument for autocracy, but supports the 'raton of renoun' and the actions of the Good Parliament. The cat is John of Gaunt, and the irony is directed against his manipulation of Parliament in 1377.

366.   Bowers, R. H.
' "Foleuyles Lawes" ("Piers Plowman", C.XXII.247)', *NQ* 8 (206):9 (September 1961) 327–8.

The reference is to five Leicestershire brothers who became notorious as 'professional strong-arm men', brigands and extortioners, but who could be admired (as L admires them) for the effectiveness of their rough justice.

367.   Fisher, John H.
'Wyclif, Langland, Gower and the Pearl Poet on the Subject of Aristocracy', in Leach, MacEdward (ed.), STUDIES IN MEDIEVAL LITERATURE IN HONOR OF PROFESSOR ALBERT CROLL BAUGH

(Philadelphia: University of Pennsylvania Press, 1961)
139–57.

L seems to accept the traditional role of the aristocracy, but
it plays little part in his vision of society reformed (cf. the
role of the king); his concentration is upon the spiritual
regeneration of the individual rather than upon the common
good.

368. Mathew, Gervase
THE COURT OF RICHARD II (London: John Murray,
1968).

Idiosyncratic comment on *PP* in Chapter IX (pp. 83–91),
interesting on social background and possible audience.

369. Polak, Lucie
'A Note on the Pilgrim in "Piers Plowman" ', *NQ* 17
(215):8 (August 1970) 283–5.

Points to the great expansion of pilgrim traffic, especially
after the celebration of the first jubilee year in 1300, and how
detailed and accurate is L's picture (in A VI) of the 'professional' pilgrim.

370. Birnes, William J.
'Christ as Advocate: The Legal Metaphor of *Piers
Plowman*', *AnnM* 16 (1975) 71–93.

L conceives of law as the most important stabilising force in
society, and of adherence to law as the remedy for society's
ills. He reinforces this belief by creating a powerful metaphor in which Christ becomes the embodiment of law and
establishes law as the basis of his government. L provides a
groundwork for this metaphor by drawing an analogy be-

tween contemporary legal practice, specifically the distinction between Common Law (an inflexible set of precedents) and Chancery Law (where equity and fairness are paramount, and 'grace' a term commonly employed), and the Old and New Laws of Scripture. The conflict of Old and New Laws is dramatised in the debate of the Four Daughters, with one side citing precedent, the other appealing to what is fair and just. Christ's debate with Lucifer is deliberately framed as a legal debate, in which Christ answers one by one the legal objections to the Atonement made by Lucifer. The legalism had always been present, but L gives it special attention, emphasising the universality of law in describing Christ's submission to it.

371.   Alford, John A.
'Literature and Law in Medieval England', *PMLA* 92:5 (October 1977) 941–51.

The close association between medieval law and literature is illustrated in an analysis of literary treatments of the doctrine of the Redemption, including the legalistic debate between Christ and Satan at the Harrowing of Hell in *PP* B XVIII 277–353 (see pp. 944–5). The medieval legal concept of *bona fides*, for instance, plays a large part in L's account of the debate.

372.   Baldwin, Anna P.
THE THEME OF GOVERNMENT IN PIERS PLOWMAN (Piers Plowman Studies I) (Cambridge: D. S. Brewer, 1981).

There is in the Middle Ages an ideal of good government based on the harmony of the three estates in their subjection to the good king. L shares this ideal, and it stands as the model of government behind his portrayal of the good society, and of the threats presented to that society by the power of money (Lady Meed) and by rebellious labourers (Wastour). The answer to these threats is in the assertion of authority, of the royal prerogative. Variations within the ideal pattern of good government in respect of the role of the king are resolved by L in favour of the 'absolutist' ideal of monarchy. This conclusion is reached in C after some flirting with the idea of 'limited' monarchy in B (esp. Prol. 112–45). The king learns justice from the dictates of his own reason and conscience, not from constraints placed on him by the constitution. But he is subject, himself, unlike the 'theocratic' monarch, to the laws which he administers. L shows in his presentation of both Piers Plowman and Christ how they too are sources of absolute authority who yet acknowledge obedience to the laws of God (Piers in his attitude to his 'brothers', the labourers, and Christ in his respect for law in reconciling man and God). Baldwin brings a wealth of knowledge of contemporary constitutional and legal matters to bear on the action of the poem, providing important contexts for understanding certain aspects of its representation of historical process and change. The book is particularly strong in its emphasis on L's knowledge of the law and the minutiae of legislation. At the same time, it is selective in its emphases (this partiality reveals itself in a lack of attention to real contradictions within L's presentation of the theme of government), and it exaggerates the importance of the theme within the poem as a whole. It nevertheless provides a valuable commentary on Prol. and Passus II–IV.

Review: R. Adams, *SAC* 5 (1983) 141–4.

373.   Baldwin, Anna
'The Double Duel in *Piers Plowman* B. XVIII and C. XXI', *MÆ* 50:1 (1981) 64–78.

Discusses the traditional legalistic interpretations of the doctrine of the Atonement: how, legally, Christ could overturn the Devil's 'rights' to man's soul. L's innovation is to represent the battle between Christ and Lucifer in two ways, in close accord with contemporary legal theory (and, in some cases, practice): first, as a 'civil duel of law' (such as was usually based on a Writ of Right, to prove ownership of land) fought between Life and Death on the Cross to prove Christ's right to redeem mankind; second, as a 'chivalric duel of treason' between Christ and Lucifer at the gates of Hell, to prove Christ's right to bind Lucifer forever. The essay demonstrates yet again L's close acquaintance with the minutiae of legal language and theory.

374.   Coleman, Janet
ENGLISH LITERATURE IN HISTORY 1350–1400:
MEDIEVAL READERS AND WRITERS (English
Literature in History Series) (London: Hutchinson, 1981).

An ambitious, wide-ranging and vivacious book in which *PP* plays an important part as a document in the history of the times, against a background of cultural change, intellectual ferment and Lollard heterodoxy. Coleman describes how contemporary debate about predestination and free will, salvation by grace and salvation by works, gets into the poem, and how it reflects changes in the composition of the reading public (wider, less élite, more serious-minded), and in the concern of that public with theological questions, with contemporary social reality and the problems of social reform, and with the growing sense of individual responsibility.

375.   Gilbert, Beverly Brian
' "Civil" and the Notaries in *Piers Plowman*', *MÆ* 50:1
(1981) 49–63.

The character 'Civil' in B II represents Roman law, not 'civil law' in the modern sense. Though often complained about in the Middle Ages as inherently unspiritual, Roman law was used by canon lawyers for supplying procedural rules, especially with the increase in litigation in the ecclesiastical courts. Notaries, closely associated by L with Civil and Simony, are the functionaries of Roman law: well-paid, and much in demand, they drew the attention of satirists as being closely identified with simony and simoniacal practices (e.g. papal provision to benefices, exchange of benefices by rectors).

376. Lister, Robin
'The Peasants of *Piers Plowman* and its Audience', in Parkinson, Kathleen and Priestman, Martin (eds.), PEASANTS AND COUNTRYMEN IN LITERATURE. A symposium organized by the English department of the Roehampton Institute in February 1981 (London: Roehampton Institute of Higher Education, 1982) 71–90.

The poem is fascinating because of 'the tension within it between the understood meaning of the world, the given reality, and the contradiction of that meaning by the actual world which the poem describes' (p. 71). The author supports the traditional hierarchical model of the three estates, but his poem reveals 'the model's inappropriateness to a society that is rapidly changing under the growing pressures of the market economy and capital' (p. 73). Piers is presented as the archetypal idealised peasant, but is actually one of the better-off peasants who have an interest in maintaining the status quo – landless labourers are to him 'Wasters', a self-seeking and self-assertive group who threaten stability. But L gives full expression to the plight of the poor and to the forces of change, especially in his portrayal of London life and Lady Meed, where the traditional idealism of agricultural imagery is not present.

377.   Orme, Nicholas
       'Langland and Education', *History of Education* 11 (1982)
       251–66.

       A survey of the views on education, in the broadest sense,
       expressed in *PP*. They are conventional, though L is unusual
       in giving an account of (what seems to be) his own schooling.
       He is critical of the decline of Latin in grammar schools,
       though also rather in two minds about the value of book-
       learning.

378.   Baldwin, Anna
       'A Reference in *Piers Plowman* to the Westminster
       Sanctuary', *NQ* 29(227):2 (April 1982) 106–8.

       The reference in B XX 281–9 to abuse of the Westminster
       sanctuary by debtors freeing their creditors may allude to, or
       even echo the language of, the 1378 statute enacted to
       govern use of sanctuary there.

379.   Aers, David
       '*Piers Plowman* and Problems in the Perception of
       Poverty: A Culture in Transition', in Pearsall (1983) 5–25.

       Distinguishes a 'traditional' attitude towards poverty, in
       which the poor belong to God and are worthy of un-
       discriminating charity, and a new ethos, emerging in re-
       sponse to economic change and the growth of a large and
       unruly class of chronic poor, which recommends discrimina-
       tion in charity and the suppression of vagrants and able-
       bodied beggars. L is deeply engaged in the conflict of these
       attitudes, sympathetic to the plight of the poor and to the
       traditional ideology, yet often caught up in the pragmatism
       of the new view. In the later part of the poem he disengages
       from the latter and makes a powerful restatement of the
       place of the poor with Christ, but not without some loss of
       specificity in his record of the changing world around him.

380. Shepherd, Geoffrey
'Poverty in *Piers Plowman*', in Aston, T. H., Coss, P. R.,
Dyer, Christopher and Thirsk, Joan (eds.), SOCIAL
RELATIONS AND IDEAS: ESSAYS IN HONOUR OF
R. H. HILTON (Past and Present Publications)
(Cambridge: CUP, 1983) 169–89.

Traces the attitude to and practice of poverty in the religious
orders, and the difficulties attending the institutionalisation
of poverty, and finds signs in L of a conflict between sympathy for the poor and acceptance of a world in which they are
inevitable. Poverty may be useful as a way of ensuring
accelerated progress through Purgatory, but the more important point is that it is 'a mark of brotherhood', an integral
element in a unified society in which 'rich and poor are
bound together' (p. 186).

381. Aers, David
'Representations of the "Third Estate": Social Conflict
and its Milieu around 1381', *Southern Review* (Adelaide)
16:3 (November 1983) 335–49.

The rebellious behaviour of *wastours* (in the Tavern scene, B
V) is too powerfully represented to be confined within the
traditional ideology of the proper place of the labouring
class. But L tries to do this in the Ploughing scene (B VI),
and finds himself increasingly drawn into a conventional
condemnation of those who do not take kindly to being poor
and oppressed. He tries to take refuge, after B VII, in
reaffirmation of the traditional Christian idealisation of
poverty, but the vitality of his own poetic engagement with
the new economic individualism shows that this is anachronistic. [The essay continues with discussion of Chaucer
and Gower.]

382. Swanson, R. N.
'Langland and the Priest's Title', *NQ* 33 (231):4
(December 1986) 438–40.

The reference in C XIII 100–13 to the 'title' of priest is to the technical term *titulus* used in ordination and referring to the 'entitlement' of the ordinand to an income derived from a benefice or other source. The allusion is important in emphasising L's concern for the practical necessities of financial provision for priests.

383.   Revard, Carter
' "Title" and "Auaunced" in *Piers Plowman* B.11.290', *YLS* 1 (1987) 116–21.

Correct interpretation of these two technical terms makes it clear how emphatic L was that priests should have a financially secure status.

384.   Alford, John A.
PIERS PLOWMAN: A GLOSSARY OF LEGAL DICTION (Piers Plowman Studies V) (Cambridge: D. S. Brewer, 1988).

Alford provides entries for all words and phrases, in both English and Latin, derived from legal usage, and also for other words with legal associations and implications. For each entry he provides examples from *PP* (not, however, an exhaustive list), definitions, illustrative quotations from other sources, especially legal texts, and explanations of difficult points of interpretation or use. The book serves to indicate the poet's knowledge of law and the part he played in importing legal terms from Latin and French into English; it also marks earlier uses and senses of words than those given in the *OED* and *MED* and acts as a reference guide for legal usage in other fourteenth-century authors. In a brief Introduction, Alford points to the special importance of legal language in relation to the theology of salvation, and to L's often daring word play with legal terms and his habit of extending their range of reference in strikingly literal ways.

His book shows indeed how L's poem is 'saturated' in legal concepts and terminology, and in particular how much legal implication is hidden in apparently familiar words and phrases.

385. Baldwin, Anna P.
'The Historical Context', in Alford (1988) 67–86.

Uses 'the traditional analysis of society in terms of the three estates in order to demonstrate both Langland's historically accurate perception of how each was developing, and his interpretation of the individual's role within them' (p. 68).

386. Pearsall, Derek
'Poverty and Poor People in *Piers Plowman*', in Kennedy, Waldron and Wittig (1988) 167–85.

The fourteenth century sees a radical shift in attitudes towards poverty. Previously integrated in patterns of civic and religious almsgiving, poor people were now perceived, because of their numbers and concentration in towns, as a threat. A stricter charity must now take care to discriminate between the deserving and the undeserving. The debate about the 'poverty' of the friars adds to the demand for discrimination. Meanwhile, traditional eulogies of poverty screen out the social reality of poor people. L does not ignore their sufferings, and attempts on several occasions to come to grips with the practical problem of chronic urban poverty and what he sees as the exploitation of almsgiving by able-bodied beggars, but in the end he reinstates the traditional spiritual ideal of poverty, to which he gives moving and powerful expression on several occasions later in the poem.

Allegory

(*See* also [245]–[268] (Sources: analysis of personifications).)

387. Frank, Robert Worth, jun.
'The Art of Reading Medieval Personification-Allegory',
ELH 20:4 (December 1953) 237–50. Reprinted in Vasta
(1968) 217–31.

There is symbol-allegory and personification-allegory. The
former uses images which need to be understood sym-
bolically, where the meaning is not transparent. The latter is
to be understood more or less literally, with substitution of
the name of the abstraction (or a category, or a type) for a
real person, or at most, when personifications are set in
motion in narrative, with one simple act of translation. This
is the kind of allegory we find in *PP*. [Frank's essay does not
take account of some important modes of allegorical meaning in *PP* (see Salter 1967 [74], Aers 1975 [399]) but it is
historically important as an early attack on the methods of
fourfold exegesis practised by Robertson and Huppé 1951
[223].]

388. Mitchell, A. G.
'Lady Meed and the Art of *Piers Plowman*', Third
Chambers Memorial Lecture, University College, 1956
(London: H. K. Lewis, 1956). Reprinted in Blanch (1969)
174–93.

A very good essay on the importance of understanding L's
art of allegory, and how the significance of Meed is subtly
revealed in her every speech and act. She is often plausible
(e.g. in her claim that a king should reward his followers for

their loyalty), and she forces a realisation of the complexity of what she stands for. Her unawareness of wrongdoing (she is, so to speak, morally neutral), and her indiscriminate desire to please everyone, are the allegorical enactment of the plausible attractiveness of 'reward' in society.

389. Cejp, Ladislav
THE METHODS OF MEDIEVAL ALLEGORY AND LANGLAND'S 'PIERS THE PLOWMAN' [a summary in English appended (pp. 192–206) to the book in Czech published as Acta Universitatis Palackianae Olomucensis, Facultas Philosophica 8, *Philologica* V] (Prague, 1961).

Cejp's book, as reported in the summary, presents (i) 'a systematic analysis of medieval poetic theories concerned with allegory'; (ii) accounts of other medieval poetic visions, a translation into Czech of the Prologue and a summary and quantitative (numerological) analysis of the poem as a whole; (iii) interpretation of key symbols (plough, ploughman, field, feast, barn); (iv) analysis of relation to contemporary historical events, with specific identification of characters and events in the poem (Piers is Wat Tyler), some on the basis of anagrammatic allusion. Cejp associates L closely with the Peasants' Revolt and with Wyclif.

390. Burrow, J. A.
'The Action of Langland's Second Vision', *EC* 15:3 (July 1965) 247–68. Reprinted in Blanch (1969) 209–27 and in Burrow (1984) 79–101.

In this subtle and suggestive essay, Burrow shows that the allegorical action of B V–VII is not as incoherent as it may seem. It consists of sermon, confession, pilgrimage and pardon. The substitution of ploughing for pilgrimage, due to L's distaste for professional pilgrimages, creates a tension between the allegorical action and what it signifies, a deliber-

ate disturbance which emphasises that the life of the half-
acre is itself the life of truth. Likewise in the Pardon scene,
because of the commercialisation of pardons, and the consequent confusing of formal practice and essential meaning
(cf. Burrow 1969 [549]), he has the pardon torn, to dramatise
his rejection of 'paper pardons'. L's interference with his
allegorical action is potentially confusing but also enig-
matically powerful.

[The Introduction to Salter–Pearsall 1967 [74] has important comments on the 'allegorical procedures' of the poem.]

391.   Salter, Elizabeth
'Medieval Poetry and the Figural View of Reality', Sir
Israel Gollancz Memorial Lecture, British Academy, *PBA*
54 (1968) 73–92.

Applies the figural or typological interpretation of the Bible,
as expounded by Erich Auerbach for Dante, to *Pearl* and
PP. Events and characters in an allegory may retain their
historicity, their reality, at the same time that their full
significance is not released except through allegorical understanding. It is not the only kind of allegory in *PP*, but it
contributes to much of its power – in the representation of
the dreamer, for instance, or of Piers, or of the Good
Samaritan, as also in the importance given to certain themes
or actions, such as the motif of travelling.

392.   Strange, William C.
'The Willful Trope: Some Notes on Personification with
Illustrations from *Piers (A)*', *AnnM* 9 (1968) 26–39.

'Personification allegory' is often condemned as sterile and
schematic (e.g. Piers' wife and son in A VII 70–3). But true
personification is a figure of thought not a figure of speech,
according to the rhetoricians. It often goes unrecognised, as
in the journey through the Ten Commandments (A VI 48–

56), full of personal directness and immediacy if read in its dramatic context. Personification, properly understood, demands that the world make human sense: it is not essentially different from the idea of 'character' in fiction, e.g. the horse-riding allegory of A II 127–30. Modern resistance to it shows a reluctance to accept its commitment to the world or reality. An interesting, suggestive and wide-ranging article.

393. Jenkins [Martin], Priscilla
'Conscience: The Frustration of Allegory', in Hussey (1969) 125–42.

There is a conflict between what L wants to say and the mode of allegory. L is disturbing and complex, allegory is idealised and clear-cut. Allegory is inadequate to his vision, and his narrative often deliberately frustrates the desire for allegorical tidiness as the means to something more subtle and profound. The violation of allegory in the portrayal of Conscience at the end of the poem (as a literal confused person rather than a personification) is a striking example.

394. Wimsatt, James I.
ALLEGORY AND MIRROR: TRADITION AND STRUCTURE IN MIDDLE ENGLISH LITERATURE (New York: Pegasus, 1970).

Medieval poetry is essentially didactic, and the poet's job is to reveal the divine order behind the multifariousness of reality. The mode of allegory is well adapted to such learned teacher-poets, as is the mirror or *speculum*, the potentially all-embracing image of truth. Wimsatt has brief accounts of the First Vision (B Prologue and I–IV) as an example of personification-allegory, in which L is a virtuoso, vivid and racy yet always offering a moral commentary on human activity; of Dowel (VIII–XV) as the Allegory of Reason, imaging mental activity; and of XVI–XX, as the Allegory of

Revelation, where the practice of charity is the means to grace and vision. The nearest to a mirror in L is the treatment of the Vices.

395. Gradon, Pamela
FORM AND STYLE IN EARLY ENGLISH
LITERATURE (London: Methuen, 1971).

L is discussed at length in the chapters on Allegory and Structure. Analysis of the portrait of Covetousness at B XX 120–7 (pp. 60–2) shows the movement from the allegorical to the literal and dramatic – the secret of L's effectiveness. Comparison of Holcot's and L's portrayal of Avarice (B V 188–208) shows in the one a monster, in the other a human being, while B XVIII 10–35 illustrates L's power of combining intellectual depth and power of vivid evocation in allegorical narrative (pp. 66–77). In the dream vision, too, 'the person of the Dreamer is used to give actuality to the dream and, in a sense, himself becomes part of the reader's own experience' (p. 87). Other examples are given of this power to 'fuse the sensuous and immediate with the symbolic' (p. 89). The structure of the poem depends on patterns of symbols, particularly the evolving symbolism of Piers, here analysed as a *figura* (pp. 98–113). In the *Visio* he is a real labourer (with allegorical functions), not an abstraction, which is why he can tear the Pardon without destroying the allegory. He retains this identity throughout, Christ-like but not Christ, and closely associated with the dreamer's experience. Later in the book there are comparisons between L and later allegorical writing in Charles d'Orléans (pp. 339–40) and *Everyman* (pp. 367–8).

396. Cantarow, Ellen
'A Wilderness of Opinions Confounded: Allegory and Ideology', *CE* 34:2 (November 1972) 215–52 (with Comment by Nancy Hoffmann, 253–5).

Allegory, coming from a particular class and social order, tends to confirm conservative and authoritarian notions of society, and to be unreceptive to ideas of change. L's allegory is a vehicle of satire but the satire is directed against the abuse, not the nature, of existing institutions. Allegory is invariably didactic (where the novel emphasises personal experience and the emotional involvement of the reader), and its use of personification reinforces a static view of society. The Ploughing scene of B VI is an accurate picture of the economic and social upheavals of the time, and may have been read as an encouragement to insurgency. But L's own attitudes are clearly orthodox and conservative, and the allegory works to relate the reality of social circumstances to unchanging hierarchies and transcendent moral virtues. Piers himself is a kind of 'pastoral' figure who appears to transcend class boundaries, create a bond between rich and poor and legitimise the activities of rulers and employers. It is only peasants who are idle and recalcitrant, and Hunger, as a personification, comes to seem an instrument of justice. [This valuable article goes on to talk about *The Faerie Queene* and *Pilgrim's Progress*.]

397. Clifford, Gay
THE TRANSFORMATIONS OF ALLEGORY
(London: Routledge & Kegan Paul, 1974).

A lively and wide-ranging study of allegory, mostly post-medieval, with frequent reference to *PP*: for the concretion and visual power of its allegory (pp. 9, 79–81), the importance of allegorical transformation (e.g. in Piers and in the dreamer, p. 30), the structural clarity of the allegory (pp. 59–62), the mythopoeic power of suggesting the mysterious and timeless beyond the temporal (pp. 95–6, 99).

398. Delany, Sheila
'Substructure and Superstructure: the Politics of Allegory in the Fourteenth Century', *Science and Society* 38 (1974) 257–80.

Allegory, as a mode of analogy appropriate to an age in which social relations and political ideas (both economically determined) likewise work on principles of analogy and hierarchy, decays in the fourteenth-century, when economic conditions change. *PP* is not an allegory, but an example of estates satire (p. 266). Cf. a previous essay by Delany, 'Undoing Substantial Connection: The Late Medieval Attack on Analogical Thought', *Mosaic* 5:4 (Summer 1972) 31–52, in which the same theme is developed in an analysis of scientific and philosophical writings (but with no significant mention of *PP*).

399.   Aers, David
PIERS PLOWMAN AND CHRISTIAN ALLEGORY
(London: Edward Arnold, 1975).

Makes a distinction between the theory and the practice of medieval biblical exegesis, and emphasises the need to be conscious of this distinction in relating such exegesis to the interpretation of medieval literature. The theory maintains that medieval exegesis (the allegory of the theologians, as opposed to the allegory of the poets) is based on typology and therefore preserves the literal and historical reality of the text. But examination of exegesis in practice in specific passages (e.g. the story of Rahab in Joshua 2:6) shows that the commitment to history is superseded by the desire to enforce mechanical doctrinal correspondences (when the writer says . . . what he really means is . . .) in which the reality of events and actions is dissolved. Analysis of sermons, of poems by Deguileville and Lydgate, of the models employed for understanding the functioning of allegory and figurative language (e.g. the shell/kernel model) demonstrates likewise the rigidity of mentality and the disposability of the history or story (the shell). But there is another way of thinking about figurative language, exemplified in Dante, where it is seen not as a 'picture model' from which meanings already known to be present are simply 'read off', but as a 'disclosure model', in which metaphor and allegory are the means to achieve and express insights otherwise inaccessible. This way of thinking is implied in L's notion of the role of poet as 'maker', and, after confronting those (especially Robertson and Huppé 1951 [223]) who have argued that *PP* must be read according to the manner of medieval exegesis, Aers offers a way of interpreting L's allegorical technical techniques based on close reading of specific passages. He centres on the figure of Piers, and makes a long and very important examination of the Tree of Charity in B XVI (pp. 79–107), arguing that 'different modes of figurative expression' are being deployed 'within an organic poetic process' (p. 85). An analysis of ploughing imagery in B V–VII and XIX concludes that it is neither literal nor 'mere' personification-allegory, but that it is used by L within specific contexts in ways that transform and make new its implications.

400. Bowers, A. Joan
'The Tree of Charity in *Piers Plowman*: Its Allegorical and Structural Significance', in Rothstein, Eric and Wittreich, Joseph A., jun. (eds.), *Literary Monographs*, vol. 6: *Medieval and Renaissance Literature* (Madison: University of Wisconsin Press, 1975) 1–34.

The Tree of Charity is a source of 'imagistic unity' in *PP*. It is the climactic reference to the traditional 'tree of life' or *lignum vitae* image, allusion to which, with its allegorisation as Christ and the Church, is woven throughout the poem (in the allusions to Adam and Eve being restored through the *lignum vitae*, to the wood from which Noah's Ark was made, and to the building of Holy Church as a wooden barn). The Tree of Charity itself draws on a very rich tradition of tree-images, but essentially represents most fully what L sees as the significance of the *lignum vitae* image – its promise of hope and love as well as judgement. [A very wooden account of the poem.]

401.   Quilligan, Maureen
'Langland's Literal Allegory', *EC* 28:2 (April 1978)
95–111.

Argues (against Burrow 1965 [390]) that the problematic
nature of the relationships between the literal and metaphorical meanings of allegorical narrative in the pilgrimage-
ploughing-pardon sequences of B VI–VII is not peculiar to L
but characteristic of a 'reflexive tension' which is the essence
of the genre of allegory. L disrupts the literal level so that the
reader does not become too comfortable with his allegorical
translations (as he might with pilgrimages), and is brought
back to the words, the *letters*, the literal. So with the joust in
B XVIII, an allegorical narrative which seems to be inex-
plicably dropped. L is deliberately frustrating easy reading,
forcing the reader to make the 'transition from a metaphorical reading of a literal level to a very word-conscious *literal*
reading of the poem's *text*' (p. 103). *Jousting* is too simple a
way of thinking about the Redemption, but, if the words are
attended to, it gives way to *justice*.

402.   Barney, Stephen A.
ALLEGORIES OF HISTORY, ALLEGORIES OF
LOVE (Hamden, Conn.: Archon Books, 1979).

Important conventions in *PP* (discussed pp. 82–104) are
those of the naïve narrator, of encyclopaedic satire and of
multiple allegory. The structure of the poem is basically a
vision of the corrupted world seen in the context of a wider
and wider spiritual perspective, both personal and historical.
Summarises Dobest, and shows how the apparent chaos of
L's narrative can be better understood in the context of the
allegory of the *Psychomachia* of Prudentius, and of the
poem's allegorical development as a whole. We have a
deepened vision of the folk, who have been so chaotically
energetic a presence in the poem, in the 'division of graces';
Conscience, a complex allegorical personification through-

out, emerges more clearly as an almost literal figure in the very process of reaching out for grace; the constant recircling of the action of the poem upon itself now comes to a climax.

403. Martin, Priscilla
PIERS PLOWMAN: THE FIELD AND THE TOWER
(London and New York: Macmillan, 1979).

The poem is characterised by inconclusiveness, inconsistency and incoherence, full of uncompleted actions and collapsing allegories, abrupt shifts of locale and point of view. The dissatisfaction with allegory is patent. L can never bring his view of the *field* of human reality into a single encompassing vision with his view of the *tower* of spiritual truth. All his allegories embody a critique of the allegorical method, and often move more towards the effective embodiment of enigma than the clarification of problems. The breakdown of allegory is an attack on the fixed habits of thought encouraged by allegory. [These views of the poem are stimulatingly presented, but the book does not progress far beyond its initial proposition of 'significant formlessness'. It neglects history: historical realities of life, belief and conduct, which L transmits with such harassing urgency, are diffused into formal problems of a more comfortable kind altogether.]

Reviews: M. Carruthers, *SAC* 3 (1981) 161–5.
B. J. Harwood, *Review* 3 (1981) 323–40.
D. Pearsall, *MLR* 76:2 (April 1981) 435–7.

404. Quilligan, Maureen
THE LANGUAGE OF ALLEGORY: DEFINING THE GENRE (Ithaca: Cornell UP, 1979).

PP (pp. 58–79) is both a text and a commentary on that text, both allegory and allegoresis. Internal glossing often evolves

from punning, e.g. on *tre-* (*tri-*) in *trielich*, *treuthe*, *tresor*, *tre*
and trinity. Such word-play constantly invites interpreta-
tion, and a recognition of the way in which words may both
redeem understanding and also deceive (see Carruthers
1973 [564]). Likewise, the conflict between the literal and
the metaphorical in L's allegory creates a reflexive tension
which impresses upon the reader the vital problem of interpretation, as in the pilgrimage-ploughing-pardon sequence
of B VI–VII, where the breakdown of the literal allegory
(see Burrow 1965 [390]) involves the reader in the paradox
of faith and works. Will, missing the paradox, reads the
pardon literally and goes off looking for something or someone called Dowel. The jousting in Jerusalem is often regarded as an allegory that is similarly just dropped; but again
it acts as a stimulus to interpretation, especially through the
pun on *joust* and *justice*. A literal reading of the allegorical
meaning is not enough: there must be a literal reading of the
text and its words. The reader is induced to correct his own
sense of dissatisfaction with the development of the action.
Further comments on significant punning, pp. 162–6. [See
also Quilligan 1978 [401]]

405.   Benson, C. David
'The Function of Lady Meed in *Piers Plowman*', *ES* 61:3
(June 1980) 193–205.

L's skill and power in allegory demonstrated in an analysis of
the presentation of Meed, who is not a simple figure of evil,
but is deliberately made appealing and plausible, with a
certain approachableness lacking in Holy Church or Conscience. Indeed, Benson argues, she prefigures or acts as a
parodic anticipation of Christ, doing for bad reasons what he
will do for good (forgiving sinners, freeing those in gaol,
gaining exemption from the law, acting with undiscriminat-
ing generosity).

406. Bloomfield, Morton W.
'The Allegories of *Dobest* (*Piers Plowman* B XIX–XX)',
MÆ 50:1 (1981) 30–9.

Personification-allegory is the principal mode of allegory in
PP: but Piers is a symbol, existing on a number of levels.
Brief analysis of B XIX–XX as an example of the resultant
complex of allegorical techniques.

407. Dronke, Peter
'Arbor Caritatis', in Bennett (1981) 207–243.

Opulently learned account of the background in arboreal
allegory of L's Tree of Charity (B XVI). The enigmas and
obscurities in L, the 'disordered scenery', are taken as
characteristic of the tradition of allegorical trees, where
there was always a readiness to move freely between different kinds of allegorical activity. The allegory of L's Tree is
'less a toleration of inconsistencies than a number of instinctive contraventions of the norms of allegoresis, in order
to achieve a richness not fully explicable, a whole that is
greater than the sum of its explicit parts' (p. 213).

408. Burrow, John
MEDIEVAL WRITERS AND THEIR WORK:
MIDDLE ENGLISH LITERATURE AND ITS
BACKGROUND (Oxford and New York: OUP, 1982).

Excellent elementary discussion of allegory in L (e.g. pp.
89–90, 103–106) emphasises the importance of the literal as
the vehicle of allegorical meaning: the former must be
relished before the latter can be understood. Allegorical
personifications have to be engaged in action and relationship before they can have meaning: 'Characters have
patience but Patience does not have a character' (p. 91). [See
also Griffiths 1985 [591], on personification-allegory.]

409.   Aers, David
'Reflections on the "Allegory of the Theologians",
Ideology and *Piers Plowman*', in Aers, David (ed.),
MEDIEVAL LITERATURE: CRITICISM,
IDEOLOGY AND HISTORY (Brighton: Harvester,
1986) 58–73.

The 'historical criticism' of D. W. Robertson and his followers was essentially dogmatic, idealising and unhistorical,
like the medieval biblical exegesis whose methods it imitated. 'The allegory of the theologians was a literary form
well-shaped to impose orthodox ideology' (p. 62), to confirm
the power of the church as an institution and to contain
criticism. L's relation to such allegory is *problematic*: he
resists the assimilation of contemporary social struggles
(exemplified in a discussion of wasters in B VI) to clerical
allegory. Reality is not to be dissolved into nor problems
solved by allegory. Even when clerical allegory is fully
deployed, as in the agricultural scenes of B XIX, it is then
exploded in the return to intractable historical reality at the
end of the Passus.

410.   Finke, Laurie A.
'Truth's Treasure: Allegory and Meaning in *Piers
Plowman*', in Finke, Laurie A. and Shichtman, Martin B.
(eds.), MEDIEVAL TEXTS AND CONTEMPORARY
READERS (Ithaca and London: Cornell UP, 1987)
51–68.

The traditional view is that 'allegorical texts produce stable
meanings and mirror unequivocal truths'. Post-structuralist
criticism suggests that 'allegory verges on being a self-
canceling trope, that it simultaneously holds out the promise
of truth and demonstrates the inadequacy of its linguistic
formulations' (p. 52). '*Piers Plowman*, at times, seems almost an allegory of the impossibility of discovering either
significance or truth within language . . . The more human

language strives to represent the world, the more it is trapped and frustrated by its own failure to assume referentiality' (p. 57). Language continually proclaims its own inadequacy; interpretation is resisted. The poem 'explores the process of coming to terms with its own unreadability' (p. 67). Yet in the end the acquiescence in the mystery of meaning is part of the required leap of faith. [The deconstructionist argument is as clearly presented here as may be.]

411. Allen, David G.
'The Premature Hermeneutics of *Piers Plowman* B', in Russell (1988) 49–65.

The way allegory works is a topic that increasingly interested L. He talks about the problems of allegory more and more, and often revises from B to C where he sees that an allegory has got out of hand (e.g. in Ymaginatif's example of Christ's writing in the sand as a confirmation of the value of learning). But the hermeneutic freedom of B may itself be part of a desire to be more spiritually daring, to draw closer to Christ; the censoring in C may be a loss.

412. Barney, Stephen A.
'Allegorical Visions', in Alford (1988) 117–33.

PP seen in the context of 'the traditions of allegory and visionary literature' (p. 118).

413. Blythe, Joan Heiges
'*Transitio* and Psychoallegoresis in *Piers Plowman*', in Russell (1988) 133–55.

'The allegory of *Piers Plowman* is not a catechetical effort enervated by a closed-down system of signification, but rather a labyrinthine, encyclopedic, metaphoric-inferential network of inward and outward epistemic access – always becoming' (p. 147). 'The fog of Lacan can be as dense as that on Malvern Hills' (p. 135).

414.   Manning, Stephen
'William Langland and Jean Piaget', in Russell (1988) 89–106.

Difficult allegorical moments in *PP* (e.g. the problem the dreamer has with Dowel, etc.; the tearing of the Pardon; the role of Piers) are actually key stages in the cognitive development of the dreamer. Understood in terms of Piaget's psychology, these dislocations and disturbances are essential to 'equilibration'.

415.   Morgan, Gerald
'The Status and Meaning of Meed in the First Vision of Piers Plowman', *Neophilologus*, 72:3 (July 1988) 449–63.

L's allegorical fictions are not confused and enigmatic, as they are often made out to be. Meed is not ambiguous: she is condemned outright by Holy Church, but she gradually gets to be spoken of, by the dreamer and others (e.g. Theology) as if she were potentially respectable. Conscience alone stands out against her, through his intuitive understanding of the good. Meed's parentage makes the scholastic distinction between subjective falseness (the falsehood inherent in the nature of a thing) and objective falseness (as induced in others, e.g. by her marriage). The development in C of the contrast between *mede* and *mercede* is intended to emphasise that Meed stands for unrighteous reward. There is development of ideas and greater clarification in B and C, but no confusion.

Dream vision and the role of the dreamer

416. Frank, Robert W., jun.
'The Number of Visions in *Piers Plowman*', *MLN* 66:5
(May 1951) 309–12.

The first serious attempt to count the dreams. There are
three in A, ten in B, including two inner dreams (B XI,
XVI), and nine in C, the second inner dream being elimi-
nated (though L inadvertently keeps the double
awakening).

417. Martin, Jay
'Wil as Fool and Wanderer in *Piers Plowman*', *Texas
Studies in Literature and Language* 3:4 (Winter 1962)
535–48.

Local satire is incorporated into a total structure which is
only partly adequate. The structuring mode of the narrator-
as-fool (the 'I' of the poem being entirely conventional)
works well, since the traditional wisdom and licensing of the
Fool make him an apt vehicle for satirical comment, but the
idea of the narrator-as-wanderer leads to difficulties, since
the credentials of the wanderer as truth-teller are so doubtful. The poem becomes confused.

418. Kane, George
THE AUTOBIOGRAPHICAL FALLACY IN
CHAUCER AND LANGLAND STUDIES. The

Chambers Memorial Lecture delivered at University College London, 2 March 1965 (University College: H. K. Lewis, 1965).

The work of writers such as L and Chaucer, of whose lives little is known, creates a powerful impression of their personalities. This may lead to inferences concerning their life, the assumed nature and events of which then form the basis of further speculation concerning the autobiographical nature of their writings. Bright 1928 [129] is a notorious example. But the 'presence' of authors like L and Chaucer in their writings is nevertheless strong, because of the circumstances of oral delivery, the absence of 'any convention of detached, impersonal narrative' (p. 10) and above all the expressly personal nature of the dream-vision poem, in which verifiable biographical detail relating to the poet will often be attached to the dreamer. This identification of poet and dreamer is often intended to be ironically understood, but it is also something in which the poet is genuinely engaged, an imaginative creation of the narrator as an object of interest in his own right. The narrators are 'constructs' and 'their ultimate reality is imaginative only'. 'The poets invite us to identify the narrators with themselves, and then, by the character of what is narrated, caution us not to carry out the identification' (p. 15). The first-person narrator is a way of defining, in a complex way, the relation between poet and audience, as well as between poetry and reality. Such narrators offer the powerful illusion of intimacy, understanding and self-revelation. But 'externally unsupported biographical inference' (pp. 16–17) from such writings is bound to be fallacious. [See also Kane 1965 [143].]

419.   Holleran, J. V.
'The Role of the Dreamer in *Piers Plowman*', *AnnM* 7 (1966) 33–50.

The narrative is built around the character of the dreamer, a kind of fourteenth-century Everyman, and its structure is simple when seen in terms of the three stages of his progress from the young idealist searching for justice and truth (B *Visio*), through disillusionment, rejection of a life of the spirit which cannot be come to by mental exercise, and giving over of the self to the world and Fortune (VIII–XI), to renewal of the quest, as death comes nearer, with a new sense of urgency and a new spiritual orientation. A good stage-by-stage account of the poem.

420. Hieatt, Constance B.
THE REALISM OF DREAM-VISIONS: THE POETIC EXPLOITATION OF THE DREAM-EXPERIENCE IN CHAUCER AND HIS CONTEMPORARIES (De Proprietatibus Litterarum, Series Practica 2) (The Hague: Mouton, 1967).

In *PP* (pp. 89–97), loose syntax contributes to the ambiguous and dreamlike effect, as does the dreamer's confusion, the mixing of literal and allegorical, the presence of dreams-within-dreams (characteristic of actual dream-psychology), the blurring of sleeping and waking (though certain waking episodes are importantly distinguished), discontinuity, abrupt shifts, 'condensation' (of several figures into one) and 'transference'.

421. Mills, David
'The Role of the Dreamer in *Piers Plowman*', in Hussey (1969) 180–212.

The dreamer is not L, thinking aloud and struggling with the problems of spiritual understanding, nor is he an allegorical abstraction. He is a representative of earthbound man, demonstrating the limitations of such a man's language, power of reasoning and view of reality in the search for spiritual truth, a dramatic focus for the intellectual and imaginative activity of the poem. Piers is a visionary embodiment of the divine potential in man, almost inexpressible in words. Will and Piers together are L. [See also Mills 1980 [348].]

422.   Riach, Mary
        'Langland's Dreamer and the Transformation of the Third Vision', *EC* 19:1 (January 1969) 6–18.

        The dreamer's experiences are often close to the poet's own life, it seems (see Kane 1965 [143]): examples are the meeting with Need, the opening description of the narrator, his contentiousness, and above all the sense of personal humiliation in the rebuke offered to intellectual pride in B X.

423.   Palmer, Barbara
        'The Guide Convention in *Piers Plowman*', *LSE* 5 (1971) 13–27.

        A quest is a narrative with an educational purpose, and it requires that the dreamer be guided and instructed by an authoritative figure, as in *Pearl* and Dante. The lack of such an authority-figure, and the 'inconsistent use of the guide convention' (p. 13), reduce the coherence of *PP*. In contrast with Dante, L is confused and naïve, and his poem is enigmatic because it is structurally weak. The handling of dream-structure, of personification and of the quest motif are all inconsistent. Potentially important guide-figures such as Holy Church and Piers prove unreliable.

424.   Higgs, Elton D.
        'The Path to Involvement: The Centrality of the Dreamer in *Piers Plowman*', *Tulane Studies in English* 21 (1974) 1–34.

Much of the success of L's poem springs from 'his ability to harness for literary purposes the vagaries and changing directions characteristic of dreaming' (p. 1). It presents 'a highly individualized Dreamer, whose personality . . . gives coherency to the form and the content of his visions' (p. 2). 'The central experience of the poem . . . takes place in the mind of Will' (p. 3) and the reader's involvement comes through following the development of that mind. An account of the poem, based primarily on C, with the eight dreams grouped in three main sets (1–2, 3–5, 6–8), illustrates these arguments, showing the dreamer's developing understanding of himself, of Charity, Christ and the Church, and of the need to 'pay what we owe'.

425. Spearing, A. C.
MEDIEVAL DREAM-POETRY (Cambridge: CUP, 1976).

Quite full summaries (pp. 138–62) of A and of the B continuation, showing the function of the dreams in *PP* as a means of allowing L to talk about himself and to dramatise his own problems as a man and a writer, to show himself 'implicated in the subject-matter of his vision' (p. 147), thus turning the dream-poem 'from an objective into a reflexive form' (p. 151). Dreams are a device to break 'the tyranny of chronological narrative' (p. 153), but the poem is also genuinely dreamlike in the way the characters shift and merge, in the apparent inconsequence of the narrative and in the bizarre and mysterious nature of some events.

426. Russell, J. Stephen
'Meaningless Dreams and Meaningful Poems: The Form of the Medieval Dream Vision', *MSE* 7:1 (1978) 20–32.

The dream-frame is genuinely important and rhetorically functional in a unique way. The dreams, in poems like *Pearl* and *PP*, are not oracular visions but the personalised projections of troubled men. It is this that creates the double perspective, and draws the reader to interpret what the dreamer seems unable to understand. At the end, the dreamer's perturbation, which the reader comes to realise he suffers from too, is transformed into a directed longing.

427.   Arn, Mary-Jo
'Langland's Characterization of Will in the B-Text', *DQR* 11:4 (1981) 287–301.

Will is characterised more fully than other medieval dream-narrators and therefore operates more complexly as the 'lens' through which the reader perceives his experience. In the *Visio* he is mostly a 'window' through which we see, but from *Dowel* onwards he takes an essential part in the action, enters into disputes, talks about himself, shows self-awareness and provides the continuity that sustains the poem and makes sense of the sequence of episodes. Will is 'the locus and embodiment' of the poem's meaning (p. 301).

428.   Bridges, Margaret
'The Sense of an Ending: The Case of the Dream-Vision', *DQR* 14:2 (1984) 81–96.

In *PP*, one of several works studied here in the light of Kermode's book, 'the dialectics of closure are both enlightening and brilliantly confusing' (p. 89). John But, in adding a conclusion to A XII, associates the end of the poem with the death of the poet, but L himself constantly undermines closure, especially that seemingly imposed upon dreams by waking. [See Middleton 1988 [355].]

429.   Economou, George D.
'The Vision's Aftermath in *Piers Plowman*: The Poetics of

the Middle English Dream-Vision', *Genre* 18:4 (Winter 1985) 313–21.

The settings of the eight dream visions are important, particularly the second and seventh, both of them visions in which the dreamer falls asleep in church and also speaks explicitly about studying and setting down his dream (so too with the sixth). They are the dreams that become texts (like Chaucer's), metaphors for the creative process, a final harvest (or 'aftermath') from experience.

430. Schmidt, A. V. C.
'The Inner Dreams in *Piers Plowman*', *MÆ* 55:1 (1986) 24–40.

Regards the obscuring in C of the second inner dream of B XVI as achieving some clarification of the line of thought, but at a loss. Lost, through the omission of Piers, is the experience of potent mystery at that point, the moment of emotional intensity which leads to the inner dream, which is an opening up of spiritual mysteries. The first inner dream (B X–XI) is a first premonition of this deeper understanding, beginning in recognition of the importance of *suffraunce*.

431. Lawton, David
'The Subject of *Piers Plowman*', *YLS* 1 (1987) 1–30.

'Almost all critics actively appreciate that the first-person subject of *Piers Plowman* is indeterminate, flexible, and dynamic; yet their characterization of it, for the most part, inclines heavily to the determinate and static' (p. 1). Modern critical theory helps in the formulation of an approach to *PP* which will recognise the multiple meanings of and discontinuities in L's presentation of his dreamer/narrator, and avoid the tendency to see a unity of authorial intention in the progress of Will towards enlightenment. It is essentially a dialogic poem, constructed from the many monologic discourses that clamoured for the author's attention; the subject or subjectivity of the poem (the 'I') is itself constituted at the intersection of contradictory discourses. Lawton gives examples of the portrayal of the dreamer-subject, e.g. as a mouthpiece of a discourse of power concerning penance which is a major theme in the poem and an important agent in the construction of subjectivity, as a proxy for those holy fools and minstrels who seem to have a direct access to God and as essentially a figure from those margins of society (Margery Kempe is another) where a new kind of non-traditional non-hierarchical subjectivity was being constructed.

432.   Weldon, James F. G.
'The Structure of Dream Visions in *Piers Plowman*', *MS* 49 (1987) 254–81.

The dream visions of B are carefully structured and are of deliberately different kinds, so that the poem as a whole is really 'an interconnected sequence of dream vision poems' (p. 255). The eight dreams form three groups: dreams of attachment (dreams 1–3, Prol.–XII), preoccupied with the world and with secular literary themes; dreams of detachment (4–6, XIII–XVIII), more remote from society, more unworldly in space and theme, more pensive; and dreams of spiritual advance (7–8, XIX–XX), where the dreamer is spiritually transformed in being directly illuminated by or involved in essentially mystical visions. The 'prologues' to the dreams are analysed in detail, as the key to the dreamer's spiritual state and progress recorded in the dream.

Use of language; style, metaphor, imagery and word-play

433. Traversi, Derek
'The Vision of *Piers Plowman*', *Scrutiny* 5:3 (December 1936) 276–91. Revised and reprinted as 'Langland's *Piers Plowman*' in Ford, Boris (ed.), THE AGE OF CHAUCER (Pelican Guide to English Literature I) (London: Penguin Books, 1954) 129–47. Reprinted in Ford, Boris (ed.), MEDIEVAL LITERATURE, PART ONE: CHAUCER AND THE ALLITERATIVE TRADITION (The New Pelican Guide to English Literature I) (Harmondsworth: Penguin Books, 1982) 188–207.

Interesting on immediacy, concreteness and vitality of poetic language, instinct for realistic description, firm grasp of the particular.

434. Huppé, Bernard F.
'*Petrus id est Christus*: Word Play in *Piers Plowman*, the B-Text', *ELH* 17:3 (September 1950) 163–90.

Word-play is important in *PP*, both structurally and thematically. Illustrates first its frequency in *PP* (some of the examples are pretty far-fetched); then how it is used to develop a theme over a long passage, or even through the whole poem; and how the names of both the dreamer (Will) and Piers (*Petrus*) are examples of word-play.

435. Kaske, R. E.
'The Use of Simple Figures of Speech in *Piers Plowman*
B: A Study in the Figurative Expression of Ideas and
Opinions', *SP* 48:3 (July 1951) 571–600.

How figurative expressions are used for descriptive, structural, narrative and atmospheric effect, but more importantly to express and reinforce certain intellectual attitudes,
to illustrate or support arguments by the use of similitudes,
and above all to put abstract ideas in concrete form. Many
examples are cited.

436. Spearing, A. C.
'The Development of a Theme in *Piers Plowman*', *RES*
NS 11:43 (July 1960) 241–53.

PP is shot through with a network of recurrences and
repetitions, through which ideas are often developed, not
merely restated. This thematic organisation is often more
fully brought out in C, as in the example chosen for analysis –
recurrence of ideas of hunger and bread, in the 'autobiographical' passage of C VI, the Hunger episode in C IX
and the speeches of Patience in C XVI. Bread in C IX seems
to be the natural symbol of a material solution to material
problems. In C XVI we realise that 'Not by bread alone . . .'
and that man must trust to God for his livelihood as for all
things (*Fiat voluntas tua*). These themes are alluded to but
latent in C IX, and there is a foretaste of them in C VI.

437. Kaske, R. E.
' "*Ex vi transicionis*" and its Passage in *Piers Plowman*',
JEGP 62:1 (January 1963) 32–60. Reprinted in Blanch
(1969) 228–63.

The Latin tag at B XIII 151 is the most baffling single crux in the poem. Relating it to the surrounding lines, Kaske finds in it a grammatical metaphor and allusion to the idea of transitivity in verbs: Patience 'governs' Dowel. The mass of biblical and patristic sources that he cites encourages Kaske to speak of the complexity of intellectual texture in the poem. He comments also on the revision of the passage in C.

438. Spearing, A. C.
'Verbal Repetition in *Piers Plowman* B and C', *JEGP* 62:4 (October 1963) 722–37.

Verbal repetition, of both single words and phrases, is an important part of the rhetoric of *PP*, and the patterns of repetition are consistently intensified in C, particularly in the interests of reinforcing structurally important allegorical meanings. Particular attention is given to repetition in C XVIII 126–64 and throughout C XXI, notably lines 404–15. L's practice is perhaps influenced by the *artes praedicandi*, where there is a similar overriding need to make things clear. But it is not clarity in an analytic sense, the making of intellectual distinctions, that L aims at, but a 'potent vagueness . . . the building up of large theologically undefined ideas which will have the power to stir men's emotions and move them to action' (p. 737).

439. Kean, P. M.
'Langland on the Incarnation', *RES* NS 16:64 (October 1965) 349–63.

Analyses the complex imagery of the 'triacle of hevene' passage in B I 146–56, tracing the synthesis of traditional material from sources in the Bible, biblical commentary and mystical theology.

440.   Ryan, William M.
'Word-Play in Some Old English Homilies and a Late
Middle English Poem', in Atwood, E. Bagby and Hill,
Archibald A. (eds.), STUDIES IN LANGUAGE,
LITERATURE, AND CULTURE OF THE MIDDLE
AGES AND LATER (Austin: University of Texas, 1969)
265–78.

There are links between the use of two-word puns, or
annominatio, and of the device of 'the alliterating matched
pair' in certain Old English homilies and in *PP*. L is very
fond of word-play, and uses it to create an effect of sub-
thematic continuity; it tends to increase in revision. There is
also an increase in the use of playful and mostly private
intertextual punning.

441.   Chessell, Del
'The Word Made Flesh: The Poetry of Langland', *The
Critical Review (Melbourne)* 14 (1971) 109–24.

An appreciation of L's poetry, especially that quality in it of
'thought discovering itself only as it finds words, actively
shaping and defining itself in and through the poetry' (p.
109). It is a poetry of incarnation, that constantly fuses the
spiritual and the physical, most notably in the 'plant of
peace' (B I) and 'lord of life' (B XVIII) passages.

442.   Amassian, Margaret and Sadowsky, James
'Mede and Mercede: A Study of the Grammatical
Metaphor in "Piers Plowman" C: IV:335–409', *NM* 72:3
(September 1971) 457–76.

Like Alanus de Insulis, L uses grammatical metaphor as an
important structure of meaning, specifically in a finely poetic
and effective addition in C that distinguishes between appropriate reward and bribery, and between that kind of giving of

reward which respects law and equity (*mercede*) and that which establishes a bond of love (*mede*). Conscience, the speaker, uses the technical language of grammar (e.g. the notion of direct and indirect relationship, the relation of substantive and adjective, of relative pronoun and antecedent) to throw light on the relationship between giver and recipient in true and false reward, and between man and God.

443. Middleton, Anne
'Two Infinites: Grammatical Metaphor in *Piers Plowman*', *ELH* 39:2 (June 1972) 169–88.

As 'infinites' (B XIII 127–8), Dowel and Dobet are in themselves imperfect and unintelligible: this point is illustrated from speculative grammar, as also the related 'redditive' pronoun and its connection with the theme of restitution in the poem, embodied in Dowel and Dobet. 'As verbs, *ex vi transicionis*, "carry" the dependence of one noun to the other, so Dowel and Dobet, perfected in Dobest, "carry" and "restore" man to God' (p. 181). This kind of obscurity is not infrequent in L: it is deliberate, drawing attention as it does to the interpretative process and its problems, especially in allegorical fictions. Grammar is appealed to as something definite, something that relates mind and reality in a universal way.

444. Dale, Judith
'The Poet in *Piers Plowman*', *Parergon* 4 (December 1972) 3–10.

L's use of language is essentially allegorical, often on a series of levels, as in the imagery of Christ's battle with Death, or of the Tree of Charity. The dreamer has an important place in these verbal structures, as one who is shown struggling to find the right language for his vision of truth.

445. Hill, John M.
'Middle English Poets and the Word: Notes Toward an
Appraisal of Linguistic Consciousness', *Criticism* 16:2
(Spring 1974) 153–69.

Examples of problems in the understanding of language that
are used thematically by Middle English poets. The passage
from *PP* that is analysed (pp. 154–7) is Holy Church's
conversation with the dreamer, where there is a gap between
her words, with their figurative meaning in relation to truth,
and the dreamer's demand for reference to the real world.
The problem is linguistic. Will does not understand how
words are being used: he is resolutely literal.

446. Schweitzer, Edward C.
' "Half a Laumpe Lyne in Latyne" and Patience's Riddle
in *Piers Plowman*', *JEGP* 73:3 (July 1974) 313–27.

Takes '*ex vi transicionis*', in the context of Patience's riddle,
as a punning reference to *transitus*, the word used to gloss
Pascha in the Hebrew bible. It means '*ex vi Paschae*' and is a
reference to the events of Easter as the sum of teaching on
charity. The 'half a laumpe lyne' is a reference to the use of
the candle in the baptismal liturgy, which is the means,
through confirmation, to sacramental participation in
Christ's gift of love. L's lines have 'all the imaginative force
and density of intricate metaphor' (p. 327). But cf. Kaske
1963 [437], Middleton 1972 [443].

447. Mann, Jill
'Eating and Drinking in "Piers Plowman" ', *E&S* NS 32
(1979) 26–43.

Images are not merely a way of giving vivid concretion to
things abstract or not present, but themselves embody
meaning, as can be seen in images of food and drink, hunger

and thirst. The need for food and the means of supplying it described in B VI embodies an important concept of the relationship between physical need and moral laws; gluttony epitomises social waste and corruption; the close association of gluttony and other (verbal) sins of the mouth (contrasted with 'chewing on' the Scriptures) is illustrated in the Feast in B XIII. Spiritual feeding is another major theme embodied in images – in the Eucharist, in the idea of Christ thirsting for man's redemption, an image of God's need to redeem man.

448. Mander, M. N. K.
'Grammatical Analogy in Langland and Alan of Lille',
NQ 26 (224):6 (December 1979) 501–4.

Suggests that L, in his use of grammatical metaphor to describe 'right relation' in C IV 335–409, is drawing on a tradition well represented in Alan of Lille (see Schmidt 1982 [207]) in the *De Planctu Naturae*, where grammatical analogy is similarly used to speak of right and wrong sexual relations.

449. Schmidt, A. V. C.
'Langland's Structural Imagery', *EC* 30:4 (October 1980) 311–25.

Examination of the imagery of food and drink to show its systematic structural relation to the main themes of the poem. Recurrent descriptions of overeating and gluttony (e.g. the fat Doctor) are images of spiritual disorder, while accounts of spiritual food (e.g. what Patience offers Haukyn) are figures of the Eucharist. [See Mann 1979 [447].]

450. Dillon, Janette
'*Piers Plowman*: A Particular Example of Wordplay and its Structural Significance', *MÆ* 50:1 (1981) 40–8.

Considers that there is word-play on 'Will' and 'Dowel' (this seems unlikely) which throws light on the relationship between man's will, God's will and the Good Life.

451. Alford, John A.
'The Grammatical Metaphor: A Survey of its Use in the Middle Ages', *Speculum* 57:4 (October 1982) 728–60.

Illustrates how widespread the use of grammatical metaphor was in the Middle Ages, not just for puns but as a structure of thought, since grammar had universal correspondences in the nature of things. Grammatical distinctions could be used therefore to expound theological and philosophical problems, grammatical solecisms to figure moral ones. Grammar could also be used in allegory, as in Alain de Lille's *De Planctu Naturae* and *PP*. Alford shows (pp. 754–9) how frequently L uses grammatical metaphor but concentrates on the extended grammatical metaphor of C IV 335–409, particularly on the close analogies between grammar and the law.

452. Donaldson, E. Talbot
'Apocalyptic Style in *Piers Plowman* B.XIX–XX', in Pearsall (1983) 74–81.

Comparison of style of B XIX–XX with that of the biblical Apocalypse: onrush of half-formed images, violation of time-sequence, mixing of literal and metaphorical levels of allegory.

453. Spearing, A. C.
'Langland's Poetry: Some Notes in Critical Analysis', in Pearsall (1983) 182–95.

The case for 'close reading' of L's poetry, demonstrated in

analysis of B I 179–209 (concrete realisation of abstract ideas, done with swift strokes, bafflingly elusive), B V 135–63 (allegory and metaphor constantly dissolving and re-forming, deep punning, dramatic vividness) and B XII 131–53 (juxtaposition of prosaic and sublime).

454. Schmidt, A. V. C.
'*Lele Wordes* and *Bele Paroles*: Some Aspects of Langland's Word-Play', *RES* NS 34:134 (May 1983) 137–50.

L knows the power of language, both to communicate spiritual truth through '*lele wordes*' (B XVI 6) and to obscure it in '*bele paroles*' (B XV 115). Word-play (on healing and salvation) reveals the corrupting effects of the latter in the flattering speech of the friar at B XX 347–8. Further analysis, of B XVI 108–10, shows how word-play releases significant spiritual meanings. [See also Schmidt 1987 [603.]

455. Overstreet, Samuel A.
' "Grammaticus Ludens": Theological Aspects of Langland's Grammatical Allegory', *Traditio* 40 (1984) 251–96.

In discussion of *mede* and *mercede* in C III, confusion has arisen because of the failure to see that *relacion rect* and *indirect*, in the grammatical allegory, do not correspond to *mede* and *mercede*; *mede* refers to gifts, *mercede* to payments; either may be *rect* or *indirect*, good or bad. 'He defines two rewards (meed and mercede) and two relationships (*rect* and *indirect*), evaluating various transactions in the light of each' (p. 279). Further problems arise because of L's habit of linking theological doctrine and grammatical allegory through word-play rather than by making systematic analogies; because of the abrupt shifts between social and theological reference; and because of his way of using side by side terms from elementary and advanced grammar.

456.   Gray, Nick
'The Clemency of Cobblers: A Reading of "Glutton's
Confession" in *Piers Plowman*', *LSE* NS 17 (1986) 61–75.

The Tavern scene in the Confession of Glutton has been
much praised for its comedy and gross realism. It seems,
indeed, to be almost a digression from the serious business of
Repentance. But there are reminders of the offices of the
Church, and Glutton's vomiting, on his knees, is itself a
figure of oral confession; Clement the Cobbler, who tries to
help him out, is a mock-confessor (cobblers were notorious
for getting above themselves). His staggering and stumbling
and obscured vision are likewise metaphors for sin. The
scene is a mirror image of confession.

457.   Peverett, Michael
' "Quod" and "Seyde" in *Piers Plowman*', *NM* 87:1
(1986) 117–27.

'Quod' and 'seyde' are usually thought of as synonymous
words in Middle English, but their usage in *PP* is carefully
controlled. 'Quod' is always used except when 'seyde' is
necessary for alliteration or near the end of the line. The
discovery of the regularity of this practice has consequence
for some editorial decisions. Further, the use of 'quod'
indicates, and appears only in the context of, dramatic
narrative: this may help clarify certain vexed questions of
speech-attribution in the poem.

458.   Donner, Morton
'Agent Nouns in *Piers Plowman*', *ChauR* 21:3 (Winter
1987) 374–82.

L uses an unusually large number of agent nouns. His
'penchant for agent nouns manifests his sense of man's world
as a fair field of folk busy at work, emphasizing an idea

central to his poetic conception by emphasizing the linguistic forms which literally assert that idea' (p. 374). It emphasises his sense of individual life and activity, even with allegorical personifications of states and qualities, the energy of both work and wrongdoing.

459. Hill, Thomas D.
'Seth the "Seeder" in *Piers Plowman* C.10.249', *YLS* 1 (1987) 105–8.

L uses subtle word-play on Seth, *seth* ('then, since') and 'seed' in making analogies between the miscegenation of the offspring of Cain and Seth and modern kinds of bad marriage for money.

460. Matheson, Lister M.
'*Piers Plowman* B.13.331 (330): Some "Shrewed" Observations', *YLS* 1 (1987) 108–16.

An example of the potential grammatical and lexical ambiguities in a line from B, arising especially through the lack of indication of direct speech, which has caused problems for both medieval scribes and modern editors. The sense is clarified in C.

461. Shoaf, R. A.
' "Speche that spire is of grace": A Note on *Piers Plowman* B.9.104', *YLS* 1 (1987) 128–33.

L's bold punning often subverts simple notions of the way in which language operates. Speech is both the offspring and the breath of grace, but it is also potentially impure. Speech may be 'spilled', and poetry too can be onanistic.

462.   Adams, Robert
'Mede and Mercede: The Evolution of the Economics of
Grace in the *Piers Plowman* B and C Versions', in
Kennedy, Waldron and Wittig (1988) 217–32.

B tries to evolve a theology of economic motive which will
allow some legitimate activity to *mede*. C develops this,
introducing a new term, *mercede*, in an attempt to clarify the
nature of a morally proper form of recompense, where a
proper chronology of reward (payment after service) and a
proper congruent relationship between giver and recipient
can be insisted upon. The grammatical analogy offered for
the latter is analysed by Adams, and paraphrased in full in
Modern English.

463.   Bland, Cynthia Renée
'Langland's Use of the Term *Ex vi transicionis*', *YLS* 2
(1988) 125–35.

The terminology of *regimen*, a system for analysing syntax,
was well known, and taught in English grammar schools. It
shows how words are related in a sentence, how a verb
governs its direct object, for instance, *ex vi transicionis*
('through its transitive power'). It is a system of terminology
well suited to metaphorical application.

464.   Green, Eugene
'Patterns of the Negative in *Piers Plowman*', in Russell
(1988) 67–88.

A semiotic approach. L's use of the negative is part of a
coherent symbol-system: 'in its broad function it offers
access to those impulses that move the spirit, that direct it
towards a full acceptance of faith, that deflect it as well
toward a self-regard pernicious for communion' (p. 69).

465. Tarvers, Josephine Koster
'The Abbess's *ABC*', *YLS* 2 (1988) 137–41.

Analysis of B VII 138–9 shows how complex is L's use of words, and what a wide variety of meanings and associations he draws upon.

Discussion of the general significance in the narrative of particular episodes and passages

The Pardon episode

466. Coghill, Nevill K.
'The Pardon of Piers Plowman', Sir Israel Gollancz
Memorial Lecture, British Academy, 1945, *PBA* 30 (1946,
for 1944) 303–57. Reprinted, with some abridgement, in
Blanch (1969) 40–86.

The A text 'was undertaken by the author, under the stimulus of *Wynnere and Wastoure*, as a topical narrative allegory about the moral condition of England; his narrative
went vigorously forward to its climax, which was a Pardon
for that moral condition, granted to the Field of Folk' (p.
337). But the Pardon was enigmatic, and in the present state
of society seemed to be on offer to very few. L struggled on
in the A *Vita*, but only got as far as rejecting learning. Long
musing brought the realisation that the reordering of society, which preoccupies A, must give way to the quest for
salvation. The movement to this different plane, the anagogical or spiritual, causes L some trouble, and the B
revision of the A *Vita* is confused, but he regains his sureness
of touch when he comes to new material (Ymaginatif),
keeping the form of the allegory but changing the course of
the argument. Meanwhile, revisions of the A *Visio* provide
'foretastes' of the new themes of B, especially 'the supernal
things of eternal glory'. As to the Pardon, B mitigates its
apparent ruthlessness by concentrating even more closely on
the offer of mercy and redemption through the love and

sacrifice of Jesus Christ and the grace of the Holy Ghost. This wonderfully clear, fresh and vivid account of the whole poem (the Pardon acting as the hinge on which it turns) has had considerable influence on English readers. There is an important review by Morton W. Bloomfield in *Speculum* 22:3 (July 1947) 461–5.

467. Lawlor, John
' "Piers Plowman": The Pardon Reconsidered', *MLR* 45:4 (October 1950) 449–58.

The Pardon, which is no more than a statement of what is required of man for salvation, makes Piers realise the difference between the goodness he has achieved and the perfection for which he must strive. Characteristically, it is the process of finding this out that L enacts so dramatically, making us share in the enigma. The story in its unfolding must be attended to. The earning of the Pardon is a recognition of shameful inadequacy, personal and social, an act of penitence, but also shows that the age when such documents were necessary is past. But L differs from mystics such as Julian in his continued concern for right conduct in this life.

468. Frank, Robert Worth, jun.
'The Pardon Scene in *Piers Plowman*', *Speculum* 26:2 (April 1951) 317–31. Reprinted in Vasta (1965) 169–93.

An important and sensible essay, with a valuable survey of previous opinions. Argues that the Pardon is a valid pardon; that Piers' reaction in tearing it is a dramatic gesture (against 'paper pardons'), not the primary meaning of the episode (the tearing is omitted in C); that Piers accepts the Pardon. The episode does not mark a turning from the Active life (whether or not misinterpreted as Dowel) to the Contemplative, but the recognition of the pre-eminent importance of the spiritual life and the search for Dowel over the care of the body.

469.   Fowler, David C.
'The "Forgotten" Pilgrimage in *Piers Plowman*', *MLN*
67:8 (December 1952) 524–6.

The pilgrimage is not forgotten; it was to follow the ploughing of the half-acre, but Truth, hearing the warning of
famine, tells Piers to stay at home and work his land, and in
doing thus receive Truth's Pardon. [Fowler does not really
solve the problems here, it seems: see Burrow 1965 [390].]

470.   Reidy, John
'Peris the Ploughman, Whiche a Pardoun He Hadde',
*Papers of the Michigan Academy of Science, Arts, and
Letters* 50 (1965: 1964 Meeting) 535–44.

An interpretation of the Pardon episode in A, with a review
of previous opinions. Piers receives what is literally an
indulgence, though allegorically the general pardon from sin
offered to mankind. It is clearly valid. The tearing is a
mystery, for what Piers goes on to is not a repudiation of the
Active life in the world but a completion of it in that higher
Contemplative life which is also the lower part of the Contemplative life, as defined in *The Cloud of Unknowing*.

471.   Walker, Marshall
'Piers Plowman's Pardon: A Note', *English Studies in
Africa* 8:1 (March 1965) 64–70.

The tearing of the Pardon is not a rejection of the Active life:
the *Visio* was an essential beginning, and *doing* remains
central to the life that is to be pursued. It is the priest who
misunderstands the Pardon, thinking it not a pardon because
it does not offer exemption from continuing in the doing of
good works.

472. Mroczkowski, Przemyslaw
'Piers and his Pardon: A Dynamic Analysis', in Brahmer
(1966) 273–92.

Describes the problems presented by B VI, where coercion
seems the only alternative to idleness, and B VII, where the
Pardon episode may dramatise a possible inner conflict in L.

473. Woolf, Rosemary
'The Tearing of the Pardon', in Hussey (1969) 50–75.
Reprinted in Woolf (1986) 131–56.

The Pardon is not a pardon in the usual sense, like a royal
pardon, but a quasi-legal document confirming the offer of
Redemption, at the same time clearly stating the consequences, at the Last Judgement, of rejection of that offer.
It is thus a sentence of death for nearly all the inmates of the
poem we have met: but it becomes a pardon after Piers has
torn it up. Woolf gives an excellent account of the theological background to the episode, and her interpretation of the
tearing is a brilliant *tour de force* which seems to tap the
extraordinary mythic power of Piers' act. The omission of
the tearing in C is a serious obstacle to the acceptance of her
interpretation.

474. Schroeder (Carruthers), Mary C.
'*Piers Plowman*: The Tearing of the Pardon', *PQ* 49:1
(January 1970) 8–18.

There is nothing wrong with the Pardon: it is not untruthful
or excessively rigorous. Comparison with another angry
destruction of a written covenant between God and man –
Moses' breaking of the tablets of the Law – reveals a close
dramatic correspondence (the anger is not directed at the
covenant as such). Furthermore the biblical episode was

traditionally interpreted as the move from the Old to the New Law, and this fits in with the typological pattern of the poem: the *Visio* shows fallen man trying to live by the law without grace, and failing – as in the Ploughing scene – because of his reliance on his natural faculties. To represent Christians as living under the Old Law is not anachronistic: it has to be understood typologically, in terms of the movement of the individual soul from unredeemed natural law to its fulfilment in the law of charity.

475.   Trower, Katherine Bache
'Temporal Tensions in the *Visio* of *Piers Plowman*', *MS* 35 (1973) 389–412.

Building on the interpretation of the Pardon episode offered by Woolf 1969 [473], suggests that the episode dramatises the transition in salvation history from a time before the New Law to the Age of the Church, in which Piers figures in a multi-temporal way as prophet and preacher (the importance of agricultural imagery is stressed here), as apostle, and as man seeking salvation through Christ. The C text changes (e.g. of the perfected number of years, fifty, to the unperfected, forty, in C VIII 188), interpolations, and omission of the tearing of the Pardon emphasise that the episode does not take events out of the present into (apocalyptic) future time, or offer a release from time, but presages a time in the future when doing well will be possible on this earth. The Pardon was the 'reprieve', not the tearing of it. Piers acts here as spokesman for Christ.

476.   McLeod, Susan H.
'The Tearing of the Pardon in *Piers Plowman*', *PQ* 56:1 (Winter 1977) 14–26.

Summary of previous views. The early part of the passus (B VII 9–105) does not specify the terms of a pardon but merely relays a *message* sent by Truth (including a special *letter* to merchants). The contents of the message are thought by Piers to be the terms of the Pardon, which is why he is exasperated and tears it, but the reader recognises that Piers is mistaken: the meaning of the two documents is essentially the same.

477. Baker, Denise N.
'From Plowing to Penitence: *Piers Plowman* and Fourteenth-Century Theology', *Speculum* 55:4 (October 1980) 715–25.

L does not intend Truth's Pardon to be understood as a true pardon, since to accept it as such would be to accept that men can be saved by good works, which would be contrary to orthodox Augustinian teaching on the necessity of pre-venient grace, and more in accord with the semi-Pelagianism of fourteenth-century nominalist thinkers, who believed that the man who does what is in him (*facit quod in se est*) must be granted grace. The tearing of the Pardon thus initiates the shift from ploughing (good works) to penitential pilgrimage (acknowledgement of the need for grace), and shows that Piers recognises that the ability to obey the Law and win salvation is not in man's power alone. In other words, the priest who impugns the Pardon is right. L intends the audience to be momentarily misled, and shocked into a recognition of what the nominalist heresy may lead to. [Whatley 1984 [490] criticises this view as seeming to fix the shifting patterns of L's thought in a premature rigidity, and to ignore the later part of the poem.]

478. Ames, Ruth M.
'The Pardon Impugned by the Priest', in Levy, Bernard S. and Szarmach, Paul E. (eds.), THE ALLITERATIVE TRADITION IN THE FOURTEENTH CENTURY (Kent, Ohio: Kent State UP, 1981) 47–68.

The argument over the interpretation of the Pardon episode stems from differences of emphasis between the prophetic and priestly interpretation of the relation of the Old Law and the New Law. L's view is illustrated chiefly from later episodes in the poem. Love (Piers) fulfils the Old Law (harshly interpreted by the priest), but the Old Law is still part of Truth.

479.   Lawton, David A.
'*Piers Plowman*: On Tearing – and not Tearing – the Pardon', *PQ* 60:3 (Summer 1981) 414–22.

The Pardon is a true pardon, yet Piers does not act wrongly in tearing it, since he tears it horizontally, separating the two verses in which it consists and thus dramatising its point. Not tearing it in C does not therefore involve the loss of anything integral to the movement of the poem. [This is more ingenious than convincing.]

480.   Baker, Denise
'The Pardons of *Piers Plowman*', *NM* 85:4 (1984) 462–72.

Truth's message is not a true pardon: its role in the poem is dynamic, a stage in the quest for salvation, not static. The shock it gives to the reader makes him look more closely at what follows. Its emphasis on good works as the means to salvation is shown to be inadequate in the subsequent introduction of other documents: the 'acquitaunce' given by Patience to Haukyn (B XIV), which shows that penance is the only good deed man is capable of and the true means to salvation; the letters patent brought by Peace (B XVIII) that supersede the old law of Truth's Pardon and announce the new law of love; and finally the true pardon that Christ gives to Piers (B XIX) to absolve man from sin.

The Dowel debate

(*See* also [245]–[268] (Sources: analysis of personifications), and [416]–[432] (Dream vision).)

481. Chambers, R. W.
'Long Will, Dante, and the Righteous Heathen', *E&S* 9 (1924) 50–69.

The rejection of the Pardon in favour of the words of hope of the Psalmist (*Si ambulavero* . . .) is understandable, but the A *Vita* cannot solve the problems of predestination, the fate of the righteous heathen and the relation of learning to salvation. B inserts the inner dream of the poet's own life, which refers to the fifteen-year interval between A and B (on this use of 'autobiographical' material, cf. Hulbert 1948 [137], Burrow 1981 [146]), and plunges back into the debate, which is finally resolved by Ymaginatif. Comparison of L's treatment of Trajan with Dante's treatment of Ripheus, another virtuous pagan. Chambers is chiefly arguing for the intelligibility of B and its continuity from A, as a way of answering those who said it was confused and incoherent and not the work of the author of A.

482. Dunning, T. P.
'Langland and the salvation of the heathen', *MÆ* 12 (1943) 45–54.

L's views on the fate of the righteous heathen are completely in accord with the common theological teaching of his time (cf. Marcett 1938 [153]). Salvation needs faith and baptism: but Christ died for all, and no adult is damned but by his own fault. The theological answer to this dilemma was in the theory of divine inspiration leading the infidel of good will to faith; and in two substitutes for baptism – by blood (martyrdom) and by fire (Baptism of the Holy Ghost).

483.   Maguire, Stella
'The Significance of Haukyn, *Activa Vita*, in *Piers
Plowman*', *RES* 25:98 (April 1949) 97–109. Reprinted in
Blanch (1969) 194–208.

As the poem moves from intellectual questioning to matters
of practical morality, L gathers up themes from the *Visio* in
Haukyn. He has affinities with Piers – industry, scorn for
wasters – but he is the Active life in its superficial aspect
(being 'busy'), the merely practical man, and shows the
inadequacy of that life for salvation. The sins of the Folk
remain in Haukyn's coat, and he recapitulates their penitence and their desire to seek God.

484.   Longo, Joseph A.
'*Piers Plowman* and the Tropological Matrix: Passus XI
and XII', *Anglia* 82:3 (1964) 291–308.

PP is an allegory of the quest for the salvation of the soul, in
which B XI–XII represent a crucial stage, a spiritual and
intellectual climax in which Scripture and Ymaginatif refute
point by point the objections earlier made by Will against
Clergy and learning generally. The inner dream is the passage to this deeper understanding, bringing the dreamer to
the edge of desperation at the nature of his life in the world.
Humbled, he is receptive to the teaching of Trajan and
Reason, and finally of Ymaginatif, the faculty in which is
stamped the image of God in man. Ymaginatif directs this
stage in Will's spiritual education, answering his earlier
doubts and questions, and emphasising the importance of
love and grace.

485.   Russell, G. H.
'The Salvation of the Heathen: The Exploration of a
Theme in *Piers Plowman*', *JWCI* 29 (1966) 101–16.

In B X, Will is driven to a denial of the value of learning, if such as Aristotle and Solomon, because unbaptised, are condemned to hell. C, having removed references to baptism as a guarantee of salvation, makes the argument more extreme by giving it to Recklessness. The account of Trajan is also somewhat altered in C so as to emphasise that baptism is not necessary to salvation: Trajan is not said to have been baptised. C's revisions of B XV extend a fuller promise of salvation, without baptism, to Saracens, suggesting that they may come to belief in the moment of death. In these changes L seems to be influenced by the unorthodox views of the fourteenth-century theologian Uthred of Boldon (one of whose opponents was Friar William Jordan who may be alluded to in the banquet scene), particularly that which affirms the possibility of a clear vision of God available to any soul, Christian, unbaptised child, or heathen, at the moment of death. The revisions of C seem to have been part of a consistent attempt to play down the necessity of sacramental baptism and to put forward, tentatively, a version of Uthred's theology.

486. Wittig, Joseph S.
' "Piers Plowman" B.Passus IX–XII: Elements in the Design of the Inward Journey', *Traditio* 28 (1972) 211–80.

The progress of the dreamer in these passus is related to the tradition of spiritual ascent through self-knowledge as it is represented in the *Meditationes Piissimae* (cited by L) and the *Liber De Spiritu et Anima*. Self-knowledge is derived from the recognition of the self as *imago Dei*. The Castle of Kynde is based on this psychology of the mental faculties, especially the relative role of cognitive and affective knowledge. Many of the dreamer's problems arise from subduing the latter to the former. The inner dream of XI dramatises the obscuring of the image of God, the 'unlikeness' that results, in the mistaking of the nature of the vision of the mirror of Middle Earth (it is a mirror of the dreamer's own folly rather than of God's purpose) in contrast with the mountain vision. Cf. Augustine, *Confessions*, Books 7 and 8, where a similar process of self-recognition and conversion is described. Trajan and the praise of patient poverty are introduced to affirm the value of works (as against learning) and the importance of the affective disposition. Ymaginatif (discussed at length) is essentially a figure in whom the *intellectus* and *affectus* have been restored to their proper relationship, much more than a mere remembrance and recombination of sense images. The course of events of preceding passus is reviewed, and it is affirmed that knowledge is given meaning by love. A detailed and important essay.

487.   Harwood, Britton J.
' "Clergye" and the Action of the Third Vision in *Piers Plowman*', *MP* 70:4 (May 1973) 279–90.

The vision of B VIII–XII records the dreamer's attempt, in a crisis of belief, to seek a 'kynde knowyng' of Christ, but it leaves him little the wiser. One reason is that Clergy, an important character throughout the vision, represents a mode of knowledge and an object of knowledge that is in itself an obstacle to him, being that cultivated understanding that unlocks the Scriptures through *allegoria*. The dreamer tends to separate this activity from belief and love, and see it as a merely intellectual exercise, which is why he is preoccupied with the message of Trajan (and sometimes perilously close to advocating 'cheap grace', 'sinlessness for want of opportunity') and why he undervalues Clergy at the Feast of Patience.

488.   O'Driscoll, Philomena
'The *Dowel* Debate in *Piers Plowman* B', *MÆ*, 50:1 (1981) 18–29.

Dowel, if it is the way to salvation, cannot mean what it says, since good deeds are insufficient without grace, and grace depends on baptism. It is rather an index to the elements (merit, grace, reason, faith) in a debate about who is saved, a debate which concludes in the offer of Redemption through Christ. It is a university debate, in which the issues are those fought over by the followers of Ockham and Bradwardine. The various spokesmen are not in themselves authoritative, since they represent only one view in the debate. What they do *not* say is as important as what they do say.

489. Gradon, Pamela
'*Trajanus Redivivus*: Another Look at Trajan in *Piers Plowman*', in Gray, Douglas and Stanley, E. G. (eds.), MIDDLE ENGLISH STUDIES PRESENTED TO NORMAN DAVIS IN HONOUR OF HIS SEVENTIETH BIRTHDAY (Oxford: Clarendon Press, 1983) 93–114.

The question of how Trajan could be saved, though damned and in hell, was a difficult one for medieval theologians. One answer was that he remained in hell with his pains mitigated, or went into limbo. L does not avail himself of these explanations, nor does he suggest a special form of baptism for Trajan (cf. Dunning 1943 [482], Russell 1966 [485]), nor that there was an act of faith like that of the penitent thief on the cross. Trajan seems to have been saved by merit and good works alone, a clearly Pelagian position, and there seems to be no use of the *moderni* (cf. Coleman 1981 [304]) to escape this position. The general emphasis on merit throughout this episode, as well as the interpretation of *salvabitur vix iustus* by Ymaginatif, reflect the fourteenth-century debate on Pelagianism, though there is also emphasis on poverty and humility in a passage (B XI 154–319) that Gradon attributes to Trajan,

490.   Whatley, Gordon
'The Uses of Hagiography: The Legend of Pope Gregory
and the Emperor Trajan in the Middle Ages', *Viator* 15
(1984) 25–63.

The legend of Trajan was not traditionally used in discussion
of the fate of the 'just pagan' (cf. Chambers 1924 [481]),
since Trajan lived in the Christian era and had access to the
Christian faith. His was an exceptional case, demanding a
return to life, however briefly, to live as a Christian and be
baptised before dying in the faith. But Dante does use him as
an example of the 'just pagan', influenced by the humanist
ideal of the exemplary just ruler, and certainly extending the
hope of salvation at the expense of the Church. L (discussed
pp. 50–6) is even more insistent on the idea that Trajan was
saved by the spirit of love and active commitment to the
moral life; he does not mention the resuscitation motif, and
sets aside the Church and its sacraments. An appendix (pp.
61–3) takes issue with the interpretations of the episode in
PP offered by Russell 1966 [485], Coleman 1981 [304] and
(implicitly) Baker 1980 [477] (see also Baker 1984 [331]).
Whatley is close to Gradon 1983 [489].

491.   Whatley, Gordon
'*Piers Plowman* B.12.277–94: Notes on Language, Text,
and Theology', *MP* 82:1 (August 1984) 1–12.

Interpretation of *allowed* in line 290 as 'rewarded' rather
than 'commended' makes the promise of salvation more
emphatic to those who live a just and moral life according to
their lights; the Kane–Donaldson emendation of line 291
likewise helps to clarify this point. The final comments on
Trajan (see also Whatley 1984 [490]) do not offer him
salvation on the basis of some kind of baptism but again
directly because he was a good man. L is unorthodox in thus
offering salvation to an unbeliever who lived in the Christian
era.

492. Collins, Marie
'Will and the Penitents: *Piers Plowman*, B X 420–35', in Collins, Price and Hamer (1985), *LSE* NS 16 (1985) 290–308.

Gives theological background and vernacular examples of the theme of contrite sinners redeemed (the penitent thief, Mary Magdalene, the apostle Paul), and shows how they are used as encouragement to hope for mercy and persuasion to repent. Will, however, uses them in an aggressive, controversialist way to support an argument (the uselessness of learning for salvation) to which they are irrelevant. C makes Will's wilfulness more explicit by giving the speech to Recklessness.

493. Simpson, James
'The Role of *Scientia* in *Piers Plowman*', in Kratzmann and Simpson (1986) 49–65.

Terms referring to human learning, book-learning, are used in *PP* in an often mocking way to contrast with that intuitive knowledge which is won through 'reading in the book of conscience'. The speech of Study in B X acts as a transition from an understanding of learning as passive absorption to a recognition of the need for active, 'kynde' understanding of God, a movement from *scientia* to *sapientia*; but she recognises that *scientia* has its place in this process. Ymaginatif offers further enlightenment on the relation between acquired and natural learning, but it is at the Feast of Patience that the distinction is made clearest, at the same time that the necessity of both, of Clergy to Conscience, is reiterated.

Later episodes

494. Frank, Robert W., jun.
'The Conclusion of *Piers Plowman*', *JEGP* 49:3 (July 1950) 309–16.

Discussion of the conclusion of *PP* has neglected the vital importance of the theme of the friars' poverty. The lack of provision for friars is the source of their neediness (Need is not correct, at the beginning of B XX, in elevating need above all morality other than temperance), and makes them a danger to the community, since they corrupt the sacrament of penance to win money. In the final lines of the poem, L looks to a day when an ideal pope (Piers) will take action so that the friars have a *fyndyng*, and so destroy Pride. The ending of the poem is thus not apocalyptic nor pessimistic, but proposes a specific remedy for a specific ill, through which the hope of grace may be made real again through true penance.

495.   Tillyard, E. M. W.
MYTH AND THE ENGLISH MIND, FROM PIERS PLOWMAN TO EDWARD GIBBON (London: Chatto & Windus, 1961).

A myth is a story that has become 'a common possession, the agreed and classical embodiment of some way of thinking or feeling' (p. 12). The Harrowing of Hell exerted a powerful hold on the medieval mind because, as a myth, it enacted, in concrete form, the meaning of the act of Redemption. L's daring innovation (pp. 39–41) was to link it with the Debate of the Four Daughters, as well as making the Harrowing itself echo universal myths of light fighting against darkness, life fighting death.

496.   Paull, Michael R.
'Mahomet and the Conversion of the Heathen in *Piers Plowman*', *ELN* 10:1 (September 1972) 1–8.

The Introduction to Dobet is centrally concerned with the failure of contemporary clergy, especially in their mission to convert the heathen. Mahomet is presented as the false prophet and excommunicated Christian who has led heathens away from Christ, and also as a type of the Antichrist who has perverted the clergy.

497. Adams, Robert
'The Nature of Need in "Piers Plowman" XX', *Traditio* 34 (1978) 273–301.

The scene is enigmatic, given that Need's advice is often orthodox in content yet also suspect in tendency, but the enigma is in its complexity not in any lack of conviction on L's part of what he wants to say. Need is neutral in condition but not in effect, and here he has fallen into bad company (the brewer, etc. from the end of XIX). The clue is in Job 41:13 and the commentary especially of Gregory in his *Moralia*, where Need goes before Antichrist (as in *PP*). His plausible strategy (necessity needs only the constraint of temperance) is thus in fact devious. L also alludes to Proverbs 6:9–12 and 30:8–9, which were used by antimendicant writers in attacking begging friars. 'Langland never shifts his basic principles on the issues associated with poverty' (p. 289). What he does is to represent the debate in all its complexity, and also in a 'dialectical' way that unfolds its complexities gradually, so that the reader may be drawn into traps of self-discovery. He wants to tell the reader the truth, but also to re-enact the process by which truth is grasped. Finally, the Job commentary, as also a debt to the *Liber De Antichristo*, makes it clear that the Antichrist who follows Need is the genuine figure of apocalyptic tradition, seen in a prophetic vision, not a metaphor. A learned and important article.

498. AlKaaoud, Elizabeth
'*Caro*, *Caritas*, and the Role of the Samaritan in *Piers Plowman*', *Proceedings of the Patristic, Mediaeval and Renaissance Conference* 7 (1982) 39–45.

The Latin pun on *caro* and *caritas* corresponds to the psycho-spiritual integration Will achieves after he meets the Samaritan. Intellectual understanding of charity is completed through practical experience of charity in action, the humbly physical and the loftily spiritual being symbolised in the lowly mule of the Samaritan.

499.   Ashley, Kathleen M.
'The Guiler Beguiled: Christ and Satan as Theological Tricksters in Medieval Religious Literature', *Criticism* 24:2 (Spring 1982) 126–37.

The theory of the Atonement that has Christ tricking the trickster Satan and so overcoming him was not popular with later medieval scholars, nor has it been popular with modern scholars. But it appealed to a medieval mentality that was closer to folklore and to its love of tricksters, and is notably present in *PP* (pp. 133–4), side by side with the later interpretation based on the divine motivation of love.

500.   Tavormina, M. Teresa
' "Bothe two ben gode": Marriage and Virginity in *Piers Plowman* C.18.68–100', *JEGP* 81:3 (July 1982) 320–30.

Revision of this passage in C, though not disturbing the traditional hierarchy of virginity, widowhood and marriage, gives increased value to marriage and affirms its positive sanctity. The 'furste fruyte' blessed by God in line 94 is marriage, not virginity.

501.   Arn, Mary-Jo
'Langland's Triumph of Grace in *Dobest*', *ES* 63:6 (December 1982) 506–16.

The ending of the poem is not pessimistic. As an individual,

Will has learnt how to do well, better and best, and now finally, after some difficulties with Need and in the battle against Pride, he attains to the freedom to be a receptor of divine grace. In the last passus he ceases to be Will, 'wilful', and comes to be represented as Conscience. Conscience's crying out for Grace at the end is not despairing, for Grace has been and is to be found thus.

502. Bertz, Douglas
'Prophecy and Apocalypse in Langland's *Piers Plowman*, B-Text, Passus XVI to XIX', *JEGP* 84:3 (July 1985) 313–27.

It is the inner dream of the Tree of Charity, concerned with looking into the future, that introduces the prophetic and apocalyptic visions of B XVI–XIX. These are visions of the future that work with the past, and partial visions of the future (Abraham, Moses), and from that past onwards. The exposition of the life of Christ is an account of the past, but one that is suffused with visions of the future drawn from the Apocalypse.

503. Waldron, R. A.
'Langland's Originality: the Christ-Knight and the Harrowing of Hell', in Kratzmann and Simpson (1986) 66–81.

B XVIII is not just a confirmation of what was always expected, but a challenge to imagination and intellect in its complexity and originality: in the handling of the figure of the Christ-Knight, with much emphasis on the imaging-forth of the transcendental in the feudal and chivalric (and some further parallels with Bozon); in the unusual placement of the Debate of the Four Daughters; and in the dramatic emphasis, here and in the Harrowing, on the legality of the Redemption (influence from *Le Chasteau d'Amour*).

General interpretative studies

504. Warton, Thomas
HISTORY OF ENGLISH POETRY FROM THE
TWELFTH TO THE CLOSE OF THE SIXTEENTH
CENTURY, ed. W. Carew Hazlitt (London: Reeves &
Turner, 1871).

Section VIII, on *PP*, was communicated by W. W. Skeat,
and superseded what Warton and earlier editors had said
about the poem. It is Skeat's most important early statement
about *PP*, the end of the 'myth' of the poem, and the
beginning of a more accurate historical appraisal of it. Skeat
deals first with the title, author, date, and three versions of
the poem. He accepts the characterisation of the poem as a
satire on the vices of the age, especially those of the clergy,
but argues that the poem is 'something more than a satire'
(p. 250): it is an account of 'the whole history of the religious
life of man', with Piers representing 'the spiritual part of
human nature which ever wars against evil, but which can
never wholly triumph in this world' (p. 251). Lengthy extracts exemplify the imaginative vividness, good sense, observation of life, picturesque humour and occasional
sublimity of the poem.

505. Jusserand, J. J.
PIERS PLOWMAN: A CONTRIBUTION TO THE
HISTORY OF ENGLISH MYSTICISM. Translated from
the French by M.E.R., revised and enlarged by the author
(London: T. Fisher Unwin, 1894; reprinted, New York:
Russell & Russell, 1965).

After some preliminary historical background, Jusserand gives a summary of the poem (though 'no analysis can give a satisfactory idea of the mingling of realities and shadows', p. 23), which becomes very brief after the *Visio*; an account of the contents and date of the three versions; a speculative biography of the poet, drawn from internal allusions, with much fanciful reconstruction; a description of the social and political world portrayed in the poem, with much emphasis on the vividness of that portrayal, and on the grandeur of L's idea of the constitutional role of the Commons (p. 107); a description of the Church as it appears to L, with stress on his moderateness and orthodoxy, as well as his urgent impetus towards reform. Chapter VI deals with L's art, which is marked above all by sincerity (his words 'flow in a burning stream, and could no more be checked than the lava of Vesuvius', p. 153), and a power of giving concrete expression to spiritual realities, and his aims, which are those of a passionately sincere teacher, opposed to all sham and show. Chapter VII speaks of L's popularity in his own time and at the Reformation; of the relation of his ideas to those of the Wycliffites; and of the similarities between L and continental writers, especially mystical writers, and between L and earlier and later English writers, including Rolle and Blake. L has the passionate and mystical quality of the Anglo-Saxon, Chaucer the lucidity and logic of the Latinized Celt (p. 219). There is an appendix of selected passages. Jusserand's Langland was the dominant image of the poet at the turn of the century and for many years thereafter. [See also Jusserand 1909 [105].]

506. Ker, W. P.
ENGLISH LITERATURE: MEDIEVAL (Home University Library) (London: Hutchinson, 1912).
Reprinted, as MEDIEVAL ENGLISH LITERATURE, with Bibliographical Notes by Pamela Gradon (London: OUP, 1969).

Careless construction, some tedious allegory, good poetry (1969, pp. 106–9).

507. Legouis, Emile, and Cazamian, Louis
A HISTORY OF ENGLISH LITERATURE. Translated from the French by Helen Douglas Irvine, 2 vols. (London: Macmillan, 1927).

The authors admire L's boldness, realism, energy and fervour, but consider him to be 'entirely without the art of construction or arrangement' (p. 72). Confused at the start, the poem becomes more incoherent in revision, especially in the long second part. 'His work is of first-rate value to social historians, his literary merit is barely second-rate' (p. 75).

508. Wells, Henry W.
'The Construction of *Piers Plowman*', *PMLA* 44:1 (March 1929) 123–49. Reprinted in Vasta (1965) 147–68 and in Vasta (1968) 1–21.

The appearance of roughness and incoherence in *PP* is illusory. The *Visio* is concerned with the primary duties of the ordinary Christian in his life in the world, the *Vita* with the specialised spiritual life improper to the layman. Wells finds correspondences between *Visio* and *Vita* in a division into three parts, with many parallels and echoes (some of them fanciful). The three lives of the *Vita* (Dowel, Dobet, Dobest) correspond to the theologians' division of the lives of the active and the contemplative, and a third life in which the contemplative returns to the world to serve others; also to the three persons of the Trinity: Father, Son and Holy Spirit. The poem is 'a really finely built structure, the nave for the people, the choir for the clergy', though it has its digressions, as a church has its clutter. An historically important essay.

509. Coghill, N. K.
'The Sexcentary of William Langland', *The London Mercury* 26:151 (May 1932) 40–51.

L's poem seems disorderly and chaotic, but it is in fact 'a comprehensive and highly integrated achievement such as only long consideration and labour could have brought about' (p. 40). Coghill's characteristically vivacious account of the poem concerns itself with four main attributes: 'intensity of tone; power to imagine and organise great structural myths or images to include and complete his thought; an awareness, very profound, both of the practical world and of the enfolding kingdom of God; and power to invent characters that are spiritually alive' (p. 43).

510. Troyer, Howard William
'Who is Piers Plowman?' *PMLA* 47:2 (June 1932) 368–84. Reprinted in Blanch (1969) 156–73.

Analyses the appearances of Piers, and argues, none too clearly, that Piers is to be allegorically understood, according to medieval principles of exegesis, as a symbol with multiple meanings: as a man with needs in the natural world, as man with his obligations in the moral world, and as a representation in human form of the divine agency of Christ the redeemer.

511. Coghill, Nevill K.
'The Character of Piers Plowman considered from the B Text', *MÆ* 2:2 (June 1933) 108–35. Reprinted in Vasta (1968) 54–86.

The poem is in four parts. The *Visio* is the allegory of human life in the active world, Piers acting as the embodiment of Faith and Work. The *Vita de Dowel* is the exposition of the virtues that underlie the Active, Contemplative and Pontifical lives, where we see L offering successive definitions of the Three Lives, feeling for his ideas, ruminating upon them. Piers reappears in the *Vita de Dobet*, the life of the contemplative who teaches, heals, suffers and lives as he preaches: Piers is the human aspect of Christ, who represents this life in its highest form. The *Vita de Dobest* is the allegory of salvation through the spiritual authority of the Church, embodied in Piers as Peter (and the Holy Ghost). It is the cumulative nature of the Three Lives that makes them suitable for embodiment in a character who develops but who still retains the traits with which he first appeared. A very important early essay. [See Wells 1929 [508], Hussey 1956 [529].]

512.   Carnegy, Francis A. R.
THE RELATIONS BETWEEN THE SOCIAL AND DIVINE ORDER IN WILLIAM LANGLAND'S 'VISION OF WILLIAM CONCERNING PIERS THE PLOWMAN' (Sprache und Kultur der Germanischen und Romanischen Völker, Anglistische Reihe, Band XII (Breslau, 1934).

Salvation is to be attained only through work. Piers as a labourer represents the noblest type of manhood, but his attempt to put the world to work (which reflects contemporary social unrest) is a failure. The 'labour problem' allegorises human sinfulness: Piers is saved, but not the rest of mankind, as the Pardon shows. The *Vita* brings an understanding of the importance of love, patience and humility ('to see much and suffer more'), but the poem continues to be concerned with the life and work of Christians on earth and in society. The solution of the labour problem is in the centring of life and work in Christ.

513. Dawson, Christopher
'The Vision of Piers Plowman', in his MEDIEVAL
ESSAYS (London: Sheed & Ward, 1953) 239–71.
Originally published in his MEDIEVAL RELIGION
(London: Sheed & Ward, 1934).

'At once the most English of Catholic poets and the most
Catholic of English poets: a man in whom Catholic faith and
national feeling are fused in a single flame. He saw Christ
walking in English fields in the dress of an English labourer .
. .' (p. 240). In an age of social unrest and spiritual upheaval,
his poem, though formless and lacking in literary artifice, is
urgent in its spiritual vision. Realism bursts out of the
creaking machinery of allegory: it is the first authentic voice
of the English people, almost the only utterance of the cry of
the poor. His aim is to bring religion back to common
humanity, as embodied in Piers. Like Wyclif he is a fierce
critic of the established Church, but he has the faith of an
orthodox Christian and apocalyptic hope of spiritual renewal. He is 'thoroughly English in the way in which he
combines an intense class-consciousness and a hatred of
social injustice with a strong conservatism and a respect for
the established order' (p. 261).

514. Lewis, C. S.
THE ALLEGORY OF LOVE: A STUDY IN
MEDIEVAL TRADITION (London: OUP, 1936).

Remarkably influential brief remarks (pp. 158–61) on *PP*.
'Its only oddity is its excellence; in *PP* we see an exceptional
poet adorning a species of poetry which is hardly exceptional
at all . . . Even as a moralist he has no unique or novel
"message" to offer . . . the defence of the universally
acknowledged . . . a poem every way unsuitable for recita-
tion . . . excellent satiric comedy' (pp. 158–9). 'What is truly
exceptional about Langland is the kind, and degree, of his

poetic imagination . . . sublimity is frequent . . . a Lucretian
largeness' (quotes C XXIII 80ff). 'This power of rendering
imaginable what before was only intelligible is nowhere . . .
better exemplified than in Langland's lines [C II 149ff] on the
Incarnation' (p. 160). 'He lacks the variety of Chaucer, and
Chaucer's fine sense of language: he is confused and monotonous, and hardly makes his poetry into a poem. But he can
do some things which Chaucer can not . . .' (p. 161).

515.   Dunning, T. P., CM
PIERS PLOWMAN: AN INTERPRETATION OF THE
A-TEXT (London: Longmans, Green & Co., 1937;
reprinted Westport, Conn.: Greenwood Press, 1971).
Second edn, revised and edited by T. P. Dolan, with a
prefatory memoir by J. A. W. Bennett (Oxford:
Clarendon Press, 1980).

The theme of A is the right use of temporal goods, demonstrated first in expository fashion by Holy Church and then
through the allegorical picture of Cupidity, of the improper
use of these goods, in the Lady Meed passus. The Confession of the Folk is dominated by the theme of the abuse of
worldly goods, as in the Ploughing of the Half-Acre, despite
the momentarily wider spiritual implications of Piers' directions to the Castle of Truth. The Pardon episode is a
recognition that attention must be turned away now from
worldly to spiritual things. The *Vita*, which follows, is really
a separate and not very important poem, briefly declaring
that perfection is to be sought in faith, simplicity and obedience to God's law. The purposes of the A *Vita* are misun-
derstood in B, which is badly constructed and lacking in
drama and concrete visualisation. In the revised edition,
Dolan has removed, in accord with Dunning's changed view
of the matter (see Dunning 1956 [530]), the comments on B
and its authorship. He has also improved the apparatus and
systematised the practice of quotation.

Reviews: J. A. W. Bennett, *MÆ* 7:3 (October 1938) 232–6.
J. A. Alford, *Speculum* 57:2 (April 1982) 367–70.

516. Wells, Henry W.
'The Philosophy of Piers Plowman', in *PMLA* 53:2 (June 1938) 339–49. Reprinted in Vasta (1968) 115–29.

The Three Lives (of Dowel, etc.) are the Active, Contemplative and Mixed (or Pontifical) lives. There are correspondences with the *Visio*: the pragmatic analysis of civil and social corruption (I–IV) corresponds to the intellectual analysis of moral and theological problems (Dowel); the move to the inner life through confession of sins corresponds to the exposition of the mysteries of the faith (Dobet); and the summary of the virtues of the Christian community (B VII) corresponds to the account of the establishment of the corporate body of the Church (Dobest). But the Lives are not to be interpreted narrowly or exclusively: they are states of the soul, not estates of society, and each Christian will pass and repass through them.

517. Chambers, R. W.
MAN'S UNCONQUERABLE MIND: STUDIES OF ENGLISH WRITERS, FROM BEDE TO A. E. HOUSMAN AND W. P. KER (London: Jonathan Cape, 1939).

PP is an attempt to understand and expound the ways of God in relation to England and the soul of the individual, written by a devout non-radical Christian, well versed in the Bible and liturgy but not learned. The movement from the concerns of the *Visio* to those of the *Vita* (and from A to B) is inevitably a move from the vivid concretion of display of the world's ills to a greater abstraction and circuitousness, but the progression is a natural one and does not argue for multiple authorship (Chambers reserves his position on C). The Pardon marks the transition from the world of commandments and pardons to the inward quest for salvation, at first confused, but clarified through Ymaginatif. Dowel is the life of honest labour in the world (though the presentation of Haukyn shows how the idea of the active life has to be spiritually understood), Dobet that of contemplative charity and ascetic poverty, Dobest the apostolic or mixed life, the righteous rule of the united Church. (On this, see Hussey 1956 [529].) The ending is grim, but the breaking of the outward bulwarks only drives L inward to the fundamentals of his faith – the search of the individual soul for Christ. Chambers' two essays here (pp. 88–171) are, with all his work on authorship, text, etc., the fullest account of his view of the poem *as* a poem. They are the distillation of a deep and fruitful reading, and a landmark in the history of the reception of the poem.

518.   Rauch, Rufus William
'Langland and Medieval Functionalism', *Review of Politics* 5 (October 1943) 441–61.

L shows that the reform of society depends upon the redemption of the individual. Only through the latter can society be restored to that order in which its different parts function as a whole organism, in which hierarchy is maintained and the divine order made manifest. Paraphrase of *PP*, with lengthy quotation in translation, illustrates these points.

519.   Baugh, Albert C.
A LITERARY HISTORY OF ENGLAND (New York: Appleton-Century-Crofts, 1948).

Baugh (pp. 241–7) gives an account of the authorship question, and a summary of A which praises the author's powerful, yet wayward and rhapsodic imagination, his vivid realism and trenchant satire, but he refuses to summarise the new material in B and C on the grounds that the plan of the poem, if any, is completely obscured by L's constant parentheses and digressions: he is 'powerless to resist the impulse to pursue any idea suggested by another idea or even by a word that he happens to use' (p. 244).

520.   Gerould, Gordon Hall
'The Structural Integrity of Piers Plowman B', *SP* 45:1 (January 1948) 60–75.

The turning-point of the *Vita* is the mention of Piers by Clergy in B XIII, and the revelation of the importance of love, above all of Christ's love. Faith and Hope are meaningless until crowned in Charity (Piers, Christ). The final passus returns with this revelation to the present world. The poem as a whole is a pilgrimage in time, through which L allows the reader to share in Will's religious education as he struggles towards righteousness.

521.   Donaldson, E. Talbot
PIERS PLOWMAN: THE C-TEXT AND ITS POET (Yale Studies in English, 113) (New Haven: Yale UP, 1949; reprinted with new preface and revised MS lists, Hamden, Conn.: 1966). Excerpt (156–98, on religious allegory) reprinted in Vasta (1968) 130–89.

Aims to reinstate C in its properly important position, and to demonstrate that it is by the same author as B. Deals first with the authorship controversy and the generally inferior place of C in critical tradition, and then with the mathematics and methods of the C revision, especially the variation in the scale of revision from line-by-line retouching and thorough rewriting (e.g. of B IX–XI) to mere insertion of added passages. Changes in passus numbering and alliteration are also treated. In his chapter on 'The Art of the C-Reviser', Donaldson shows how C is castigated as unimaginative, abstract, lacking in B's vivid visualising power, cautious, moralistic, generalising, prone to repeat certain words. Such qualities are present, but where they distinguish C from B they are often the result of attempts to make an argument more clear and coherent, to remove potential understandings that may arise from the use of figurative language, to dispense with merely traditional poeticising (as in the opening lines), or else they relate to modern notions of what is 'poetic'. They certainly do not argue that the C-reviser was a different person; new material is often full of characteristically Langlandian poetic power. The supposed discrepancy between B's radicalism and C's ultraconservatism is seen, on examination of C's changes in passages dealing with kingship, knighthood, the commons, or with topical events of 1376, to be the product of misinterpretation of B by democratic sympathisers. In the representation of the occupations of the Folk there is a considerable degree of consistency from B to C (e.g. towards clerics, including bishops), and even where there is difference (e.g. on beggars and minstrels, discussed at length) it is the product of a greater complexity and intensity of treatment (perhaps due to L's increasing sense of his perilous closeness to both groups) and certainly not of inconsistency.

Changes in C affecting the interpretation of the religious allegory are also discussed, after systematic categorisation of the Three Lives has been dismissed as impossible (rather the movement of the whole poem, from *Visio* to *Vita*, hinges on Matthew 19:16–22, and Christ's successive injunctions to the young man: 'Keep the commandments', and, 'If thou wilt be perfect . . .'), namely: the change in the Pardon episode (the tearing had to be removed, whatever the dramatic loss, since it shows Piers to be disobedient to Truth; but the general thematic transition to the *Vita* is the same); the expansion of the role of Recklessness (to point to both the good and bad aspects of what he stands for, as also his closeness to the dreamer); the near-obliteration of Haukyn (because the C-reviser now wanted to stress patient poverty above everything to do with the renewal of interest in the life of labour); and the allocation of Anima's role to Liberum Arbitrium, as well as Piers' role as proprietor of the Tree of Charity (this gives much-needed clarity to the relationship of Piers and Christ). A final chapter attempts a reconstruction of the author's life, chiefly from the evidence of the 'auto-biographical' passage in C VI. Appendices include a list of *PP* MSS and an account of the textual situation of C. In many ways, though it is a pity Donaldson had to be so preoccupied with the authorship question, this is still the most sensitive, eloquent, subtle and 'literary' account of the poem.

Reviews: J. A. W. Bennett, *MÆ* 21:1 (1952) 51–3.
M. W. Bloomfield, *MLQ* 12:2 (June 1951) 230–1.
G. R. Coffmann, *Speculum* 24:3 (July 1949) 422–7.

522. Smith, A. H.
PIERS PLOWMAN AND THE PURSUIT OF POETRY. Inaugural Lecture at University College, London, 1950 (London: H. K. Lewis, 1951). Reprinted in Blanch (1969) 26–39.

Obsession with the question of authorship, which is not really in doubt, has distracted attention from the singular merit of *PP* as a poem. Its theme is the search for truth and salvation, its form that of a pilgrimage. The author is congratulated for his 'appreciation of what we call moral standards' (Blanch, p. 38).

523. Meroney, Howard
'The Life and Death of Longe Wille', *ELH* 17:1 (March 1950) 1–35.

Argues that the Three Lives correspond to the purgative, illuminative and unitive aspects of the mystical life (cf. Hussey 1956 [529]). Also offers a new view of the authorship question: 'The A-Text is an abridgement for a non-clerical audience by a redactor of the B-Version, who abandoned his project when the poem became too esoteric' (pp. 22–3). The evidence is in the omission of Latin in A, the avoidance of difficult words and the failure to comprehend 'the original'.

524. Bennett, J. A. W.
'Langland's World of Visions', *The Listener* 43:1101 (2 March 1950) 381–2.

L is not an itinerant rustic preaching the gospel of hard work, nor a learned theologian, but a poet trying to communicate his vision through images and symbols – 'a field, a plowman, a pilgrim'. The poem progresses in a series of spirals in its search for truth, self-knowledge and spiritual purification.

525. Kane, George
MIDDLE ENGLISH LITERATURE: A CRITICAL STUDY OF THE ROMANCES, THE RELIGIOUS LYRICS, *PIERS PLOWMAN* (London: Methuen, 1951).

Part II (pp. 182–248) is on *PP*. Argues against any attempt to separate the plan or meaning of the poem from its poetry; discusses its relation to alliterative tradition (more direct, less precious), the nature of the poet's personality (fiercely outspoken, stern yet tender, intensely idealistic, full of intellectual curiosity, wryly ironic), and the qualities of his poetry (uneven, capable of sublimity, fluent, visually vivid, boldly metaphorical, verbally violent) as they reflect the combination in L of religious, moral, emotional and intellectual impulses. Kane sees no systematic programme of symbolic meaning in the poem, but rather a succession of flowerings of significance; the poem is driven by a series of powerful impulses rather than structured according to any prepared design, though there is an important turning-point at B VII 117, from the life of the Christian in the world to a higher kind of spiritual life.

526. Tillyard, E. M. W.
THE ENGLISH EPIC AND ITS BACKGROUND
(London: Chatto & Windus, 1954).

The discussion of the three versions of the poem (where Tillyard makes interesting comparison with Wordsworth's *The Prelude*) concludes that each has its merits, though the total effect is to increase the reader's bewilderment. The poem has the quality of 'epic' in its versification, where L shows his power of enriching sense through sound, and of sententious utterance, and not only in short passages. The poem speaks for a great body of people, on subjects of great importance; the religious motive of the poem makes of it a 'heroic poem, a Christiad' (p. 163). In the main theme, of salvation and the earthly pilgrimage, the allegory has sometimes a kaleidoscopic and shifting quality, but the melting of one allegory into another gives its own kind of continuity. Structurally, there is too much repetition, too much of the accretion of didactic material that bespeaks the moralist rather than the artist, and the division between the *Visio* and the Life of Dowel is not sufficiently clear-cut. But there is much that is masterly in the handling of key transitions and in the sense of movement towards a goal. '*Piers Plowman* emerges as the undoubted, if imperfect, English epic of the Middle Ages' (p. 171).

527. Suddaby, Elizabeth
'The Poem *Piers Plowman*', *JEGP* 54:1 (January 1955)
91–103.

PP is neglected as a poem. Its style and point of view are
important aspects of L's poetic power, and both reflect his
personality. Passages are analysed to demonstrate the effectiveness of L's use of alliterative verse, the striking manner
in which he moves from the general to the particular or
embodies the abstract in the concrete, his power of commu-
nicating physical reality. In larger things, too, he has an
instinct for selecting the important things to put his emphasis
on – the Harrowing of Hell rather than the medieval vision of
hell – and for displaying those qualities of humanity and
compassion which make the poem permanently durable.

528. Schlauch, Margaret
ENGLISH MEDIEVAL LITERATURE AND ITS
SOCIAL FOUNDATIONS (Warsaw: Polish Scientific
Publishers [PWN]; London: OUP, 1956).

Discussion of *PP* (pp. 213–17) follows the older view that the
Visio is clear and vivid while the *Vita* is confused and
baffling; identifies L as 'essentially conservative' in his political and religious attitudes, but 'democratic in his broad
human sympathies'. 'His positive conclusion is reached in an
atmosphere of increasing mysticism which becomes more
obscure as it becomes more rapturous' (p. 216).

529. Hussey, S. S.
'Langland, Hilton and the Three Lives', *RES* NS 7:26
(April 1956) 132–50. Reprinted in Vasta (1968) 232–58.

Argues against Wells 1929 [508] and Coghill 1933 [511]. A
reading of Hilton shows that the Contemplative life is not
superseded by the 'Mixed'. Nor does L ever mention the

Mixed life; nor is his Contemplative life at all retired or enclosed; nor is the Active life anyway to be identified with hard work in the world. The triad offered by Meroney 1950 is equally unsound. The Lives are not to be understood in any systematic or restrictive way: they are ways of talking about the degrees in the effort to live the Good Life in whatever state the Christian is called to. An important landmark in *PP* criticism.

530.   Dunning, T. P., CM
'The Structure of the B Text of *Piers Plowman*', *RES* NS 7:27 (July 1956) 225–37. Reprinted in Vasta (1968) 259–77, and in Blanch (1969) 87–100.

The interpretation of the Three Lives offered by Wells 1929 [508] and Coghill 1933 [511] needs to be refined. The 'active life' is not the life of hard work in the world, but the first stage of the spiritual life proper. The *Visio* is the allegory of the discipline of natural appetite through measure: it has to do with the needs of life and the moral order of society. The Pardon is the clear call, of the individual, to the spiritual life, which is then described in its three phases – the active, the religious and the prelatical – as the increase, perfecting and overflowing (into the apostolate) of love.

531.   Frank, Robert Worth, jun.
PIERS PLOWMAN AND THE SCHEME OF SALVATION: AN INTERPRETATION OF *DOWEL, DOBET, AND DOBEST* (Yale Studies in English 136) (New Haven: Yale UP, 1957). Extract (pp. 19–33) reprinted in Vasta (1968) 298–318.

Rejects the interpretation of the Three Lives made by Wells 1929 [508] and Coghill 1933 [511]. Dowel, etc. are not three concepts or separate ways of life, but simply the law of love carried to an ever higher degree. Dobet and Dobest are divisions within the generic term Dowel. Meanwhile Piers represents the divine in man, man's capacity for salvation: but it is God's scheme that makes salvation possible. 'It is the implications of the divine plan for human salvation that give the poem its direction; and it is the spectacle of man now blundering and now moving forward within the framework of this plan that gives the poem its drama' (p. 18). The Pardon scene marks the move on to a different level after the *Visio*, prompted by Piers' anger that pardons, pieces of paper, should be a substitute for 'doing well'. The three divisions of the *Vita* have a general association with the three persons of the Trinity, as also, chronologically, with the time of Law, the life of Christ and the time of Grace. The theme of Dowel is the moral soul, the power that God gives man to *know* the Good Life, the role of intellect and learning in the scheme of salvation. The second vision of Dowel (B XIII–XV) shows how man *does* well, through the active virtues of love, patient poverty and penance. Dobet leads up to Christ and shows how, through him and his teaching of love through his death, man is better able to know and obey the law of love. Dobest completes the scheme of salvation with the gifts of the Holy Ghost – grace, the gospels, Holy Church. The scene is again the Field Full of Folk, but now recognised as a vast battleground in which man's soul is contended for. The greatest evil is within the Church, in the person of the friars, and the ending of the poem, so far from being apocalyptic, is a practical plea for reform (that friars should have a 'fyndyng').

Reviews: T. P. Dunning, *RES*, NS 11:41 (January 1960) 67–9.

S. S. Hussey, *MLR* 54:1 (January 1959) 84–5.

R. E. Kaske, *MLN* 74:8 (December 1959) 730–3.

D. W. Robertson, *Speculum* 33:3 (July 1958) 395–7.

T. Silverstein, *MP* 56:3 (February 1959) 204–5.

532. Lawlor, John J.
'The Imaginative Unity of *Piers Plowman*', *RES*, NS 8:30 (April 1957) 113–26. Reprinted in Vasta (1968) 278–97 and in Blanch (1969) 101–16.

Accepts the interpretations of the Three Lives offered by Dunning 1956 [530] and Hussey 1956 [529], but argues further for a real unity between 'doing well' in the world and 'doing well' in the spiritual life. The unity is maintained imaginatively, in a poem which can be categorised neither as spiritual autobiography nor as strategically planned revelation of an already apprehended grand design, through the dreamer. He embodies the quest for truth, with all its stubborn attachment to the world and its ways of seeing, to the idea of intellectual answers to spiritual questions, and to false images of the self which can only be exposed by the satiric intelligence. What the poem does is to re-enact, through the dreamer and the reader, the processes of growing spiritual awareness, the movement from knowledge to 'realisation'. An epoch-making article.

533. Bloomfield, Morton W.
'*Piers Plowman* and the Three Grades of Chastity', *Anglia* 76:2 (1958) 227–53.

The subject of the poem is Christian perfection, and references to the three grades of perfection (marriage, widowhood and virginity) are woven through the poem, notably in B XII 31–52 (where there is a list of those guilty of lechery and therefore opposed to virginity; the list includes Lucifer, whose sin of pride signifies also Lechery) and in the Tree of Charity (B XVI), which is really a Tree of Perfection, influenced by Joachite tree-symbolism. The passage is analysed, and the changes in C XIX noted.

534.   Pepler, Conrad
THE ENGLISH RELIGIOUS HERITAGE (St Louis: Herder, 1958).

Treats the poem (pp. 40–66: gathered from earlier essays in *The Life of the Spirit* 1 (1946–7), 101–5, 136–41, 169–72, 198–204) very simply as an account of the conversion of the poet from sin, and sinful attachment to the things of the world, to the life of the spirit, progressing through the Three Lives to the perfected Contemplative life.

535.   Moe, Henry Allen
' "The Vision of Piers the Plowman" and the Law of Foundations', *Proceedings of the American Philosophical Society* 102:4 (August 1958) 371–5.

Why should 'foundations' go on for ever and not pay taxes? Because they serve the public good, and it is interesting to find L anticipating this argument in his account, in the Pardon episode, of the charitable uses (hospitals, roads, bridges, the support of scholars, etc.) to which merchants may properly give their money. He does not mention those religious covenants more commonly associated with the good of the donor's soul.

536.   Daiches, David
A CRITICAL HISTORY OF ENGLISH LITERATURE, 2 vols. (New York: Ronald Press, 1960).

The standard brief critical account of *PP* (pp. 122–7): praise of vigorous handling of alliterative line, social realism, satire, religious visionary power; full summary of *Visio*; dismissal of rest as rambling and long-winded. 'The author seems to be allowing his moral views and his religious emotion to deflect the poem at any point, and lively contemporary references, grand moments of religious passion, and flat didactic passages jostle each other. The author does not seem to have been able to subdue his material to an adequate literary form' (p. 126).

537. Coghill, Nevill
'God's Wenches and the Light that Spoke (Some notes on Langland's kind of poetry)', in Davis, Norman and Wrenn, C. L. (eds.), ENGLISH AND MEDIEVAL STUDIES PRESENTED TO J. R. R. TOLKIEN ON THE OCCASION OF HIS SEVENTIETH BIRTHDAY (London: Allen & Unwin, 1962) 200–18. Reprinted in Newstead (1986) 236–54.

He has 'a great poet's stunning-power' (p. 201). Among his unique gifts are the fluidity of narrative movement (e.g. in terms of space and time), the vivid authenticity of satirical portraiture, the mysteriously evolving power of his symbols (e.g. Piers), the fusion of allegory and symbolism (e.g. in the landscape of the Field), the suggestiveness and lightness of touch of his allegory (e.g. when taking the Castle of *Caro* from, probably, the drily allegorical *Castle of Love*), the sudden shafts of illumination that come from an unexpected image or pun, the mixing of homely naturalism and mystery (e.g. God's wenches, B XVIII 13, the light that spoke, B XVIII 315, the book with eyes, B XVIII 228). The union of opposites (cf. William Blake), of the mental and material worlds, is the heart of his poetic technique. A brilliantly suggestive essay.

538. Lawlor, John
PIERS PLOWMAN: AN ESSAY IN CRITICISM (London: Edward Arnold, 1962).

Insists on the importance of reading the poem as a poem, in its own sequence and according to its own rules. Therefore the first half of the book (pp. 17–186) is given over to a step-

by-step account of the poem (it is one of the best there is) for
the comparative newcomer. This account pays attention to
the development of major themes, but concentrates more on
the embodying of those themes in poetic form: the way the
dreamer draws us into the experience of searching and
thinking (L 'gives us thinking rather than thought', p. 11);
the dramatisation of argument in moments of great poetic
power (e.g. Conscience kneeling to the King, B III 229;
'Thanne spak *Spiritus Sanctus*', B XVI 90; Christ at the gates
of hell); the 'exact delineation of a complex and ambiguous
reality' (e.g. in the Confession of the Sins), p. 47; the
enforcement of the distinction between knowledge and realisation (or theory and practice) where vision must supersede
discourse; and the juxtaposition of ironic penetration with
visionary ardour, and of solemnity with lightness of tone and
more humour than is usually recognised. The second part of
the book analyses specific poetic techniques: the flexibility of
the alliterative line (extensively demonstrated) that goes
with the fluidity of the structure, and of its resources of
diction (the essential quality of which is 'language as speech',
p. 223) and imagery; the vivid dramatic sense of movement,
gesture, turn of speech and timing. The quality of the
allegory is in the strength of the literal, and the graphic visual
power; there is much word-play to bring before us the
riddling complexity of the world that is portrayed, but no
question of systematic four-level allegory (cf. Robertson and
Huppé 1951). The final chapter returns to Lawlor's main
argument, concerning the role of the dreamer. All his perplexities are set before us, the problems he cannot solve as
well as the truths he can triumphantly affirm; so too are his
inadequacies, and his recognition of them. He is the fallible
guide (valuable comparison with the dreamers of Chaucer
and Gower), full of doctrinaire assurance, literal-minded,
inexperienced, whose coming to understanding despite
continual rebuffs dramatises the progressive argument and
central truth of the poem. It is not the answers that are
important, but the answers as painfully arrived at by the
dreamer: his recognition of the truth that lies within and that

must be constantly sought (in *doing* well) is both the theme of the poem and its method. The return to the world after finding this self-knowledge is also crucial. Lawlor also discusses the relationship between the poet and the dreamer, and the various interpretations of Dowel, etc. (pp. 295–306). Throughout the book there are interesting comparisons with later English literature.

Reviews: M. W. Bloomfield, *Speculum* 38:2 (April 1963) 369–70.
J. Burrow, *CQ* 5:4 (Winter 1963) 380–1.
P. M. Kean, *RES* NS 14:56 (October 1963) 395–7.

539. Salter, Elizabeth
PIERS PLOWMAN – AN INTRODUCTION (Oxford: Basil Blackwell, 1962).

The first part of this short but valuable book places emphasis on *PP* as a work of art, as evidenced in its handling of the alliterative line, its variety of diction, its use of repetitive verbal devices of echo and anticipation to create an imaginatively coherent structure (the analysis here (pp. 49–52) of B XVIII 362–70 is particularly notable). Yet the real centre of L's energy is spiritual, and the poetry serves this dedication: unsystematic as it is, the poem is dominated by the urge to communicate the truth as L sees it, and is given added urgency by the dream and waking sequence. The second part of the book discusses the range of allegory in the poem, and the varieties of allegorical texture: there are many-layered allegories, and other passages more or less literal, but the characteristic form is improvisatory and suggestive, and has the nature of an organic growth (as illustrated in a fine analysis of the Tree of Charity, pp. 73–6). Through the allegory is mediated the central theme of the poem, the journey through love to truth (God), in which Piers comes to play a semi-mystical role, while the dreamer is the means through which the reader is drawn to participate in the activity of the quest. The book, which ends with a reading of the poem (pp. 95–105) as a version of the mystic's progress, centred on the figure of Piers, is enriched throughout by references to a wide range of background materials – other alliterative poems, works of religious instruction, mystical writings and the visual arts.

Reviews: M. W. Bloomfield, *MP* 62:1 (August 1964) 62–4.
T. P. Dunning, *MÆ* 33:2 (1964) 147–9.
R. W. Frank, *Speculum* 40:4 (October 1965) 750–3.
S. S. Hussey, *RES*, NS 14:55 (July 1963) 279–80.

540.   Adams, John F.
'*Piers Plowman* and the Three Ages of Man', *JEGP* 61:1 (January 1962) 23–41.

Discusses the various interpretations of the Three Lives, and shows their weaknesses. The *Vita* is better understood as the story of the growth of the dreamer from youth, through middle age, to old age, facing the temptations and problems incident to each. The characters that he meets in Dowel correspond to his own increasing understanding of the limitations of intellect. The Tree of Charity itself epitomises the three ages, and there are parallels in the life of Christ as it is first unfolded, and in the successive temptations of the world, the flesh and the devil. At the end the dreamer is explicitly shown as an old man: the life being fought over is his life.

541.   Woolf, Rosemary
'Some Non-Medieval Qualities of *Piers Plowman*', *EC* 12:2 (April 1962) 111–25. Reprinted in Woolf (1986) 85–97.

PP is different from usual medieval allegory in its lack of a sustained literal level. It is not clear what Piers symbolises: the combination in him 'of uncertain significance with deep emotional power' (p. 114) is unmedieval. Related to this is the lack of the visual quality so characteristic of medieval literature (e.g. there is no visual image of Piers). The dreams too have the vagueness of real dreams, the abrupt shifts of time and place, combined with a sense of constant vigorous movement. The role of the dreamer is unusual too in that it relates so closely to the life of the poet, who is indeed 'exploring the perplexities of his own mind' (p. 121). He has 'the earnestness typical of the amateur' and does not write with 'the assurance of professional ease' (p. 121). L's passionate engagement with his own problems gives the poem its driving force, but also contributes to a sense of confusion. [Brief comment on this essay is made by Jasodhara Sen Gupta (*EC* 13:2 (April 1963) 201–2), who points to analogies with twentieth-century art and cinema; and by Ojars Kratins (*EC* 13:3 (July 1963) 304), who says that mysterious significance is often attached to figures in Arthurian romance, and is not unmedieval.]

542. Coghill, Nevill
LANGLAND: PIERS PLOWMAN (Writers and their Work No. 174) (London: Longmans, for The British Council and the National Book League, 1964).

Summary of information about authorship and date, followed by an account of the *Visio*, seen as announcing the theme of the whole poem, the search for the true nature of the love of our Lord, and of the *Vita*, in which the search for the definition of the three good lives gradually accumulates 'a quite unsystematic yet feeling body of Christian wisdom' (p. 29). Ends with comparisons with Chaucer (also with Bunyan and Beckett), contrast of their use of irony, and how the two together give 'a binocular, stereoscopic vision of the body and soul of their Age' (p. 39). There is nothing in

Chaucer like Piers, in whom L gives form to the idea that 'man is made in God's image of Truth and Love' (p. 41).

543.   Kean, P. M.
'Love, Law, and *Lewte* in *Piers Plowman*', *RES*, NS 15:59 (July 1964) 241–61. Reprinted in Blanch (1969) 132–55.

Gathers references to *Lewte* to show that it is an index to an important political theme in *PP*, namely, how observance of law by king (ruling well) and people (recognising the just use of material goods in society) is the acting out on earth of obedience to God's law, which is love. *Lewte* is 'living truly', justice in the fullest sense.

544.   Colledge, E., OSA and Evans, W. O.
'Piers Plowman', *The Month* 218, NS 32:6 (December 1964) 304–13.

Review of previous scholarship, and an account of the poem which stresses its nature, not as 'a treatise in mystical theology, or a Scriptural key' (p. 308), but as 'a highly emotional account of the stages of thought and feeling encountered by a Christian striving to live as best he can' (p. 309), with a 'constant concern to bring all men into his scheme of salvation' (p. 312).

545.   Vasta, Edward
THE SPIRITUAL BASIS OF *PIERS PLOWMAN* (Studies in English Literature vol. XVIII) (The Hague: Mouton, 1965).

PP deals with the mystic's way of salvation – personal perfection and union with God – and not that of the ordinary Christian. As an allegory it dramatises the soul's journey to union with God. It is this essentially mystical quest that gives unity to the poem. This argument is illustrated from analysis, in C, of a number of passages, but especially of the dreamer's conversation with Holy Church, where it is personal 'conversion' that is sought, not that of society, and personal perfection through grace. Holy Church concentrates not on the sacraments or commandments, but on the operation of truth and love within man that brings him through *kynde knowyng* to perfection, and to 'deification', C II 86 (union with God through restoration of likeness: through becoming like him). The key to this interpretation is in the deeper significance of the *Deus caritas* verses (C II 82): the soul is in the way of union when it responds truly to God's love. The goal of Piers' journey to Truth in C VIII is similarly to find Truth indwelling in one's heart; passing through the purgative and illuminative stages of contemplation to the unitive. Further examples of the mystical meaning of the poem are in the dreamer's experience of contemplation at the Eucharist (C XXII), and in the role of Piers as the Bride of Christ of Bernard's Sermons on Canticles. [Vasta surely exaggerates the mystical element in *PP*.]

546. Vasta, Edward
'Truth, the Best Treasure, in *Piers Plowman*', *PQ* 44:1 (January 1965) 17–29.

The Truth of which Holy Church speaks does not have to do with the ordinary gift of grace and salvation, but with the higher spiritual perfection sought by the contemplative. Truth designates the ultimate goal of man's aspiration: it conforms man to God, makes union with God the whole object of man's will. This union results in the mystical 'deification' of man.

547. Howard, Donald R.
THE THREE TEMPTATIONS; MEDIEVAL MAN IN SEARCH OF THE WORLD (Princeton: Princeton UP, 1966).

The three temptations are the World (lust of the eyes, avarice), the Flesh (lust of the flesh, lechery) and the Devil (pride of life). *PP* is seen as specially preoccupied with the needs of the world (e.g. the ploughing) and the unjust distribution of its goods through avarice (Meed, the Confession of the Sins). 'The problem of supplying the needs of the body is the central concern of *PP*' (p. 198). It continues to be a main theme in the *Vita*, e.g. Haukyn, and the last passus. The solution is in the ideal Christian body politic, ruled by love, law and *leaute* in the person of the good king. But L is aware of the inherent dilemma of Christian man, living in the world and dedicated to a perfection beyond it, and the dream form enables him to express this with special personal intensity. The moments of awakening are particularly important, moments when outer and inner are united and when the meaning of the vision is fully focused.

548.   Ryan, William M.
WILLIAM LANGLAND (Twayne's English Authors Series) (New York: Twayne, 1968).

Primarily offered as a work for beginners, with emphasis on the character of the poet as it may be deduced from the poem, and on the development of his ideas as they may be discerned in the three versions, especially (as Ryan eccentrically maintains) in certain patterns of word-usage (increased use of *all* in B and C suggests 'an enlargement of spirit', p. 35). There are further chapters on the handling of allegory (Meed, the Sins), on the targets of L's social satire, and word-play (Ryan's other speciality).

549.   Burrow, J. A.
'Words, Works and Will: Theme and Structure in *Piers Plowman*', in Hussey (1969) 111–24.

One of L's chief concerns is to expose hypocrisy and formalism (preoccupation with words and external observances), all that is 'bogus', in religion and religious language. This concern penetrates to his very self-consciousness of himself as a poet, and to his organisation of his poem, where he continually rejects the easy accommodations of allegory and worries about the unstable relation of words and works.

550. Dunning, T. P.
'Action and Contemplation in *Piers Plowman*', in Hussey (1969) 213–25.

In *PP* the Contemplative life is not what the Christian progresses to from the Active life (cf. Wells 1929 [508], Coghill 1933 [511]). Action and contemplation are integral, non-sequential aspects of the life of all Christians. Valuable background from theological writing and pastoral manuals.

551. Elliott, R. W. V.
'The Langland Country', in Hussey (1969) 226–44.

An account of the 'terrain' of *PP*, its landscape, sense of space and movement, and how it relates to spiritual terrain (cf. Muscatine 1963 [320]). Particular attention to topographical words.

552. Evans, W. O.
'Charity in *Piers Plowman*', in Hussey (1969) 245–278.

A disquisition on the nature of Charity, seen as the principal theme and message of *PP*, as it is recurrently attended to and described in the poem.

553.   Kean, P. M.
'Justice, Kingship and the Good Life in the Second Part of
Piers Plowman', in Hussey (1969) 76–110.

Analysis of the nature of the Good Life, as expressed in the
various definitions of Dowel, Dobet and Dobest. These
refer primarily to: (i) observance of Law; (ii) active charity
towards one's neighbour; (iii) charity fulfilled through grace
and Christ's Passion. This corresponds to the Law, *Lewte*
and Love of the *Visio* (see Kean 1964 [543]), the concern of
which with the commonwealth and the Good Ruler remains
a subtext in the *Vita*, finally made explicit in the presentation
of Christ as King (B XIX). The reformation of the individual
and the reformation of Church and State are not to be
separated.

554.   Raw, Barbara
'Piers and the Image of God in Man', in Hussey (1969)
143–79.

Piers guides Will to the understanding of the inner life of
man and his responsibilities in society. He is not Christ, but
the perfected representative of that image of God implanted
in man through which he can attain, by reason, to knowledge
of God. The restoration of the divine image in history and
the individual soul is the unifying theme of *PP*. Important
account of aspects of the theological background to the
poem.

555.   Bourquin, Guy
'PIERS PLOWMAN': ÉTUDES SUR LA GENÈSE
LITTÉRAIRE DES TROIS VERSIONS. Thèse présentée
devant la Faculté des Lettres et des Sciences Humaines de
Paris, 1970, 2 vols. (Lille: Université de Lille III, 1978).

PP cannot be understood as a series of three self-sufficient texts, each composed in the order in which it now appears, but only in terms of an organic process of development, the stages of which are revealed by the 'genetic approach'. This shows the 'poems' of *PP* as a series of accretions around thematic nuclei, an ensemble of works on related themes, ordered into unity by retrospective processes, not all of them fully achieved. Bourquin's criteria for determining the stages of composition are inadequate, though his thesis of composition is not in itself implausible. Meanwhile, in this vast, sprawling and unmanageable book, he is always interesting on the nature, extent and development of L's reading (one of the best accounts of this difficult subject), on L's intellectual and spiritual progress as reflected in his poems and on the theological background (especially Franciscanism). His account of C is particularly full of good things: he sees here a more rigorous awareness of the self-delusions of hypocrisy and the 'banalisation' of religious language, a more abstract and monolithic conception of the political order, a more urgent concern with the question of ecclesiastical possessions, a more absolute exaltation of poverty, and above all an emphasis on the power of free will to rectify man's life and enable him to realise his divine potential.

Reviews: G. Kane, *Speculum* 55:3 (July 1980) 526–9.
R. W. Lister, *RES*, NS 31:123 (August 1980) 336–8.
D. Pearsall, *MLR* 77:4 (October 1982) 915–19.

556. Hobsbaum, Philip
'Piers Plowman through Modern Eyes', *Poetry Review* 61:4 (Winter 1970/71) 335–62.

It is really two poems, the *Visio* and the *Vita*, the first a 'secular sermon packed with examples, always vivid and sometimes scarifying' (p. 338), the second a theological dialogue, much inferior as poetry, with different methods and preoccupations. Isolating the *Visio* reveals its true greatness: it can then be presented in 'slightly rationalised spelling' so as to be accessible to the modern reader as 'England's greatest allegory', (p. 343). Since C constantly spoils B, and A omits much, B alone should be read. It is a poem that reveals a radical conscience at work, a fire kindled in the same way as William of Ockham's, repudiating the corruption of institutions and expressing its vision of decay and reform with a gift for 'minute particulars' (p. 357), as in the portrayal of the Sins. 'We should be indignant at the way in which our greatest non-dramatic poem has been treated by its scholars . . . English poetry is at its best when, like Langland, it is pithy, proverbial, local, alliterative. Therefore it is true to say that he who does not know Langland does not know English' (p. 362).

557. Davlin, Sister Mary Clemente, OP
'*Kynde Knowyng* as a Major Theme in *Piers Plowman* B', *RES*, NS 22:85 (January 1971) 1–19.

Kynde knowyng is commonly recognised to be important in the *Visio*, but its importance in the poem as a whole has been neglected: *kynde knowyng* is in fact the purpose of *PP*. Established in the *Visio* as meaning a personal, loving, deep knowledge of Truth or God (experiential or affective wisdom, *gnosis*, *sapientia*), it is used ironically in Dowel of Will's quest for thorough (intellectual) knowledge. His teachers keep trying to redirect him, but he does not truly acknowledge his error until rebuked by Anima (B XV 50). From here on he recognises that the mode of *kynde knowyng* is not intellectual but in love, suffering and prayer. The two inner dreams are gifts to help him know *kyndely*. The debate of the Four Daughters dramatises the two approaches to knowledge of God's purposes. The basis of the Incarnation is God's desire to know man *kyndely*, humanly. The theme is not forgotten in Dobest: Kynde's parting advice is 'learn to love' (B XX 210).

558. Bowers, R. H.
'The Comic in Late Medieval Sensibility (*Piers Plowman*
B.V)', *ABR* 22:3 (September 1971) 353–63.

The juxtaposition of the sacred and profane seems to be
relished in the Middle Ages, and it needs to be understood,
in the context of medieval religion, as an expression of
positive optimism. So, in the confession of the Sins, the
raucous comedy of Gluttony's Tavern scene exists side by
side with the serious business of Repentance.

559. Kirk, Elizabeth D.
THE DREAM THOUGHT OF *PIERS PLOWMAN*
(Yale Studies in English 178) (New Haven and London:
Yale UP, 1972).

Despite appearances, *PP* is a carefully structured poem: its
structure is one that reveals itself in the process of reading.
'The key to almost every enigma of *PP* is a sense of its
sequence' (p. 11). It actualises through its dramatic structure
'the process of trying to be a human being and a Christian
without jettisoning the essence of either' (p. 14). Kirk
proceeds by a sequential analysis of A, with comments on
the new kind of structural integrity achieved by the changes
in B. The kaleidoscopic realism of the Prologue (given an
important dimension in history in B) gives way to a statement by Holy Church of the ethical and religious absolutes
so far unmentioned, and a development of the contrast
between knowing the truth and experiencing its reality
(*kynde knowyng*). After Lady Meed, the Confession scenes
show the reordering of society taking place at the level of
individual experience: B skilfully clarifies the role of Robert
the Robber, and also expands the spiritual potential for the
future in the prayer of Repentance. Piers is something new –
an honest man – but he can only take the premises of the
Visio to their necessarily unsuccessful conclusion. The shock

value of the Pardon (important analysis, pp. 80–100) is that it does not explain but overrides what has gone before, creating awareness of a different and mysterious new state of being. This awareness is not present in the A *Vita*, which, with its knotty poetry of ratiocination, carries forward the patterns of thought of the *Visio*, only to disintegrate in confusion over the question of learning. B does not abandon the A *Vita* but rewrites it so as to work through the problems from a new perspective, less preoccupied with the dreamer. B XIII marks the end of the reworking of themes first advanced in A, and the introduction of a new kind of allegorical narrative, in the Feast, where intellectual awareness is integrated into a fuller experience. From B XV the poem opens out into a much wider visionary landscape, with Piers taking on a new role, and Dowel, etc., being released from their limiting existence as intellectual categories. The poem develops through the life of Piers-Christ, the unfolding of history and the demonstration of the fulfilment of the original Pardon in Crucifixion and Pentecost, with added unity given by allusion to the Easter liturgy, and moments of powerful dramatic imagery (e.g. the Tree of Charity) marking key points of advance. The last passus return, through many parallels with the *Visio*, running in reverse sequence, to the Field Full of Folk in B XX. The poem thus has two blocks of allegorical action flanking a central section of intellectual analysis, with much echoing of theme and imagery to give unity. Kirk's is a subtle and carefully integrated account of the poem, particularly strong on B VII–XII.

Reviews: D. C. Fowler, *MP* 71:4 (May 1974) 393–404.
            P. M. Kean, *RES*, NS 25:97 (January 1974) 72–3.
            K. B. Trower, *Costerus*, NS 1 (1974) 151–64.

560.   Muscatine, Charles,
            POETRY AND CRISIS IN THE AGE OF CHAUCER.
            University of Notre Dame, Ward-Phillips Lectures in

English Language and Literature, vol. 4 (Notre Dame: University of Notre Dame Press, 1972).

The brilliantly suggestive Lecture III, on 'Piers Plowman: The Poetry of Crisis', is at pp. 71–109. 'Its form and style are symptomatic of some sort of breakdown' (p. 72). There is no well-defined structure, the debates are never concluded, even the pattern of quest is obscured by digressions and changes. The poem seems to embody rather than represent the frustrations of the search. The different levels of allegory, the literal and the metaphorical, are not consistently maintained: 'Langland's sense of the present reality rends the curtain of allegory' (p. 82), he is 'incurably concrete and local' (p. 84), his 'space is surrealistic' (p. 88). The poem's procedures are throughout startling, abrupt, enigmatic, digressive; this can be related to sermon technique, or regarded as an imitation of the experience of exploration and discovery, of a prolonged spiritual struggle on L's part. Yet L is a great poet – in his range of tone, from the vividly familiar and concrete to the simple sublimity of his 'incarnational' style; in his gift for the arrestingly incongruous image; in his sharply satirical asides. It is a poem in which 'anything might have happened', yet it retains 'a strange integrity and coherence' (p. 105), a surrealistic merging of the concrete and the spiritual. It suggests, despite the orthodoxy of the thought, instability and imminent collapse, and in this it enacts the social, intellectual and spiritual crisis of the late fourteenth century.

561. Robinson, Ian
CHAUCER AND THE ENGLISH TRADITION
(Cambridge: CUP, 1972).

The chapter on *PP* (pp. 201–18) defends L against the charge that he is a preacher rather than a poet: we must respond to 'the language', where we shall find L 'struggling for a vision of life truer than his pre-existing moral beliefs' (p. 206).

562.   Davlin, Sister Mary Clemente, OP

'*Petrus, id est, Christus*: Piers the Plowman as "The Whole Christ" ', *ChauR* 6:4 (Spring 1972) 280–92.

The 'whole Christ' has to do with the doctrine of the mystical body of Christ, in which the Church and all its members are embodied. It is this doctrine that allows the partial revelations of Piers throughout the poem to be meaningfully related in a single coherent concept.

563.   Crewe, J. V.
'Langland's Vision of Society', *Theoria* 39 (October 1972) 1–16.

L's concern with the world is not merely with problems of social justice, but with the relation between the temporal and the eternal, and the baffling nature of the overlap between them. This relationship is most fully expressed, historically, in the Incarnation, of which L writes, in the 'plant of peace' passage, with full recognition of its physical as well as spiritual nature. So his analysis of society is always done from the standpoint of an ideal society of Christian love and truth. The Lady Meed episodes show the discord between Christ and man, heaven and earth; the Sins are 'placed', even in their noisy comedy, in the context of a single set of values; the 'common man' is seen in both worldly and idealised aspects (Waster, Piers). Where Chaucer is a 'fox' (one to whom 'a sense of the endless multiplicity of life is all-important'), L is a 'hedgehog' (to whom 'a single, inclusive vision is all-important') (p. 15).

564.   Carruthers, Mary
THE SEARCH FOR ST. TRUTH: A STUDY OF MEANING IN *PIERS PLOWMAN* (Evanston: Northwestern UP, 1973).

The analysis of words as ambiguous tools of thought, capable of revealing truth but also of generating misunderstanding, is a chief concern of *PP*, 'an allegory which devotes its primary energies to redeeming its own *littera*' (pp. 4–5). It is a search, a pilgrimage, more specifically a search for St Truth: the problem is to know what Truth is. To know truth will be to free the will to act truly. '*PP* is not basically a moral poem, or a social one, or even an apocalyptic one; it is an epistemological poem, a poem about the problem of knowing truly' (p. 10). Language has continually to be re-examined and remade, e.g. by using different kinds of expository technique, of allegory: the confusion or fluidity of the poem's processes is real. There are thus many different angles of vision and kinds of language in the Prologue. The unequivocal language of Holy Church is a barrier, not a help, and gives way to a picture of the world in which language is systematically corrupted. Conscience fails because he tries to manipulate the same language. With Piers is introduced a new kind of allegory (figural) and a new kind of understanding, one that can truly relate letter and spirit, as Piers shows in his interpretation of the Pardon. B VIII–XII are dominated by the dreamer's search for *kynde* knowing, i.e. a knowledge of the essential nature of Dowel which lies beyond mere words and definitions. From B XIII on, meaning is conveyed through figurally significant action (the Feast, Haukyn) and image (the Tree of Charity), culminating in the Harrowing of Hell, where language, like history, is redeemed through its identification with the Word. B XVIII ends in complete harmony, and passes beyond language. Divine truth and human language are not compatible, as B XIX–XX show: language is totally subverted, everyone misuses it, the Church collapses, and the poem too, in the ruin of language, though Piers remains as a figural image of what can be. A highly intelligent book, clearly written if rather narrowly focused.

565. Kaske, R. E.
'Holy Church's Speech and the Structure of *Piers Plowman*', in Rowland, Beryl (ed.), CHAUCER AND MIDDLE ENGLISH STUDIES IN HONOUR OF ROSSELL HOPE ROBBINS (London: Allen & Unwin, 1974) 320–7.

The divisions of Holy Church's speech in B I provide a structural pattern for the poem as a whole, especially the movement from the well-ordered material life to the well-ordered spiritual life, and from there to love.

566. Wittig, Joseph S.
'The Dramatic and Rhetorical Development of Long Will's Pilgrimage', *NM* 76:1 (1975) 52–76.

The poem is not a confused searching, but a series of allegories and figures developed consistently for a definite purpose. That purpose is to show first, in the *Visio*, the inevitable failure of attempts to reform society from the outside, without the reform of the individual will. The first dream of the *Vita* shows 'Will' in the process of struggling towards that reform, through reluctance, frustration, casuistry and despair to acknowledgement of fault and acceptance of the need for the affective remaking of the will (the turning-point of the poem, B XI–XII). *Intellectus* must give way to *affectus*, words to work. The reader shares in this process, this awakening of the will to do well, and in the extension in subsequent passus of the idea of reform and renewal to other Christians (Haukyn), to mankind in salvation history and to the life of L's own time. The end of the poem is not in frustration but in the call to the reader to reform his own will.

567. Tristram, Philippa
FIGURES OF LIFE AND DEATH IN MEDIEVAL ENGLISH LITERATURE (London: Paul Elek, 1976).

Frequent scattered reference to *PP* in this closely inter-
woven account of a wide range of medieval images of Life
and Death, e.g. to the imaging of youth in the Pride of Life
(Lady Meed), Kynde and seasonal allusion, to age and
physical decay, and to death, paradoxically man's enemy
and, as the warning of mortality, God's ally. There is particular attention to the triumph of Life over Death in L's
account of the Harrowing of Hell.

568. Thompson, Claud A.
'Structural, Figurative, and Thematic Trinities in *Piers
Plowman*', *Mosaic* 9:2 (Winter 1976) 105–14.

'The structure, movement, and meaning of the poem are
shaped by trinities; its versification, its images, and its
themes are dominated by triads, triplets, and triplicities
which intertwine like labyrinthine trefoils in a medieval
tapestry' (pp. 105–6). The Holy Trinity is *the* organising
principle of the whole poem, in all three texts. Examples are
the number of dreams (nine), the number of alliterating
words per line, the Three Lives (of Dowel, etc.) and the
three figures of Will, Piers and Christ. [After the excite-
ments of the opening, this essay is rather general and
commonplace.]

569. Nolan, Barbara
THE GOTHIC VISIONARY PERSPECTIVE
(Princeton: Princeton UP, 1977).

PP (discussed in Chapter 6, pp. 205–58) is a poem near
breakdown in the face of intolerable contemporary pressures – corruption in the church, confusion in its teaching,
the moral formlessness of political and social life – yet still
full of eschatological idealism, of apocalyptic hope in a
history beyond the present. It differs from the traditional
visionary quest in its determination to include all society.
Nolan gives a sensitive account of the poem, fully alive to its

unfolding drama, divided into seven 'meditations', with special emphasis on the role of Will as the 'filter' for our perceptions, sleepy and fallen, attached to the world, constantly missing the point, yet with the potential of vision; on the twofold movement of the poem, inward and heavenward but also through time; on the importance of the narrative as the *process* of revealing truth; on the significance of Piers, in the midst of all the complexities of the narrative, as the promise of spiritual understanding and salvation; and on the central importance of the theme of penitence, of the poem as the means to bring people to examine their own souls (e.g. in Haukyn), as Will does in the inner dream (B XI) of his own spiritual emptiness. There are valuable comparisons with French allegorical vision poems and with *Pearl*.

570. Aers, David
'Imagination and Ideology in *Piers Plowman*', *Literature and History* 7 (1978) 2–19.

The theme is the conflict between L's apparent acceptance of the established ideologies of his time, and the way his imaginative vision continually works against them. L accepts the traditional hierarchy of the estates, with its quiet harmonies, but embodies with great vigour the forces that deny it (the market economy, economic individualism). He disapproves of the *wastours* in B VI, but their historically irresistible vitality is transmitted through his poetic imagination, as is the increasing irrelevance of the knightly class. The Pardon scene, too, with its acquiescence in traditional moral hierarchies, is a clash between L's desire to accept orthodoxy and his imaginative revulsion from it (the tearing). Aers uses the same technique of analysis, less successfully, to expose inadequacies in Patience's exhortations and to contrast them with 'the striking specificity of the imagination's loving engagement with the material conditions under which life had to develop' (p. 13), that is, in Haukyn. So too, at the end of B XIX, the generalised recommendations of a harmonious Christian society are countered by the poetic and imaginative force of dissent, of energetic individualism (the brewer).

571. Jennings, Margaret, CSJ
'Piers Plowman and Holychurch', *Viator* 9 (1978) 367–74.

Piers is a figural representative of Holy Church. Objections to this view (e.g. that there is already a character called Holy Church, or that Piers has a family) are mentioned [but hardly disposed of].

572. Murtaugh, Daniel Maher
PIERS PLOWMAN AND THE IMAGE OF GOD
(Gainesville: UPs of Florida, 1978).

The tradition of seeing man as created in the image and likeness of God is an important nexus of thought and structuring principle in *PP* (cf. Raw 1969 [554], which Murtaugh appears not to know), especially as it moves towards the full expression of the idea in the Incarnation. The presence of the divine (and God's self-fulfilment) in man, of anticipations of Christ, of, always, two kinds of truth, are drawn out in analysis of the discourse of Holy Church, the castle of Inwit, the Tree of Charity. L's portrait of society, likewise, is constantly pressed upon by the ideal order (apocalyptic, the Heavenly City) in which it is transcended rather than reformed. L gives a vivid picture of those forces of cupidity that pervert the image of God in man, and how the image is restored (Conscience's speech on *mede* and *mercede* in C). L never abandons the actuality of the world he sees, and the conflict it creates in his poetry (e.g. B XX). In the *Vita de Dowel*, L examines the value of learning to the Christian who seeks salvation, the chief problem being the discontinuity between God and man introduced by contemporary theology (God cannot be known, or bound, pp. 76–82; cf.

Coleman 1981 [304]). L refuses the mystic's answer, and tries to restate the idea of man and the world as reflections of the divine (the fleeting image of Christ as a poor man, B XI 186, is a powerful one), to heal the breach between God and creation and, more specifically, to relate learning and grace. The Pardon is an attempt to link God and man through a promise, to make, as with Trajan, 'an underground connection between good deeds and the Redemption' (p. 103). The connection is later rebuilt through Abraham, Moses and the Samaritan, to Christ, in whom Piers, the principal representation of the image of God in man, of the search of man for God, but also of God for man ('God needs man for the full expression of His love', p. 122), is finally embodied.

Review: B. J. Harwood, *Review* 3 (1981) 323–40.

573.   Clopper, Lawrence M.
'Langland's Trinitarian Analogies as Key to Meaning and Structure', *Medievalia et Humanistica*, NS 9 (1979) 87–110.

L used trinitarian analogies in constructing major sections of his poem and as models for key concepts such as Dowel, Dobet and Dobest. He takes over traditional images of the Trinity as a taper and as a hand (B XVII), and also extends and amplifies patristic writing in which the Trinity was identified with the virtues of Faith, Hope and Charity, with the attributes of Power, Wisdom and Goodness, and with the three ages of history (of nature, law and grace). The various definitions of the Three Lives (of Dowel, etc.) embody these formulae, representing them both as hierarchies and as linear progressions, at the same time that they assert the unity of the Three Lives. All of these patterns are embodied in the structure of the poem, where the *Visio* is linked with the Father, Dowel with the Son, Dobet with the Holy Spirit and Dobest with the Unity of the Godhead finally revealed. This overlaps with another structure, in which the *Visio* has to do with Truth, and the Three Lives with the three Persons of the Trinity. The transformation of Will's understanding is what gives the quality of revelation to this structure. [See Thompson 1976 [568].]

574. Lawler, Traugott
'The Gracious Imagining of Redemption in "Piers Plowman" ', *English* 28:32 (Autumn 1979) 203–16.

The 'plant of peace' is the finest example of L's representation of the Redemption as a vigorous, swift and graceful action, rather than as a patristic concept or an element in a grand design. It is associated with freedom and lightness and, throughout the poem, with those who are similarly unencumbered (birds, children, lunatics, minstrels, knights errant, etc.). Sin by contrast is burdensome, a body in chains. Trust in God's grace (Dismas, Trajan, Longeus) is not hard work, but inspires a kind of light-hearted confidence.

575. Aers, David
CHAUCER, LANGLAND AND THE CREATIVE IMAGINATION (London: Routledge & Kegan Paul, 1980).

Chapter 1, 'Imagination and Traditional Ideologies in *PP*', is an expansion of the themes of Aers 1978 [570]. Chapter 2, 'Langland and the Church: Affirmation and Negation', argues that, though L accepts the traditional role of the Church in the individual's quest for salvation, nevertheless his imaginative engagement with the realities of the Church in his day (the way the spiritual benefits of the Church have become a commodity in the hands of pardoners and friars, and how the Church has become immersed in the money economy) 'acts in ways which go beyond conventional criticism of the *status quo* to undermine the very credibility of the ideology and organization he wished to preserve' (p. 42). At the end, the quest for Piers necessitates abandoning the Church. Chapter 3, 'Langland, Apocalypse and the *Saeculum*', examines the main apocalyptic passages in *PP*, and shows that they come at points where L has reached an impasse between his willed commitment to the orthodox ideologies of his day and the power of his imaginative recognition of the practices that undermine those ideologies. Apocalypticism is a way of resolving this tension: but it lacks the historical orientation assumed by Bloomfield 1961 [283]. It is an escape route. Aers' approach, through the study of L's response to historical actualities, has been strenuously opposed, as by Nolan, below.

Reviews: V. Rothschild, *TLS* (8 August 1980) 901.
            P. Strohm, *Criticism* 22:1 (Winter 1980) 376–7.
            B. J. Harwood, *Review* 3 (1981) 323–40.
            B. Nolan, *Speculum* 58:1 (January 1983) 139–41.

576.   Davlin, Sister Mary Clemente, OP
            '*Kynde Knowyng* as a Middle English Equivalent for "Wisdom" in *Piers Plowman* B', *MÆ*: 50:1 (1981) 5–17.

L's conception of *kynde knowyng*, a significant term in *PP* (see Davlin 1971 [557]), draws on both the scriptural tradition of divine wisdom, where an association between wisdom and 'knowledge' (knowing God, *gnosis*, a personal loving experience of God) is well-established, and also on the rich meanings attached to 'natural', *kynde*, in the literary tradition of the goddess Natura (where *kynde* is often associated with the divine) and divine love.

577.   Boitani, Piero
            ENGLISH MEDIEVAL NARRATIVE IN THE
            THIRTEENTH AND FOURTEENTH CENTURIES,
            trans. Joan Krakover Hall (Cambridge: CUP, 1982).

On pp. 72–96, in the chapter on 'Dream and Vision', there is one of the best short introductions to *PP* one could imagine. The poem is seen as 'the expression of the crisis of the fourteenth-century English and European intellectual, the tormented search for rational systems that can no longer be constructed, the total reliance on will, grace and love' (cf. Coleman, 1981 [304]). Boitani insists on the indivisibility of the poetry of the poem and its religious significance, and makes illuminating comparison with the *modus tractandi* explained in Dante's *Epistle to Can Grande*.

578. Bourquin, Guy
'The Dynamics of the Signans in the Spiritual Quest (*Piers Plowman*, the Mystics and Religious Drama)', in Glasscoe, Marion (ed.), THE MEDIEVAL MYSTICAL TRADITION IN ENGLAND. Papers read at Dartington Hall, July 1982 (University of Exeter, 1982) 182–98.

Signs, in pointing to meanings (*signans*), rather than explaining what is meant (*signatum*), are non-referential. The very apprehension of reality is similarly the product of non-referential sign-systems. But in the Word of God *signans* and *signatum* are united, so that man may know God, as God participated in man through the Incarnation. This is Dobest (pp. 191–3).

579. Carruthers, Mary J.
'Time, Apocalypse, and the Plot of *Piers Plowman*', in Carruthers and Kirk (1982) 175–88.

Argues that the autobiographical mode of *PP* is an excellent medium for meditation on faith and the Christian meaning of history, the changes of direction which form the 'story' corresponding to the growth of understanding of the 'plot' of Christian history, and the time passed through corresponding to scriptural time.

580.   Colaianne, A. J.
'Structure and "Foreconceit" in *Piers Plowman B*: Some
Observations on Langland's Psychology of Composition',
AnnM 22 (1982) 102–11.

Modern critics see *PP* as a dramatisation of the problem of
knowing truly, of the failure of allegory; older critics thought
the problems were those of the poet in controlling his
materials and his own fervour. But the discontinuities of the
poem may be otherwise explained: it is not a poem that
works according to a planned design, but 'a work in progress
with an open-ended structure' (p. 106); it adopts the conventions of many genres, but is consistent to none, maybe
doubtful of the intrinsic worth of any fiction. L did not want a
plan or 'foreconceit'.

581.   Kane, George
'The Perplexities of William Langland', in Benson and
Wenzel (1982) 73–89.

L's perplexities are those of an ordinary Christian, respond-
ing with some vehemence to the abuses within the Church,
especially among the friars, in his day. What he has, in
especial, is a penetration of insight into the implications of
such abuse, and a keen recognition of the dilemmas inherent
in contemporary theology. His reaction ranges from forceful
condemnation, to apocalyptic versions of history, to apoc-
atastasis, or the assertion of belief in universal salvation. He
is always ready to renew the act of faith and begin again.

582.   Middleton, Anne
'Narration and the Invention of Experience: Episodic
Form in *Piers Plowman*', in Benson and Wenzel (1982)
91–122.

The relation between the narrative of *PP* and its meaning,

between 'what happens' and 'what it is about', is remarkably indirect, but analysis of the function of the series of episodes, which is what the narrative consists of, shows that they are informed by a basic pattern of action. This takes the form of a combat, in which the forces that meet are commonly those of authority and personal experience. Episodes tend to develop to a climax in which the experience of the event is at odds with the assertions that are made by authority about it (e.g. the Pardon episode). The 'disrupted episode' is L's 'poetic signature' (p. 119). Overshadowing all is anxiety about the poetic endeavour itself, with constant questions about what kind of poem this is, and why L is writing it. 'The literary annexation of first person experience' (p. 116), an activity fraught with peril at this time, is what the conflict is about. 'This way of conceiving literature as subjective testimony was perhaps the major literary invention of the fourteenth century' (p. 121).

583. Brewer, Derek
ENGLISH GOTHIC LITERATURE (Macmillan History of Literature) (London: Macmillan, 1983).

Chapter 10 on *PP* (pp. 181–212) has a lively account of the content of the three texts; discussion of the process of poetic composition through structures of association, of metonymy; and accounts of the kinds of allegory in the poem, of its nature as spiritual autobiography and of the materials that go to its making.

584. Dove, Mary
'Perfect Age and Piers Plowman', *Parergon*, NS 1 (1983) 55–67.

The important question about the Ages of Man, seven or otherwise, is how they answer man's need to see the sequence of ages. One need is to keep mutability at bay by

conceiving of a perfect age, commonly thirty, the age of
Christ at the Crucifixion. L's three references to the
dreamer's age do not portray a steady and intelligible process of ageing (cf. Burrow 1981 [146]). The references in the
dream of Fortune and Ymaginatif's opening speech are
intended rather to create a sense of the crisis at the turning-
point of life from youth to age. There is no perfect age in
man's life, only in the life of Christ which he strives to imitate
in the spirit.

585. Harbert, Bruce
'Truth, Love and Grace in the B-Text of "Piers
Plowman" ', in Boitani, Piero and Torti, Anna (eds.),
LITERATURE IN FOURTEENTH-CENTURY
ENGLAND. The J. A. W. Bennett Memorial Lectures,
Perugia, 1981–2 (Tübingen: Gunter Narr Verlag;
Cambridge: D. S. Brewer, 1983) 33–48.

L belongs to the Augustinian tradition rather than that of
Aquinas, and sees the Will as more important to the soul
than the Intellect. Throughout the poem, the movement is
always from Intellect (and Truth) to Will (and Love), as in
Holy Church's discourse, or the account of learning in
Ymaginatif. The triadic structure of the soul is also important to the structuring of the poem, as in the subsuming of
truth and love in Charity and Christ, and in the tripartite
'lives' of Dowel, Dobet and Dobest.

586. Norton-Smith, John
WILLIAM LANGLAND (Medieval and Renaissance
Authors 6) (Leiden: E. J. Brill, 1983).

The poem has its great moments of visionary power, principally in those passages where the life and passion of Christ
are figured forth or described: the *plante of pees* (B I), the
prayer of Repentance (B V) and B XVIII. These passages

are notable for their clusters of images. The imagery of the Tree of Charity, by contrast, 'almost transcends bad taste' (p. 70). There are also vivid representations of social reality in the *Visio*, where L shows his satiric gifts (range, originality, vigour, artlessness). Beyond this, though the verse has spontaneity, variety and fluidity, and the allegory sometimes an instinctive effectiveness, the poem is digressive, repetitive and confused. L lacks the artistic skill and sense of design to create any unified or coherent structure. He is garrulous, not widely read, and naïvely fundamentalist in his approach to history and the society of his time. In B VIII–XV, which Norton-Smith likes least, and to which he returns constantly to foment his dislike of the poem, the structure is 'a depressing sequence of false turnings, cul-de-sacs, and miles of boot-sucking mud' (p. 23). It describes mental activity, but the mind we are in contact with is one 'with the experience of only a basic education. There is . . . no explicit reference to Oxford . . . or to Cambridge' (p. 111). The rhythms of accumulation, repetition and recapitulation in this part of the poem may indeed reproduce the basic learning process itself. But they do not make the poem a unity. Lewis 1936 [514] was right. [This eccentric, dogmatic and dyspeptic book has also a chapter 'The Text and its Evolution' which is substantially an attack on Kane–Donaldson 1975 [42].]

Review: J. A. Alford, *Speculum* 61:1 (January 1986) 192–5.

587.   Harwood, Britton J.
'Langland's *Kynde Knowyng* and the Quest for Christ',
MP 80:3 (February 1983) 242–55.

It is important to realise that knowledge of the way to salvation is not an obstacle to the dreamer's search for Christ, nor an opposite of love and faith; indeed it is an essential prerequisite of the act of will which is faith. His interlocutors are notably unhelpful, since the kind of knowledge they offer is inadequate: it is not 'evident knowledge', or intuitive cognition (of the kind talked about by William of Ockham and other philosophers), or *kynde knowyng*. Holy Church, for instance, is preoccupied with instructing the dreamer in ethical matters, such as moderation. Piers seems to embody in himself the knowledge that is sought, but the person sought and defined as Dowel is a distraction from the search for Christ.

588.   Finke, Laurie
'Dowel and the Crisis of Faith and Irony in *Piers Plowman*', in Schleifer, Ronald and Markley, Robert (eds.), KIERKEGAARD AND LITERATURE: IRONY, REPETITION, AND CRITICISM (Norman: University of Oklahoma Press, 1984), 119–37.

'As the question of language problematicizes the poem, it also enacts the archetypal crisis of faith, the attempt to confront the discrepancies between the world and the Word' (pp. 119–20). The frustrations of the reader in trying to find out what the poem means, especially in Dowel, *are* its meaning. It is Kierkegaard's idea of irony: the answers suck out the apparent content of the questions and leave only an emptiness. The poem 'questions and undermines its own premises . . . it celebrates, finally, its emptiness' (p. 120). But the ensuing silence makes necessary the leap of faith.

589.   Stokes, Myra
JUSTICE AND MERCY IN PIERS PLOWMAN: A READING OF THE B TEXT VISIO (London: Croom Helm, 1984).

Justice, in the sense of equity, the equivalence between desert and reward, is a fundamental principle in *PP*, in relation to secular rulers and economic life as well as to God.

Obligations both spiritual and social are conceived of in terms of exact and due repayment of debt, *redde quod debes*. The ending of the poem concentrates on the friars because they above all encourage the evasion of penance, the payment of the debt of sin. God's scheme of salvation itself is a body of law through which justice is administered: priests are in a sense legal officials. The imaginative use of these analogies between human and divine law is traced out in the B *Visio*. The authority of the State is shown to be correlated, in the Prologue additions, to that of the Church. Holy Church makes clear that the mercy and love of the New Law benefit only those who obey divine law: there is nothing higher than truth or justice. Violation and corruption of justice is the essence of Lady Meed; what Conscience restates is the principle of equity in meed. In IV and V the question throughout is what atonement or amends for offence may properly be said to justify mercy, in the response to Wrong (by Reason) and the Sins (by Repentance). Mercy must square with justice, not supersede it; mercy cannot be granted until the debt of sin is paid, until restitution is made. Piers' idea of truth is essentially of obedience to law: the pardon is granted to those who labour truly; 'earnings' are commensurate with labour. The rejection of the Pardon is in one sense the logical conclusion of the *Visio*: pardons must be preceded by doing well. But the shift from the social to the spiritual life is a radical one, and the dreamer does not fully see this until the meeting with Haukyn. Justice and law remain, however, the dominant principles throughout the *Vita*, the Old Law being not discarded but perfected in the New. The Atonement is the vindication of Justice.

590. Godden, Malcolm
'Plowmen and Hermits in Langland's *Piers Plowman*',
RES, NS 35:138 (April 1984) 129–63.

Ploughmen and hermits represent two kinds of life, the life of honest labour in the world and the life of penitential seclusion, the opposition between which preoccupies L. The Pardon episode shows Piers rejecting the one life for the other, and, though the A *Vita* never comes to grips with the consequences of this change, and still idealises honest labour, B reinforces its message – introducing Patience as a hermit, showing what the life of labour really is through Haukyn, representing the ascetic hermit as the ideal of life in Patience's speech on patient poverty. Grace endorses the life of labour in B XIX 230–37, but there is a return to the ideal of poverty when the Church comes under attack. Continued concern with these themes is an important motive for the C revision. There is some attempt to modify the position on both labour and poverty (e.g. in the 'autobiographical' passage), but the contrast between Active and Contemplative at the beginning of the Half-Acre seems to reinforce the opposition to the 'active' life. L himself was personally worried about the question as it related to his own life.

591.   Griffiths, Lavinia
PERSONIFICATION IN PIERS PLOWMAN (Piers
Plowman Studies III) (Cambridge: D. S. Brewer, 1985).

Personification is the dominant form of allegory in *PP* – over eighty abstract and inanimate nouns become persons or animate objects (e.g. trees). Strictly defined, personification is the grammatical transformation of a noun or other part of speech into a proper name. Many of L's personifications have little more than a name; others acquire personality, density and existence in time, though the discontinuity of allegory often obscures this process. In structuralist terms, there is a distinction between the existence of a personification in the *story* (what the dreamer sees or experiences) and in the *discourse* (what the dreamer writes down). 'Personifications are not sustained as actants, and their readiness to revert to discourse undermines the completeness of the represented world' (p. 9). Griffiths outlines the grammatical and rhetorical conditions under which appropriation of a metaphoric vehicle into the story takes place, and examines some key personifications: the shifting and polyvalent role of personified Truth in Holy Church's discourse, which is a valuable strategy for talking about God, about what cannot be rationally formulated; and the complex polysemeity of Meed, as the term is placed in many different metaphorical and narrative contexts, none of them transparent. With the Sins, L's personifications do not stand for abstractions, thought of as having some 'real' existence, but rather (as in nominalism) are names for individuals who stand for other individuals in a world of everyday natural experience. They are not, however, confined to this world, nor easy to interpret: through personification L exposes a wide variety of significations for the Sins, especially through an internal dynamism in their discourse. Always, however, we are conscious that they are names, conscious of their role in the discourse: they do not cohere as individuals. Other personifications grow out of the different levels of scriptural exegesis: such personifications work within a complex frame of reference, and are part of a poetry of extreme allusiveness which allows for translation from one dimension of meaning to another, as with the Tree of Charity. So too with the personifications of Faith, Hope and Charity, who force their way into the narrative structure, and have to be accommodated in a larger sweep of meaning, culminating in the Crucifixion.

Reviews: J. H. Anderson, *Speculum* 62:2 (April 1987) 419–21.
R. K. Emmerson, *YLS* 1 (1987) 144–5.
E. Kirk, *SAC* 8 (1986) 195–6.

592. Hicks, James E.
'The Eremitic Ideal and the Dreamer's Quest in *Piers Plowman*', in Johnston, Mark D. and Riley, Samuel M. (eds.), *Proceedings of the Illinois Medieval Association*, vol. 2 (Normal: Graduate School, Illinois State University, 1985), 107–30.

593.   Simpson, James
'Spiritual and Earthly Nobility in *Piers Plowman*', *NM*
86:4 (1985) 467–81.

L often uses an earthly practice (e.g. pilgrimage, ploughing)
to describe a spiritual reality and to offer a critique of that
practice in the context of that reality. His use of earthly
nobility does sometimes have this character, as with Meed's
promise of nobility to soldiers in war, which is negated in the
contrast with the ennobling of Christian 'soldiers' in the
following of Christ the Conqueror. But more often, and by
contrast with the practice of many homiletic writers and of
commentators on the Peasants' Revolt, earthly nobility is a
figure of spiritual nobility, and images of lordship and
serfdom are applied directly in a spiritual way. Thus the
traditional secular order is reaffirmed through its accom-
modation to the spiritual order.

594.   Clopper, Lawrence M.
'The Contemplative Matrix of *Piers Plowman* B', *MLQ*
46:1 (March 1985) 3–28.

Misunderstanding of the terms *Visio* and *Vita* by scribes has
obscured the quadripartite structure of the poem (each part
consists of two visions). L follows a contemplative scheme
derived from Augustine's theory of vision (as expounded in
the *Confessions* and the *De Trinitate*), in which understanding of the Trinity is sought first in the created world, then in
the mind, and then in the soul, where the *imago Dei* is
embedded, ending in the world again but seen now in its true
nature. The division of the one *Vita* into the Three Lives is a
figure of the Trinity, and Trinitarian images are present
throughout the poem. The fourfold division of the poem and
the enclosed Trinitarian analogy are further associated with
the literal and three allegorical senses of Scripture, conceived of as part of the contemplative *accessus* to God
(which in L's case, however, is obscurely understood and
finally frustrated).

595. Brooks, Harold F.
'What Happens in *Piers Plowman* and Why', *Durham University Journal* 78:1 (December 1985) 51–63.

An introduction to the poem for modern readers who are unfamiliar with Middle English and puzzled by the progression of the poem.

596. Bennett, J. A. W.
MIDDLE ENGLISH LITERATURE, ed. and completed by Douglas Gray. (Oxford History of English Literature, vol. I/2) (Oxford: Clarendon Press, 1986).

Chapter 10 (pp. 430–55) gives a good general account of the poem. L is seen as 'the most Catholic of poets' and *PP* as 'the greatest testament of faith in English' (p. 430). The structure of the poem is that of 'a helix, or a corkscrew', a spiral 'circling round four crucial conceptions' – the Field Full of Folk, Holy Church, the theme of Pardon and the Cross (p. 437). In allegory and style, the striking feature is the juxtaposition of vision and actuality.

597. Bowers, John M.
THE CRISIS OF WILL IN *PIERS PLOWMAN* (Washington: Catholic University of America Press, 1986).

The nature of human volition was fiercely debated in the fourteenth-century, especially in relation to salvation. Speculative theology, on this and other matters, induced a kind of scepticism, of which L (though not formally university-educated) is aware and which is reflected in the uncertainties and discontinuities of his poem. L's portrayal of Will is at the heart of the fourteenth-century debate. He is acutely aware of the 'crisis of Will', where urgent moral choices are put off because of *acedia* or sloth. The concept of sloth was expanded in the fourteenth-century to include a wide range of social abuses: it came to seem the most dangerous of all sins, since it resulted from a deficiency of will, and L gives it a privileged position in his analysis of the sins. The *Visio* concentrates upon social and political corruption as manifestations of laxity and neglect: Will himself seems to suffer from a similar negligence, and his apologia reveals more of his temperamental slothfulness than of his will to amend. His dedication to Dowel is always suspect. The dogged manner in which L worked at writing and rewriting his poem may be some kind of deliberate self-imposed discipline.

Review: R. Adams, *YLS* 1 (1987) 135–40.

598.   Bowers, John M.
'*Piers Plowman* and the Unwillingness to Work',
Medievalia 9 (1986, for 1983) 239–49.

Social problems in the Middle Ages tend to be viewed in spiritual terms. For L the dominant principle of corruption in the Fair Field is sloth – idleness, waste, unwillingness to work. It is a failure of will, evidenced in a lazy king, a waster, an idle beggar, perhaps the poet himself. [See Carnegy 1934 [512].]

599.   Dove, Mary
THE PERFECT AGE OF MAN'S LIFE (Cambridge: CUP, 1986).

What is 'the prime of life', the perfect age? L's answers (pp. 103–24) are, as always, unpredictable and enigmatic. His interest in the representation of the ages of man, in his portrayal of the dreamer especially, is not an interest in a gradual process but 'in the moment of crisis when one age confronts another, for at such crisis-moments a man may be urged into salutary action' (p. 107). 'Myddel age' (B XII 7) is thus a time to act, a time of momentous transition. Beyond the sequence of ages, so unsystematically represented in the poem, there is an age which stands apart, the perfect age of manhood ('hy tyme', C XVIII 138) in Christ. There is no perfect age of man's life, except in separation from the sequence of the ages and in association with the perfect age of Christ. [See Dove 1983 [584].]

600. Peck, Russell A.
'Social Conscience and the Poets', in Newman, Francis X. (ed.), SOCIAL UNREST IN THE LATE MIDDLE AGES (Medieval and Renaissance Texts and Studies, vol. 39) (Binghamton, New York: Center for Medieval and Renaissance Studies, 1986) 113–48.

The growth of a sense of individual conscience, of the individual's responsibility for choosing right or wrong, is important in *PP* ('Conscience' appears as a major figure in three important episodes), and associates the poem with a powerful late fourteenth-century penitential movement as well as with Wycliffite reformers. 'Personal conscience' remains when 'Social conscience' seems defeated at the end.

601. Simpson, James
'From Reason to Affective Knowledge: Modes of Thought and Poetic Form in *Piers Plowman*', *MÆ* 55:1 (1986) 1–23.

Formal changes of style reflect cognitive changes, changes in Will's kind of understanding. A theory for such change can be found in medieval theologians' distinctions between *scientia* and *sapientia*, between speculative knowledge (the business of the intellect) and affective knowledge (the business of the will), and the formal modes appropriate to them. Thus the Meed episodes are concerned with knowing and recognising what Meed is, the perception of truth through reason. The method is one of explicit argumentation, the language precise, satirical. The same is true of the formal, analytical mode of the early Dowel passus. But from the Tree of Charity onwards the mode is symbolic and metaphorical, directed to affective knowledge; it is heralded in Patience's speech at B XIII 151, mysterious, potently suggestive, prophetic.

602. Alford, John A. and Tavormina, M. Teresa (eds.)
THE YEARBOOK OF LANGLAND STUDIES, vol. 1
(East Lansing: Colleagues Press, 1987), vol. 2 (1988).

The editors' foreword announces the policy of the new journal: to publish articles on *PP* and related alliterative poems, ranging from lengthy essays to brief notes, and, with that, to offer reviews of books in the field and an annotated bibliography of the year's work. Volume 1 has bibliographies for 1985, by Robert Adams, and for 1986, by Vincent DiMarco; Volume 2 has the bibliography for 1987, by DiMarco. See *YLS* in the list of Abbreviated References.

603. Schmidt, A. V. C.
THE CLERKLY MAKER: LANGLAND'S POETIC
ART (Piers Plowman Studies IV) (Cambridge:
D. S. Brewer, 1987).

Schmidt writes on the poetry of *PP*, specifically versification, diction and word-play. L is a subtle, witty and intellectually strenuous poet who had worked out a way in which he could be both clerk and 'maker', and who wrote primarily for a clerical audience that would appreciate his learning and Latinity. The long chapter on versification discusses the ten variants of the alliterative line, distributed among three types, that L allows (they include the five-stave line, and lines with half-lines unlinked by alliteration), the relation between alliteration and stress, the use of enjambment (a favourite device, through which L gives conversational naturalness rather than rhetorical formality to his verse), of translinear, running and contrapuntal (e.g. *aabab*) alliteration, of pararhyme and rhyme. The next chapter deals with the Latin quotations and the often subtle manner in which they are integrated into the sense of the English in which they are embedded. The last chapter concentrates on the pun, a form of word-play of which L is especially fond: puns create a special alertness to the workings of language, and also epitomise L's view of language as something capable of being trusted (since the Word was revealed in words) but also shifting and suspect (because human). Schmidt illustrates his argument, here and throughout, with subtle and detailed analysis of specific passages.

Review: H. Duggan, *YLS* 2 (1988) 167–74.

604.   Simpson, James
'Spirituality and Economics in Passus 1–7 of the B Text',
YLS 1 (1987) 83–103.

L gives an account of the way in which contractual obligations within society, based on hierarchical bonds of love and loyalty, are giving way to money-based relations. He deplores this, and hankers for the traditional Utopia of idealised feudalism. Yet the economic imagery he uses in trying to establish analogies between spiritual and economic relations is often and quite deliberately drawn from the profit economy. This is true also of much fourteenth-century theology concerning the kinds of reward man may expect of God (where terms like 'wages' are similarly used). The logic of this imagery demonstrates an acceptance on L's part of the new forms of economic relationship.

605.   Adams, Robert
'Langland's Theology', in Alford (1988) 87–114.

Describes the general tendencies of L's thought; his attitudes on theological topics of particular fourteenth-century interest (grace, the sacraments, apocalypticism); and his associations with or suggested indebtedness to particular groups of religious writers ('monastic' philosophers, the *moderni*, Wyclif and the Lollards).

606.   Alford, John A. (ed.)
A COMPANION TO *PIERS PLOWMAN* (Berkeley, Los Angeles and London: University of California Press, 1988).

A series of essays by authorities in the field covering: The Critical Heritage, The Design of the Poem, The Historical Context, Langland's Theology, Allegorical Visions, Satire, Medieval Sermons, The Text, Dialect and Grammar, Alliterative Style, and The Legacy of *Piers Plowman*. Most essays are primarily devoted to surveys of the scholarly work done in the area that they cover. Each essay has quite a full bibliography. See further the list of Abbreviated References, above.

607.   Alford, John A.
'The Design of the Poem', in Alford (1988) 29–65.

A step-by-step summary of the sequence of events in *PP*, with elucidatory commentary. As good an introduction to the shape of the poem as could be imagined.

608.   Justice, Steven
'The Genres of *Piers Plowman*', *Viator* 19 (1988) 291–306.

The difficulty of finding continuity between episodes in *PP* is resolved if it is sought in terms of narrative genres. 'Langland enables narrative progress and approaches religious authority by discontinuous choices of genre that progressively abandon claims to poetic authority' (p. 305). He begins with satire, done from the point of view of an irresponsible *gyrovagus*; Holy Church offers a Boethian *consolatio*, but her authority is solitary, outside history; the *débat* of the Meed episodes is a more fully interpretative allegory, fully involved in the social world, but ends only in apocalyptic vision; B V is a confession-manual, centring on the act of penitence – the author is progressively relinquishing his own authority; now Piers, taking over that authority, introduces the final genre of the *Visio* – a replication of the narrative of the Mosaic books (wandering in the wilderness, rejection of discipline, breaking of the tables of the Law). But this imitation of biblical narrative has still a touch of literary hubris in it, and the adherence to genre in the *Visio* must give way to the *Vita*, which is no genre but enacted interpretation.

609. Kirk, Elizabeth D.
'Langland's Plowman and the Recreation of Fourteenth-Century Religious Metaphor', *YLS* 2 (1988) 1–21.

Petrus id est Christus (B XV 212) is characteristically daring in the way it brings together the ploughman, the Pope and Christ. But it is even more surprising than it seems, for L's ploughman (not the good shepherd or fisherman of scriptural tradition) is himself a prosperous wage-labourer, not a serf or independent farmer, and he belongs to the new world of fourteenth-century agricultural economy. He is not a traditional figure, but he rapidly established himself as a popular one, being in accord with developing ideas about the involvement of the Church with society (as ploughing is the basis of the economic life), and with the greater respect accorded to manual labour by the newer religious orders.

Piers Plowman and the visual arts

610. Tristram, E. W.
'Piers Plowman in English Wall-Painting', *Burlington Magazine* 31:175 (October 1917) 135–40.

Wall-paintings in certain medieval churches (especially Ampney St Mary's in Gloucestershire) portray the crucified Christ 'surrounded by many tools of labour, arranged so as to form a halo or glory'. The idea was perhaps suggested by the image of Piers Plowman as Christ, as 'a labourer working and suffering amongst his fellows', and suggests some sympathy for the idealisation of the common labourer in *PP* among the poorer clergy. [But Tristram is wrong: see D'Evelyn 1919 [611].]

611. D'Evelyn, Charlotte
'*Piers Plowman* in Art', *MLN* 34:4 (April 1919) 247–9.

The image of Christ the ploughman surrounded by the tools of his trade, supposed by Tristram 1917 [610] to be represented in certain wall-paintings, and to allude to *PP*, is not in any way suggested by the poem. In fact, the 'tools' are the well-known instruments of the Passion, commonly represented thus.

612. Kaske, R. E.
'*Piers Plowman* and Local Iconograph,', *JWCI* 31 (1968) 159–69.

Suggests possible associations between allusions in the poem

and iconographical remains in the Malvern area: the 'two
gredy sowes' of B V 347 appear in a bench-end at Little
Malvern, the beating of 'the bare ers' of B V 175 in a font at
Southrop. The mirror of Middle Earth (B XI 8) may be
influenced by a wall-painting of the Wheel of Life at
Kempley, the souls in Abraham's bosom (B XVI 254) by a
stone carving at Cleobury Mortimer.

613. Salter, Elizabeth
'Piers Plowman and the Visual Arts', in Hunt, John Dixon
(ed.), ENCOUNTERS: ESSAYS ON LITERATURE
AND THE VISUAL ARTS (London: Studio Vista, 1971)
11–27.

Analogies with the restless spirit and disordered spatial
relations of late Gothic, and with the enigmatic and paradox-
ical landscapes of Bosch, but most instructively with illustrations in manuals of religious instruction (e.g. British Library
MS Add. 37049) and their functional diagrammatic pictures
of, for example, allegorical trees. With illustrations.

614. Davlin, Sister Mary Clemente, OP
'A Genius-Kynde Illustration in Codex Vaticanus
Palatinus Latinus 629', *Manuscripta* 23:3 (November 1979)
149–58.

Suggestions that the illustration in this fourteenth-century
MS, showing a priestly or kingly male figure standing behind
an *arbor consanguinitatis*, may represent a male version of
the usually female Natura, related perhaps to the figure
Genius as he appears in Alain de Lille, Jean de Meun and
Gower, and provide an analogue for the personification
Kynde in B IX, XI.

Index

The index numbers refer to the number of the item. Numbers in square brackets indicate where the entry is the main subject.

281

Ancrene Riwle, 178, 190
Anderson, Judith H., 591; (1976)
[346]
anticlericalism, *see* clergy, criticism
of
antifraternal (antimendicant)
tradition, *see* friars
apocalyptic and prophetic elements
in *PP*, 283–4, 305, 310–11, 497,
502, 569, 575, 581
Aquinas, St Thomas, 247, 264, 266,
276, 280, 585
Arn, Mary-Jo, (1981) [427]; (1982)
[501]
art, relation of *PP* to, *see* visual arts
Ashley, Kathleen M., (1982) [499]
Attwater, Donald, (1930) [86], 87,
90
Attwater, Donald and Rachel
(1957) [90]
Auden, W.H., and Pearson,
Norman Holmes, (1950) [69]
audience, of *PP*, 341, 344, 349, 351,
368, 374; *see also* reception
Auerbach, Erich, 391
Augustine, St, 181, 184, 222, 231,
236, 243, 251, 261, 311, 585;
commentary on Psalms, 184;
Confessions, 486, 594; *De
Trinitate*, 251, 594
authorship controversy, 1, 2, 9, 19,
22–3, 29, 34, 65, 94, 100–147,
220–1, 271, 282, 339, 360, 481,
515, 517, 519, 521–3
autobiographical references *see*
Langland, William
Averroes, 216
Avicenna, 263; *Liber De Anima,
265*
Ayguani, 14th century philosopher,
252

Baker, Denise N., (1980) [477], 490;
(1984) [331], 490; (1984) [480]
Baldwin, Anna P., (1981) [372];
(1981) [373]; (1982) [378]; 1984

[332]; (1988) [385]
Bannister, Arthur T., (1922) [126]
Barney, Stephen A., 43–4; (1973)
[229]; (1979) [402]; (1988) [412]
Barr, Helen, (1986) [242]
Barthélemy, Renclus de Moillens,
Li Romans de Carité, 271
Baugh, Albert C., (1948) [519]
Baum, Paull Franklin, (1919) [176]
Beckett, Samuel, 542
Beckwith, Marc A., (1981) [170]
beggars *see* poverty
Bennett, J.A.W., 15, 18, 36, 42,
515, 521; (1943) [157]; (1943)
[158]; (1948) [30], 15; (1950)
[524]; (1969) [321]; (1972) [77] 64;
(1981) [235]; (1986) [596]
Benson, C. David, (1976) [231];
(1980) [405]
Benvenuto da Imola, commentary
on Dante, 183
Bernard, St, 243; Epistle 42, 208;
sermons on Canticles, 212, 546
Berry, Francis, 71
Bertz, Douglas, (1985) [502]
Bessinger, J.B., 36
Bible, biblical exegesis, and patristic
writing, allusion to and use of,
125, 141, 181–2, 184, 186–8, 196–
7, 199, 200, 202, 204–10, 217,
220–44, 246, 251, 268, 399, 409,
437, 439, 474, 591, 608; Canticles
6:10, 186; Daniel 7:10, 207;
Exodus, 184; Genesis 6, 182;
Isaiah, 187; James, 243; Job
41:13, 497; Joshua 2:6, 399;
Matthew 19:16–22, 521; Numbers
13:26, 204; 17:8, 186; Psalm 4:7,
187, 236; 18:6, 182; Proverbs 6:9–
12, 497; 30:8–9, 497
Biggs, Frederick M., (1984) [209]
Birnes, William J., (1975) [370]
Bishop, Ian, (1987) [335]
Blackman, Elsie, (1918) [22]
Blake, William, 89, 505, 537
Bland, Cynthia Renée, (1988) [463]

DATE DUE

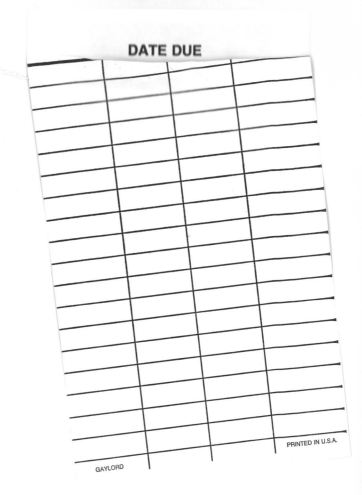

PRINTED IN U.S.A.

GAYLORD